THE STORY OF CAMARO

John Gunnell & Jerry Heasley

©2006 Krause Publications

Published by

krause publications
An Imprint of F+W Publications

700 East State Street • Iola, WI 54990-0001
715-445-2214 • 888-457-2873

Our toll-free number to place an order or obtain
a free catalog is (800) 258-0929.

All rights reserved. No portion of this publication may be reproduced or transmitted in any form or by any means, electronic or mechanical, including photocopy, recording, or any information storage and retrieval system, without permission in writing from the publisher, except by a reviewer who may quote brief passages in a critical article or review to be printed in a magazine or newspaper, or electronically transmitted on radio, television, or the Internet.

Library of Congress Catalog Number: 2006922211

ISBN 13-digit: 978-0-89689-432-7
ISBN 10-digit: 0-89689-432-0

Designed by Kara Grundman
Edited by Brian Earnest

Printed in China

Dedication

This book is dedicated to my daughter Sue, who sold me my first Camaro. Since I sold the car, I have to admit that she must have better taste in classic automobiles than I do.

— *John Gunnell*

Contents

INTRODUCTION 5

CHAPTER 1: CAMARO: CHEVY'S CONVENTIONAL CORVAIR 6

CHAPTER 2: PATTERNING THE GENERAL'S PONIES 12

CHAPTER 3: GEN I: THE ORIGINAL CAMARO (1967-68) 21

CHAPTER 4: IN A CLASS OF ITS OWN (1969) 44

CHAPTER 5: GEN II: BRIGHT NEW BEGINNINGS (1970-1977) 56

CHAPTER 6: GEN II SOFT NOSE (1978-1981) 82

CHAPTER 7: GEN III: BACK TO THE FUTURE (1982-1992) 101

CHAPTER 8: GEN IV: THE PERFECT CAMARO (1993-2002) 147

CHAPTER 9: THE 2007 CONCEPT CAMARO 199

APPENDIX: YEAR-BY-YEAR CAMARO OPTIONS 206

ACKNOWLEDGMENTS 224

Introduction

There have been four generations of Camaro. The Gen I type was built from 1967 to 1970. The Gen II type bowed in 1970 and lasted quite a long time— until 1981. The years 1982-1992 brought enthusiasts the Gen III version. The Gen IV type was built from 1993-2002 and many people thought it would be the last. Early in 2006, Chevy launched a brand new Camaro concept car and lovers of the marque have their fingers crossed on this Silver beauty, hoping it will make it to the assembly line.

Each generation of the Camaro had different specifications and body styles. The Gen I's came as hardtops and convertibles. The next Camaro came only as a coupe, with a T-top option as a running change. Gen III brought the big-glass-window fastback style—my personal favorite since I once owned an '84. It came just as a coupe and a coupe with removable roof panels until a factory ragtop was re-introduced late in 1987. (Before that there were some convertible conversions of varying quality). The best way to sum up the Gen IV models is "eye-catching." For years, every time I saw one of those cars my eyes were drawn to it a second and third time. They were like a real pretty girl who's hard not to stare at.

Some say the original Camaro was a clone of Ford's Mustang—the pioneer of "pony cars." To my way of thinking, Ford built the Mustang to steal the sports car market away from the Corvair. The Mustang was indeed better than the Corvair, and the Camaro was better than the Mustang. However, in the sense that the Mustang sprung from the conventional Falcon and the Camaro sprung from the conventional Chevy II, there is some degree of "rip off" in the way the first Camaro was constructed. Still, the idea for a four-place American sports car started at GM.

The first Camaro was a luscious little car. The '68 was nearly identical, though I like "butterfly" windows, which went the way of the Doo-Doo Bird after '67. The first six-cylinder Camaro sport coupe was cheap—only $2,466! But most buyers dipped into the options bin. You could add individual bits or the "Kalifornia Kustom" Rally Sport package or the let's-go-drag-racing Super Sport kit. If you wanted to race on a road course you sprung for the "Corvette's-kid-brother" Z/28 model-option. A pretty good '69 facelift proved popular.

The Ferrari-inspired Gen II Camaros were a little less powerful than those from the first generation, thanks to insurance companies and the smog Gestapo. After the first gas crisis in '73, the muscle car Camaro disappeared. The Z/28 was the hot ticket. It could still do 0 to 60 mph in 5.8 seconds. These cars nearly bit the bullet in the mid-'70s, but by '77 Chevrolet was selling more Camaros than Ford was selling Mustangs. The later Gen II cars were winners and made lots of moola for GM.

My wife (at the time) called my Gen III Z/28 T-Top my "male menopause machine." She was right. The car came out of Colorado, where my daughter bought it from a tooth doc who had spun the clock. We caught him and she got most of her money back (though one of his checks bounced). She got the car, too, and sold it to me. It was fast. One day in Iowa, on a long stretch of straight road, I got my first speeding ticket at over the century mark. The state boy saw me coming and just waited until I went by. The car lacked good build quality and I, like many other Americans, turned it in for a Toyota. I regret it now, but who knew the Z-car would get so collectible? The Gen III's improved after fuel-injection was introduced. And I have to admit that my car probably led a rough life, but that didn't explain why the inside door handle surrounds were crooked.

The Gen IV Camaros were better cars. They looked better and worked better, too. The '93 came as a coupe only, but convertibles returned in '94. In '98, the front end was restyled and a new derivation of the Corvette LS1 V-8 was used in SS and Z28 models. Speaking of the SS, it didn't arrive until '96, when Chevy teamed with aftermarket company SLP (Street Legal Performance) to create a new model with extra zip.

On September 26, 2001, Chevrolet announced that it would stop making Camaros. "GM loses some old muscle" said the headline in the *Detroit News*. Even though the car was going—or perhaps to move out inventory—Chevrolet celebrated the Camaro's 35th birthday with special graphics packages for the 2002 edition of the Z28 SS. Now, Camaro lovers are getting ready to celebrate when Chevy brings the Camaro nameplate back.

CHAPTER One

Camaro: Chevy's Conventional Corvair

A case could be made for tracing the Chevrolet Camaro's lineage back to the sports car boom of the late '40s. The sports car boom began when American servicemen, returning from fighting in Europe, during World War II, brought MG TCs and other foreign sports cars back to the United States. Before long, the racing and rallying of such vehicles grew into a major hobby.

Did the car that would become the mighty Camaro have its roots traced all the way back to 1961 with the funky rear-engine Corvair? Some observers would argue that is the case.

6 THE STORY OF CAMARO

By 1962, the Corvair lineup had four models, including the Monza convertible.

An equal argument could be made for following the Camaro story back to 1953, when the first Corvette arrived on the scene. That fiberglass-bodied, six-cylinder, Powerglide-equipped Chevy product was designed to combat the growing sales of imported roadsters. Over the years, Chevrolet has pushed the idea that a strong link exists between the two models. In some ways—and for certain model years in particular—the impression is true, but it wasn't Chevrolet's two-seat sports car that really inspired its four-seat sporty car back in the middle '60s.

A story passed on recently by Camaro expert Tony Hossain crystallizes the car's derivation in a very simple way. According to Hossain, in 1961, when Lee Iacoca was one of Ford Motor Company's "Whiz Kids," he obtained examples of all current Fords and Chevrolets and lined the cars up with matching models side-by-side. The only Chevrolet product that Iacocca couldn't equate a Ford model to was the Corvair Monza. That made him frustrated.

Supposedly, it was from this little exercise that the Mustang sprang and it was the Mustang that Chevy tried to checkmate—a few years later—with the '67 Camaro. The Mustang essentially had the Corvair Monza image combined with a more conventional (and perhaps less scary to car buyers) engineering layout. When it turned out to be the best-selling new car in history, the Mustang immediately became a target for Chevrolet to take pot shots at. The weapon that Chevy took aim at that target with was the first Camaro—the Ford pony car's late-arriving rival.

As author Michael Antonick noted in his *Illustrated Camaro Buyer's Guide*, "Ironically, GM itself generated signals that should have led it to the Camaro sooner. Its own Corvair, the most radical of the Big Three's 1960 entries into the compact market, was something of a dud until the Corvair Monza series came along with bucket seats and other sporty accouterments, and sold much better. The car wasn't much different, but customers responded to the image switch."

The Corvair had actually bowed in the fall of 1959 as part of the first wave of compact cars from the Big Three American automakers. Like its competitors—the Ford Falcon and the Valiant built by Chrysler—the Corvair was designed to steal sales away from small, imported cars that had gained popularity during the economic recession of 1957-1958. Smaller American car makers like AMC and Studebaker already had their American and Lark models out. Industry observers were looking to the "big boys" in Detroit for some exciting new product developments. The

The 1964 Corvair ran into some serious competition when the Mustang arrived.

buff books were filled with sketches of the never-to-arrive "Chevrolet Cadet" and "Ford Cardinal." However, the Corvair, Falcon and Valiant did materialize.

Unlike the other domestic compacts, the Corvair had been engineered along the lines of the best-selling European car—the Volkswagen Beetle. This seemed to make a lot of sense. In 1950, a total of 270 Volkswagens had been sold in the United States, but by 1960, the number had exploded to 159,995. Like the hot-selling Volkswagen, the Corvair had a rear-mounted air-cooled "pancake" engine, a fully independent rear suspension, a trunk in front and a transaxle. There was nothing quite like it available from an American manufacturer at that time. And it also trumped the Volkswagen by using a six-cylinder engine, rather than a four-cylinder job.

Car enthusiasts and automotive writers were the people who really fell in love with the Corvair. They liked its sophisticated European flavor and the idea that it offered some hot engine options and sports-car-like handling. *Motor Trend* magazine named the Corvair "Car of the Year" and presented it with the fifth annual *Motor Trend* Annual Progress Award "for engineering progress with its air-cooled engine, trans-axle and four-wheel independent suspension." The selection of the Corvair by the *Motor Trend* staff was unanimous.

"We weren't looking for the fastest or most economical, or the most lavish, or the best styled, but strictly for the most significant," said the magazine. *Motor Trend* said that the three main innovations of the new car (as listed above) "spell progress and compel us to select the Corvair as the most significant car of 1960."

With sales hovering at a quarter-million units, Chevy's "beautified Beetle" was certainly a good-selling car, but its more conventional cross-town rival—the Ford Falcon—was a real compact-car success story, with 435,676 orders filled. John Q. Public took to the Falcon's shrunken-big-car character, but just wasn't convinced that the Corvair's radical engineering was right for a family car buyer.

Mechanically, the car had some real-world problems that were hard to sweep under the carpet. Oil leaks were common. The engine had a tendency to backfire. Fan belts were prone to flying off their pulleys. The hot air heater often pulled noxious fumes into the car. Before too long, many began to consider the new Chevy a loser in the durability department. In addition, the car was a little too radical for many neighborhood mechanics asked to make repairs.

If there was a winner in Corvairland, it was the sporty Monza model that debuted—originally as a Club Coupe only—in May 1960. A show car version dubbed the Monza

Super Coupe had been displayed at the 1960 Chicago Auto Show and featured in the August 1960 issue of *Motor Trend*. The Pearlescent Blue concept vehicle had a restyled front end with "grille" moldings, an integral front bumper guard, a hand-cranked sunroof, a grain-finished top, wind-split side moldings, special upholstery, simulated air scoops, special 13-inch wire wheels with knock-off-styled hubs and a dual-outlet exhaust system.

Motor Trend tested a 1961 production-type Monza coupe in its September 1960 issue. It had a 95-hp power-pack engine, a four-speed manual gearbox and a deluxe trim package. "The Monza is a curious mixture," said the editors. "It appeals to motorists who couldn't care less about its sporting character and is certainly an excellent compromise choice for the family man-enthusiast who wants low-cost sports motoring for himself, wife and a couple of youngsters. In fact, it is a temptation to call it the Poor Man's Porsche."

Within a year of its introduction, with a four-door sedan added to the series, the luxurious bucket-seated Monza was outselling every other Corvair by a wide margin. Nearly half of all '61 models were Monzas. The sports coupe was undoubtedly the hottest-selling model, with 109,945 being made. The number of four-door sedans made in '61 peaked at 33,745.

As Michael Antonick suggested, the Monza's strong appeal to car lovers was based on its image as a four-seater combining the performance and handling of a sports car with the low price and family practicality of an economy compact. In the fall of 1963, I worked part-time in a Food Farm supermarket in Staten Island, New York. One of the slightly older, full-time workers—John Biondi—had a young wife, a new baby and a year-old Monza coupe. The car had bucket seats, a floor-mounted stick shift, room in the back for a basinet and payments low enough for a stock boy to meet. It was everything John needed to maintain his individuality, while getting used to a wedding band and fatherhood. John was our hero.

Tony Hossain describes the '61 Monza as a "very neat car that snatched success from the jaws of defeat for Chevrolet." By '62, the Monza lineup was expanded to include four body styles and a new Spyder option was added for both the club coupe and the convertible coupe. It included a special 150-hp turbocharged engine, distinctive identification features and sintered metallic brakes. Spyder equipment wasn't offered on cars with air conditioning or Powerglide transmission. The reason: Chevy was already squeezing as much out of the car as it possibly could.

The design of the Corvair wasn't as "flexible" as that of the Mustang and the copycat pony cars that followed it.

The Corvair kept rolling in 1965, but despite some improvements it was fighting a losing battle against the wildly popular Mustang and against Ralph Nader's damaging book *Unsafe at Any Speed*.

By using an air-cooled, horizontal-opposed six-cylinder engine, Chevy eliminated any possibility of offering a wide array of engine and transmission types. Other than some tuning, the use of multi carburetion and the offering of an optional turbocharger, there was little that could be done to pep up the Corvair's drive train. In addition, some of its cosmetics—such as the grille-less front end—were dictated by the engineering package as well. The Monza package was certainly a step in the right direction, but there were still definite limits on how much the car could be improved.

Production of Monzas climbed to 219,000 units in 1962 and 9,468, were Spyders. New models included an under-$3,000 convertible and a six-passenger station wagon. The carryover club coupe and the new ragtop came with front bucket seats and all-vinyl upholstery. The four-door models had a standard front bench seat and cloth-and-vinyl trim. Most sales (of the 152,000 Corvairs built) went to the club coupe.

In 1963, the station wagon was discontinued, reducing the basic Monza lineup to three body styles, but the club coupe and convertible were again available with the Spyder option (although the racing-style brake linings were deleted from the package). Out of the 254,571 Corvairs assembled in model year 1963, an amazing 205,029 were Monza types. Sports car driver John Fitch even turned out a modified Monza called the Fitch Sprint that had four carburetors instead of two, tuned dual exhausts, a modified suspension and other special features. Ultimately, his Sprint was offered for five years.

Model year 1964 brought a change in the destiny of the Corvair Monza, as reflected in a production drop off to 152,652 units. Historians assessing the Ford Mustang have said it succeeded because it filled "a market in search of a car." Until the arrival of the Mustang, in mid-1964, the Corvair Monza had served that same market. But the radical nature of the Corvair—as well as stories about handling problems and fan belt retention problems—kept Monza sales from achieving the levels that Mustang sales would hit.

After the Mustang arrived in town, the Monza's days were numbered. Says Tony Hossain, "From April 17, 1964—when the Mustang was introduced—until the fall of 1966, when the first Camaro bowed, the obvious question that everyone was constantly asking was 'What's Chevy going to do?'" General Motors and its Chevrolet division had been blindsided by Lee Iacocca's Mustang. With Chevy looking the other way, Ford stole the show. Within 12 months, 418,000 Mustangs had been sold—an awesome new world's record.

Since Chevy had nothing else to battle the Mustang with, the Corvair soldiered on with a complete redesign for 1965. A smooth new "sculptured" look, a Corvette-inspired rear suspension and an optional 180-hp turbocharged engine for a new top-of-the-line Corsa series were highlights of the model year. Monza was now the name of a mid-range car. The Corsa sport coupe and convertible took over as the fanciest, sports-oriented versions.

The year 1965 is also well known to Corvair buffs for publication of the book *Unsafe at Any Speed: The Designed in Dangers of the American Automobile*, written by safety advocate Ralph Nader. A section of the book that got wide public exposure was one criticizing the 1960-1963 Corvair for a suspension design that resulted in a tendency for the cars to oversteer if proper tire pressure wasn't stringently maintained. Although this problem was eliminated by the redesign of the suspension in 1964 models, the public came to associate the problem with *all* Corvairs and sales were permanently hurt.

In addition to redesigning the '65 Corvair to totally eliminate the suspension flaw, GM tried to harass and intimidate Nader into silence by hiring investigators to dig for skeletons in his closet. They found none and, on March 22, 1966, GM president James Roche had to make an apology to Nader before a United States Senate subcommittee.

Roche probably should have apologized to GM stockholders, too, because his product planners were immensely off base in their thinking and execution at this time. They were totally convinced that the modernized looks of the '65 Corvair were going to end the Mustang's run after just five months. They had no appreciation for the public's view of the Mustang as a brand new car (GM saw it as just a re-bodied Falcon) and they totally missed when it came to realizing that buyers much preferred a V-8 engine to a six. The base Mustang also used a six, but the V-8 model captured the bulk of sales.

After the Nader public relations disaster, Corvair production dropped to just 103,743 cars in 1966. Although the Corsa had taken over as the top-of-the-line series among the Corvair offerings, the Monza still had most name recognition with buyers and continued to sell the best of the three lines. Monza production hit 60,447 units, including 12,497 four-door sedans, 37,605 two-door hardtops and 10,345 ragtops.

"Corvair history would have ended in 1966 if not for Ralph Nader," says Hossain, who feels that the Gen II Corvair remained in production for three extra years because GM wanted to prove that Nader was wrong about the car. "You can see a styling link between it and the Camaro," he adds. "I'm sure that the Camaro was originally designed to be the successor to the Corvair, but due to politics, both cars were sold until 1969."

After the Camaro arrived in the fall of 1966, the Corvair started to look more and more like an afterthought. For '67, only the 500 and Monza series were offered, which returned the Monza to its former flagship status. A mere 27,253 Corvairs were built in the model year and 15,037 were Monzas. This was the final year for the Monza four-door sports sedan. In fact, only two-door Corvairs were sold in the 1968 and 1969 model years. The two-door sport coupe continued to be marketed in both 500 and Monza formats, along with a Monza convertible. Model year production was 11,490 in 1968 and 6,000 in 1969. The rarest Corvair of them all was the '69 Monza Convertible—only 521 were built.

As the Corvair became rarer, the first-generation Camaro grew increasingly more popular with buyers. Model-year production for the introductory year in 1967 was 220,906 cars. The little-changed '68 model saw increased output of 235,147 units. The number moved up to 243,085 Camaros built for the '69 model year. Chevy's "conventional Corvair" was off to a slow start as a rival to Ford's Mustang, but heading steadily in the right direction nevertheless. It would take a few more years before it challenged the Mustang's tight grip on pony-car market superiority, but Chevrolet had the good sense to patiently ride it up the sales charts.

There was no denying the visual appeal of the 1962 Corvair Monza convertible. It was a stylish European-looking car with no direct competition in the U.S.

CHAPTER Two

Patterning The General's Ponies

*I*f the overall theme of Chevrolet's new Camaro was that of a "conventional Corvair," then a 1964 GM show car called the Super Nova missed its opportunity to really be a winner. This one-off dream car was exhibited at the International Auto Show in New York City just a few short weeks before the Mustang arrived on the scene in April. The Super Nova was basically a conventional, Nova-sized sport coupe that blended a Buick Riviera-type frontal appearance with Corvair-like styling from the cowl section back. Chevrolet Motor Division General Manager Semon E. "Bunkie" Knudsen wanted to build the Super Nova, but the General Motors brass said no. That's too bad. It would have been a formidable competitor for Ford's hot-selling "pony car."

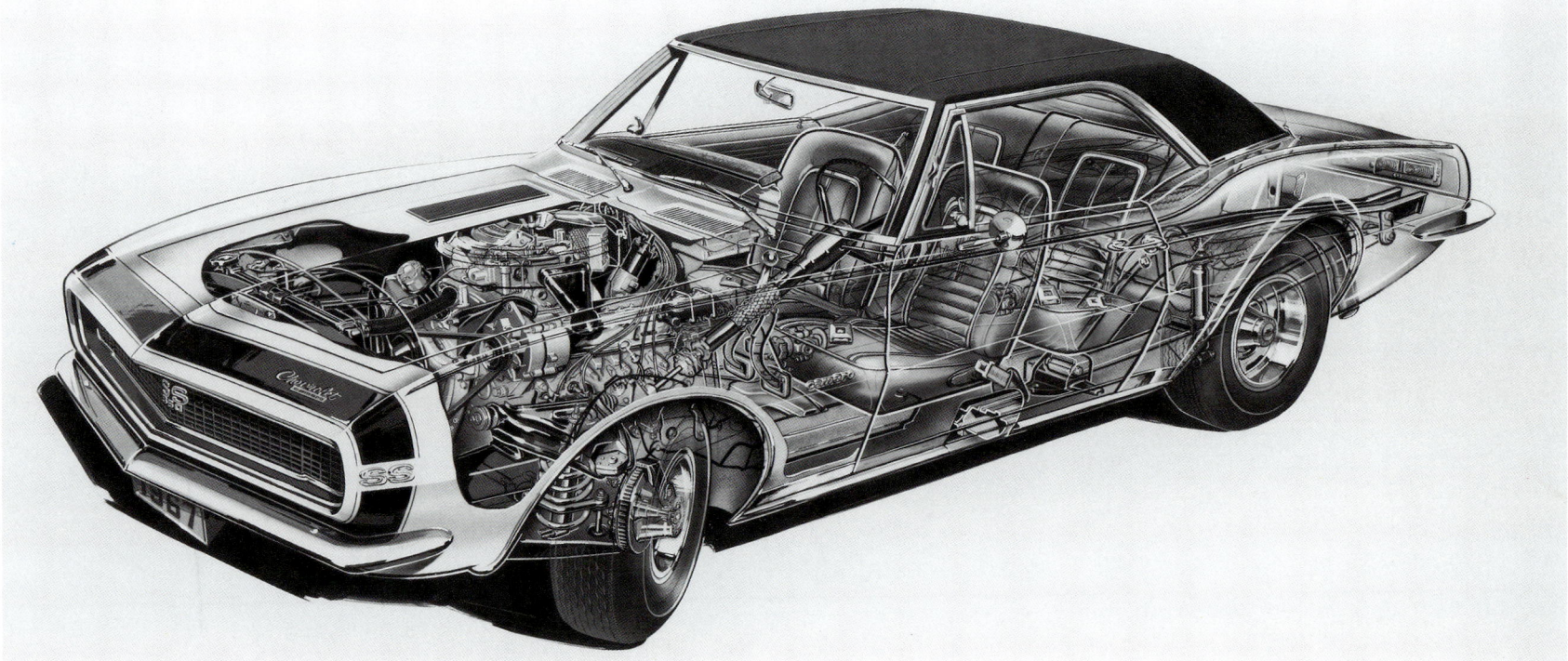

Nearly every spec on the new Camaro was slightly bigger than the rival Mustang.

12 THE STORY OF CAMARO

The sparkling new 1964 1/2 Ford Mustang meant Corvair's monopoly over the affordable personal car market in the U.S. was over in 1964.

The long hood and short trunk of the new Mustang were exactly the opposite of the Corvair.

Patterning The General's Ponies 13

The Super Nova was what GM really needed, but the '65 Corvair is what "The General" gave its Chevrolet dealers. Though GM had no reason to think the sleek new Corvair wouldn't take the ball that the '64 Monza got rolling and run with it, unfortunately, that play ended up short of the goalpost. With a little help from Ralph Nader, the popularity of the Corvair took a fast dive, while the Mustang's appeal continued to soar.

At that time, Irv Rybicki was GM styling vice president in charge of all Chevrolet products. In *The Camaro Book*, author Michael Lamm quotes Irv Rybicki as saying that no one at GM paid much attention to the Mustang until it hit 100,000 sales. "Then it shook a lot of people and off we went into designing the Camaro for Chevrolet," Rybicki confided to Lamm.

By the time GM decided to design a Mustang-type car, it was way behind the eight ball on the project and realized that completing the project would take more than two years. Unlike Ford, which based the Mustang on the current Falcon, GM did one smart thing and based the Camaro on a new-generation Nova that was in the works for 1968. This was a wise move, because the new Nova's front sub-frame was widened to accommodate big-block V-8s for muscle car fans. The Gen I Mustang had not been large enough to stuff

Ford showed it was serious about getting into the muscle car market when the new Mustang 2+2 "fastback" model debuted in 1965.

The GT option group was a popular option on the 1966 Mustangs and proved Ford was not content to let its fantastic new pony car stand still.

With the arrival of the Camaro in 1967, the Corvair was a lame duck with no future in the GM lineup.

The 1966 Nova SS was a pretty nice midsized performance car in its own right at the same time the Camaro was on the drawing board. Chevy would eventually base its Camaro on the updated 1968 Nova platform.

Phil Kunz

in the big-block engines, although Ford would change this when the Gen II Mustang arrived.

Basing the Camaro on the redesigned Nova made it a totally new car, except in the engine department. The chassis and body were not related to the previously existing Nova models. While this prevented Chevy from speeding up the car's development time to get the Camaro out earlier, it did add a great deal of excitement to the new car.

The responsibility for styling the Camaro was given to the Chevy II studio—a brand new and secretive addition to the GM Design Center's Chevrolet Studio. The late Henry C. "Hank" Haga was selected to head this new studio as chief designer. Haga's bosses were Dave Hols, the legendary Chuck Jordan and Irv Rybicki. A young 23-year-old designer who worked for him was styling great John Schinella. So it was clear that General Motors was tapping its best "talent pool" to try to make its version of the Mustang a giant success.

Haga was in charge of the Corvette and small car designs in the Chevrolet Studio from 1958-1974. Then

Prior to the arrival of the Camaro, a 396-equipped Chevelle was probably the top dog in the Chevy performance lineup.

Phil Kunz

he moved to GM's Opel branch, in Germany, where he worked for seven years. Haga was a Bugatti aficionado and owned a rare prototype 1924 Grand Prix Bugatti that had sat a long time in northern Michigan before he purchased it for $3,600. While in Germany, Haga met Bugatti expert Hugh Conway, who helped him restore the car. The Bugatti is still owned by Henry's widow Ellie and competes in vintage racing events.

With a classic car connoisseur like Haga in charge of the original Camaro's exterior appearance, it's no wonder it turned out so well, despite a couple of creative restrictions. Due to the direct link between the Camaro and the new-for-'68 Nova, certain compromises had to be made in design measurements, such as cowl height and hood length. Haga's handling of such details was magnificent, though. The job of interior styling also needed the touch of top-notch designers, and the responsibility fell to GM stylist George Angersbach and his talented team.

Hega had his design team mock-up Camaros in many different body styles, including a two-seat roadster, a two-door fastback coupe and even a sporty station wagon. The clay mock-up of the fastback was a favorite of the Chevrolet stylists, who wanted to go head-to-head with the Mustang 2 + 2 fastback, but the GM brass nixed the streamlined coupe idea.

The station wagon concept, although it seems weird, was probably prompted by a Mustang station wagon that appeared in several car enthusiast magazines. The Mustang station wagon was the brainchild of Barney Clark, a copywriter with Ford's advertising agency, J. Walter Thompson. Designer Bob Cumberford (of Griffith sports car fame) and sports car driver Jim Lieta were also involved. Frank Reisner of Intermennaica—an Italian coachbuilder—performed a few such conversions. One Mustang station wagon was loaned to Car & Driver for an article. Another was written up in *Motor Trend*. Barney

Chevrolet hit the ground running in the small-block muscle car race with the 1967 302-cid Z28 engine option.

Clark told *Motor Trend*, "Whenever Chevrolet executives see the M-Wagon on the street, it gives them a terrible shock—they think it's a production car."

No wonder a Camaro sport wagon was mocked up! However, in the end only two body styles—hardtop and convertible—were settled on to keep costs as low as possible. As for the Mustang wagon or wagons, one of them surfaced in Minnesota recently after being sold by a Colorado man.

Nearly every preliminary specification for the first Camaro was a tad "heftier" than the comparable Mustang spec, except for the height, headroom and trunk space. The Camaro was a lower car than the Mustang (by design), so the headroom inside it was less. It also had .7 cu. ft. less of trunk space. The Camaro's 230-cid/140-hp six was bigger and more powerful than the 200-cid 120-hp Mustang six, the Camaro's 327-cid/210-hp base V-8 outdid the Mustang's 289-cid/200-hp job and the Camaro's 396-cid big-block V-8 was bigger than the Mustang 390 (though the 390's 335-hp rating was 10 higher).

These specs were laid down on August 25, 1964, only 17 days after the pony car project was received the green light from GM brass. At that time, the Camaro name had not been selected. In fact, the real name would not be released until very late in the game. This, too, was done on purpose. GM wanted to generate interest in the car by its secretiveness over the name.

A day after the specs were established, the stylists went to work. Since large portions of the car were brand new, the designers had to work closely with engineers to integrate the styling concepts with real world technology. It took about a year to have "test mule" vehicles assembled. These cars looked like mutant '64 Novas. They were driven cross-country in the winter of 1965. Nobody seeing them would have rushed to their Chevy dealer to order one!

The new 1967 Camaro no doubt took some its styling cues from it's Chevy siblings (from left) the Corvair Monza, Corvette, Chevy II, Nova SS, and Chevelle Malibu SS.

A big part of the Camaro's design engineering was the use of a front sub-frame. It resembled the front section of a regular car frame, but was bolted to the cowl of the unitized body and insulated with rubber donuts. Early Chevy II's had used a fully unitized body structure, but GM engineers thought they could reduce road vibrations by using the sub frame design. They experimented with different ways to attach the sub-frame and found that the rubber mountings worked best. The result was a small car with a big car ride.

While the Camaro shared most chassis and body structure components with the '68 Chevy II, the engines and drive trains for both new cars were borrowed from the Chevelle parts bins. The single-leaf rear suspension was based on that developed earlier for Chevy II's and Oldsmobile Toronados, although the Camaro's springs were shorter. Computers were used extensively to plan a rear suspension that provided outstanding handling traits.

By the last days of 1964, the designers had the preliminary sheet metal styling wrapped up. From that point, the project moved to the stage of selecting cosmetic details like colors and trim. The designers tried various combinations and picked the best bumper, grille, headlight and taillight arrangements. Believe it or not, this ate up the better part of eight months. The basic design for the Camaro instrument panel was finally locked up in September of 1965.

The Camaro instrument panel was a nice blend of previous GM designs and new ideas. It was largely the work of interior stylist Sue Vanderbilt. She used a pair of large dials (speedometer and tachometer) sunken into the panel directly in front of the driver, as on the '68 Corvette instrument panel. But the trapezoid-shaped center panel—as well as a functional center console—looked like those used in the '64 Super Nova show car.

When Vanderbilt's work was done, other stylists took over to wrap up the bright metal body trim. The sheet metal tooling was completed by mid-November and the first hand-built prototype was completed by mid-December 16, 1965. By this time, the excitement level was really starting to build,

In *The Camaro Book*, Michael Lamm documents that engineering paperwork for the pony car project was completed on January 13, 1966. Five weeks later, purchase orders were completed. The last prototype sample car was received on May 5 and sample approval was completed by June 2. This moved the Camaro to the pilot assembly stage in which workers tested how the pieces fit together on the assembly line. This was the last step before the start of regular production on August 7, 1966.

Even at this relatively late stage of the game, the Chevy pony car still had no official name. As was usual practice, GM insiders identified it by various code names. The press frequently used the name Panther, but the names Nova and Chaparral were also hear. According to at least one source, Chevy thought about using "GM" in several formats such as G-Mini, GeMini, and Gemini, but GM was reluctant to do this, in case the car flopped.

According to other sources, "Wildcat" was considered, but this seems very unlikely. The Wildcat name had appeared on early '50s Buick dream cars, then disappeared. But in 1962, Wildcat was dusted off and used on a sporty production model; an Invicta sport coupe with all-vinyl bucket seats, a center console, special wheel covers and other custom features. Since the Buick Wildcat was already out, Chevrolet would not have used the name.

A funny thing happened at a press luncheon held during the International Automobile Show in New York in April. Chevrolet general manager Elliott "Pete" Estes was asked by a reporter whether Chevy would have a Mustang type car in 1967 and what the company might call it. Another reporter asked the first man to speak up because he couldn't hear the question. Estes chuckled and told the second reporter, "He wants to know what's the name of the Panther."

As the official Camaro launch date neared, a real media blitz began. The June 1966 issue of *Motor Trend* ran a picture of the Banshee—a well-known Pontiac show car that predicted the character of the Camaro and Firebird. "Pontiac's new Banshee is billed as a show car, but it's a dead ringer from the belt line down to the shape of Chevrolet's much-publicized answer to the Mustang," said the magazine. With a fastback roofline, articulating doors, a gull-wing roof, a flip-up-style front end, a 421-cid V-8 and independent rear suspension, the Banshee differed quite a bit from both the Camaro and Firebird, but it surely helped to generate a lot of excitement for both cars.

Soon thereafter, *Motor Trend* put artist's-conception sketches of the front and rear of the Camaro on its July issue cover above the headline "Chevy's Answer to Mustang." Inside, the new car was written up in the popular "Spotlight on Detroit" column. It noted that the "present name" of the Chevy pony car was Panther and that the dimensions might be slightly larger than original estimates, but added "the Panther has the Mustang proportions—long hood, short rear deck in a 2-door 4-passenger car." It was pointed out that rectangular tail lights had been adopted since the cover illustration was done.

A lot of the early press information about the Camaro sounded fairly "out there" at the time, although a good deal of it turned out to be true later on. For example, one report said, "Industry sources believe the top model may have hidden headlights. The top-of-the-line Panther will be called the Rally Sport. Engine lineup starts with Chevy six and may work up to the 396 V-8." While features like these seem almost ordinary now, they were almost unheard of as standard equipment in a low-priced car in 1966.

By August, *Motor Trend* updated some of its earlier drawings and information. Artist's sketches of a car that looked just like the production model appeared in an article that gave summary reports on the new 1967 models from various manufacturers. The article correctly noted that Chevy's pony car would be available in plain, RS (Rally Sport) and SS (Super Sport) series, but it incorrectly stated that only one body style—the two-door hardtop—would be available. In addition, the magazine was still using the Panther name. Finally, in its September 1966 issue, *Motor Trend* revealed the true name of the car. "Chevy's Panther to be called Camaro," read the headline.

The short item said the new name maintained Chevrolet's tradition of naming car models with a "C." According to Estes, the name Camaro meant "comrade" or "pal" in French, but *Motor Trend* pointed out, "Our French friends have never heard of the word. Could it be possible that Chevy is not only pulling words out of the air, but our legs as well?" The article clarified that a convertible was going to be offered and said that the launch date would be September 29.

On September 29, 1966, the new Camaro made its debut in Chevrolet showrooms nationwide. In October, a red Camaro SS convertible appeared on the cover of *Motor Trend*, along with photos of the restyled Mustang and the new Mercury Cougar. Of the three cars, the Camaro was the *real* news. The Mustang was an update—though a substantial one—of the original and the Cougar was viewed as little more than a fancy Mustang. The Camaro—on the other hand—was fresh out-of-the-box new.

"The Camaro is a well-engineered, carefully thought out car and a worthwhile addition to the class of machines that, in appreciative hands, yield far more than mere transportation," said *Motor Trend* after testing the Camaro. To the people at General Motors who started the pony-car project and shaped the Camaro, this type of critical acclaim was an affirmation of their ability to pattern a car that could give Ford's little pony a run for its money.

CHAPTER *Three*

Gen I: The Original Camaro (1967-68)

When they say that the first Camaro was designed and developed as a clone of the highly successful Ford Mustang, people are showing that they don't really understand the car. To state things purely and simply, the Camaro was designed and developed to be a *better* car than the Mustang! As Tony the Tiger would put it, the Camaro had to be *grrrrrrreat*!

The 1967 Camaro Z/28 quickly became a favorite of racers and performance car enthusiasts.

Gen I: The Original Camaro (1967-68) 21

The hot Z/28 small block displaced 302 cubic inches when the model debuted in 1967.

Those who worked on the development of the late-arriving Camaro *were* given the ammunition they needed to create a car capable of kicking the stuffing out of its rival. Chevy knew it was behind the curve on this project. The Mustang beat everyone else to the "pony car" market niche by several years. Ford had literally caught General Motors with its corporate trousers at half mast. A "me-too" sporty car was just not going to cut it; a "me-better" machine might.

The bigwigs at GM made a very, very big mistake in their "future think" by viewing the Mustang as just a flash in the pan. They decided they did not need a new product to fight it. The way they saw it, Chevy already had a car to compete with the Mustang when it arrived in '64. That car was the Corvair Monza, which was selling well at the time. Unfortunately, the Monza's unusual "personality" and the fact that its design was somewhat inflexible (you couldn't drop in a V-8) soon had it running far behind its rival in sales.

The signature five-slotted Camaro wheel.

22   THE STORY OF CAMARO

The GM brass had underestimated the appeal of the Mustang and over-estimated how well the hot-selling-up-to-that-point Monza could stand up to it. They watched as the Mustang became the best-selling new car in history, while Monza sales tapered off to a trickle. By then it was clear that Chevrolet needed a new car to compete with the Mustang. Ford had taught "The General" a hard lesson: traditional engineering sold better than innovation.

First, Chevy needed a "normal" car with Mustang type styling and features to knock the leader off its lofty perch.

The wide stance gave the Camaro a slight advantage over the rival Mustang, and its looks were second to none.

The SS package provided signature badging in the center of the grille and just above the rear bumper.

A console and European styling made the Camaro Z/28 interior appear race ready.

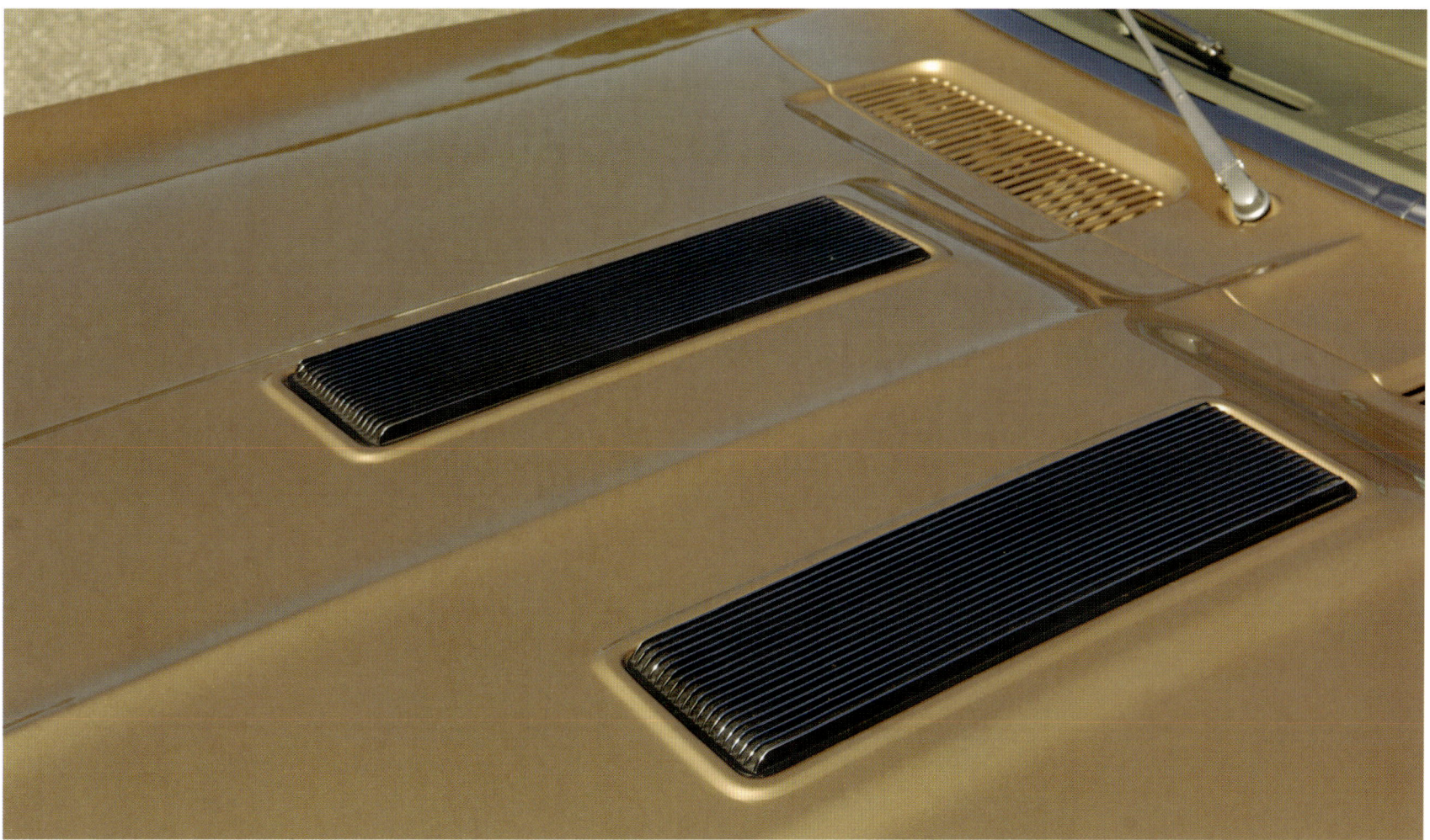
The elongated simulated hood vents were part of the 1967 SS package.

Second, to get the job done right, the Camaro would have to earn buyer respect as the "better moustrap." The Mustang had such a big lead that just building an equal car wouldn't change the sales picture enough to make developing an all-new Chevy worthwhile.

From its beginning 1967 to its end in 2002, the Camaro has always been a conventional American car featuring a pushrod engine and a rear-wheel-drive chassis. Other than styling tricks, there is really nothing exotic about any Camaro. GM simply needed a car, with the Mustang's low-price and sportiness, that was faster, fancier, sturdier, prettier, more reliable and a better overall value. Though it took a while to catch on, the Camaro proved to be just what the doctor ordered.

1967

In a sense, the Monza inspired Lee Iacocca to develop the Mustang and the Mustang inspired Chevy to give up on the Monza and build the Camaro. The Mustang platform was based on that of the compact Falcon, so it made sense to base the '67 Camaro on a forthcoming Nova platform. This was very important, because the redesigned Nova—due to be launched in model-year 1968—was made to be large enough to carry big-block V-8 engines. The early Mustangs could not accommodate big blocks.

Like the Nova, the Camaro employed a unit-body structure from the cowl rearwards. The engine was cradled in a separate sub frame that bolted to the body and had a twin-A-arms front suspension attached. At the rear, a solid axle was suspended by semi-elliptic leaf springs. Drum brakes, manual steering, a three-speed manual gearbox and a 230-cid/140-hp inline six were all standard. Sport coupe and convertible models were offered.

Being from the GM stable, the Camaro was rounder and smoother than Ford's angular Mustang, although the designers did a great job of emulating the Mustang's lean and aggressive look. As with the Mustang, accessories were part and parcel of selling the Camaro as a build-it-to-your-own-taste car, as well as a way to make a low-priced model more profitable. All-in-one Super Sport and Rally Sport packages could be added separately or combined.

Included in the arm-long list of options was a 250-cid/155-hp "big six," a 327-cid/210-hp two-barrel V-8, a higher-compression 275-hp four-barrel V-8 and 325- and 375-hp versions of the 396-cid big-block V-8. Tranny options included close- or wide-ratio three-speed and four-speed manual transmissions, Chevy's two-speed Powerglide (with smaller motors) and the three-speed Turbo-Hydra-Matic.

Rally Sport extras included deluxe interior trim and Hide-Away headlights to dress up the base Camaro. High-performance was the theme of the Super Sport kit, which added badging, a "power dome" hood with simulated air inlets, "bumble bee" stripes around the nose, a beefy suspension and fat D70-14 tires. A new-for-Chevrolet 350-cid/295-hp V-8 became the heart of an SS 350 model also

The 1967 Camaro SS came ready to run with a standard 350-cid/295-hp V-8.

Gen I: The Original Camaro (1967-68) 27

The new Camaro was immediately put into duty pacing the Indy 500.

1967 CAMARO BY THE NUMBERS

Year	Body Code	Body Type	Engine Type	W.B. (Inches)	O.L. (Inches)	Wt. (Lbs.)	HP (Gross)	Disp CID	MSP Price	Model Yr. Prod.
67	STD37	2HT	6	108.0	184.7	2,770	140	230	$2,466	49,194
67	STD67	2CV	6	108.0	184.7	3,025	140	230	$2,704	4,570
TOTAL										53,764
67	STD37	2HT	8	108.0	184.7	2,920	210	327	$2,572	88,244
67	STD67	2CV	8	108.0	184.7	3,180	210	327	$2,809	9,795
TOTAL										98,039
STANDARD CAMARO GRAND TOTAL										151,803
67	DLX37	2HT	6	108.0	184.7	2,770	140	2305	$2,561	4,329
67	DLX67	2CV	6	108.0	184.7	3,025	140	230	$2,799	715
TOTAL										5,044
67	DLX37	2HT	8	108.0	184.7	2,920	210	327	$2,667	53,998
67	DLX67	2CV	8	108.0	184.7	3,180	210	327	$2,904	10,061
TOTAL										64,059
DELUXE CAMARO GRAND TOTAL										69,103
ALL CAMARO TOTAL										220,906

Chevy called it's 1967 SS 350 the "go machine."

1967 Engine Spec's

Engine	B x S	C.R.	CID	BHP
I6	3.875 x 3.25	8.50	230	140 @4400*
V-8	4.001 x 3.25	8.75	327	210 @ 4600+

* Optional 250 CID, C.R. 8.50, BHP 155 @ 4200
+ Optional 327 CID, C.R. 10.00, BHP 275 @ 4800 up to 396 CID, C.R. 11.0, BHP 375 @ 5600
Z/28 Coupe only: 302 CID, C.R. 11.00, BHP 290 @ 4400

1967 Collector Pricing

1967 Camaro, V-8

	6	5	4	3	2	1
2d IPC	1,640	4,920	8,200	18,450	28,700	41,000
2d Cpe	1,040	3,120	5,200	11,700	18,200	26,000
2d Conv	1,280	3,840	6,400	14,400	22,400	32,000
2d Z28 Cpe	1,920	5,760	9,600	21,600	33,600	48,000

NOTE: Deduct 5 percent for Six, (when available). Add 15 percent for Rally Sport Package, (when available; except incl. w/Indy Pace Car). Add 25 percent for SS-350 (when available; except incl. w/Indy

offered a new 350-cubic-inch small-block V8 rated at 295 hp.

The SS 350 quickly gained a reputation out on the streets as a muscle car to be reckoned with. When *Car Life* magazine tested one, it ran the quarter-mile in 15.8 seconds at 89 mph. *Motor Trend* did even better with a 15.4-second run at 90 mph.

Another racy Camaro, the Z/28, debuted in December 1966. Its main selling point was a special high-compression 302-cid small-block V-8 that mated the short-stroke crank of the venerable 283 V-8 with the big-bore 327 block. Rated at 290 hp, the high-revving mill was only part of the Z/28's goodies, which also included a special suspension and custom body trim.

Since the Mustang had paced the annual Indianapolis 500-Mile Race in 1964, Chevrolet lobbied for the same promotional opportunity in 1967 and got it. Leading the pack of open-wheel cars around The Brickyard that May 30 was just about the most desirable Camaro that anyone could drool for. Chevy started with a convertible and added both the Rally Sport and Super Sport packages, as well as the SS 396 engine and hardware package. Chevrolet wound up building the actual pace car, and a pair of back ups in case of emergency. In addition, there were 101 "festival" cars made for VIP use, but most of these were SS 350 models.

1968

Only minor changes were made to the '68 Camaro. Federally mandated side marker lights were added and the grille used on the base model was revised. The grille insert had Argent Silver finish instead of Black. A front spoiler (as well as a rear spoiler) were now optional. Rectangular parking lights replaced the square ones used on 1967 models.

The SS 396 was actually quicker off the line than the Z28.

A Bolero Red Camaro RS/SS 396 with a black top made for a great-looking first-year muscle car that could really move.

There were actually four different variations of the 396-cid V-8 available for the 1968 Camaro.

The hood louvers were chromed and divided into four sections on the 1968 SS 396 models.

A new Astro-Ventilation system flowed fresh air into the cockpit and eliminated the need for "butterfly" type vent windows.

Camaro SS options grew to five. The SS 350 had the same hood as in 1967, but the SS 396 models sported a unique hood with four fake, square, bright metal intake ports on each side. The SS 396 was Camaro's muscle car and came in four "flavors." The L35, which produced 325 hp at 4800 rpm and 410lbs.-ft. of torque at 3200 rpm, was the most popular and 6,752 copies were built. Second in

The hidden headlights and small, vertical RS emblems in the center of the grille were calling cards of the beautiful 1968 Camaro RS.

popularity was the L78 edition, which 4,889 buyers ordered. It produced 375 hp at 5600 rpm and 415lbs.-ft. at 3600 rpm. The L34 version, which generated 350 hp at 5200 rpm and 415lbs.-ft. of torque at 3600 rpm went into 2,018 cars. Rarest was the L89 version with aluminum cylinder heads. It was conservatively rated for 375 hp at 5600 rpm and 415 lbs.-ft. at 3600 rpm. Due to its high $896 price tag, the L89 drew only 311 orders.

In 1968, the L35 option cost $63.20 over the base 350-cid Camaro SS engine. The L34 was $184.35 extra and the L78 was $316 extra. Other desirable SS options included the M20 and M21 four-speed manual gearboxes, both for $195.40, the M22 heavy-duty four-speed manual gearbox for $322.10, M40 Turbo-Hydra-Matic transmission for

Red was one of six interior color choices in 1968. Vinyl was the only material choice. There were 15 exterior color choices.

$221.80, a ZL2 cowl-induction hood for $79, a JL8 four-wheel disc brakes package for $500.30, a U16 tachometer for $52.70, U17 special instrumentation for $94.80 and G80 Positraction for $42.15.

Mechanically, the most significant change in the 1968 Camaro was the adoption of a new rear shock absorber setup. The shocks were mounted in a "staggered" manner, with one in front of the rear axle and one behind it. The new system was designed to counteract wheel hop under hard acceleration.

Car Life magazine road tested a 375-hp SS 396 with cold-air induction and other muscle car hardware. It did 0 to 60

The Z/28s also had badges next to the headlights, but no "bumble bee" stripes.

34 THE STORY OF CAMARO

For '69, Don Yenko was able to have 427s installed in Camaros by the factory using a Central Office Production Order. A total of 201 cars were sold. Yenko rounded out the visual package with spoilers, a cowl-induction hood, special "Yenko 427" badges, stripes and a sYc (Super Yenko Camaro) badge.

This 1968 Z/28 was dressed in LeMans Blue.

Gen I: The Original Camaro (1967-68)

mph in 6.8 seconds and the quarter-mile in 14.77 seconds at 98.72 mph. Its top speed was 126 mph.

Even though only 602 copies were made, the Chevrolet Camaro Z/28 Special Performance Package made a strong impact on muscle car fans in 1967, especially considering that it was made primarily for road racing and had only half of a selling season in the marketplace. While it did not catch the Ford Mustang in sales, the Camaro was not that far behind the original, 4-year-old pony car in racing results and that's something that rapidly enhanced the Z/28's appeal to enthusiasts.

In the hard-fought Trans-Am racing series, Roger Penske's Camaros had taken the checkered flag at Marlboro, Las Vegas and Kent, Washington, earning driver Mark Donohue some much-deserved recognition. The Camaro Z/28's image was mostly associated with this form of competition and the Z/28 was specifically designed to fit the Sports Car Club of America's small-cubic-inches formula.

As in its first year, the 1968 Z/28 came only as a two-door sport coupe. You could not order it with air conditioning or with an automatic transmission. In fact, you had to order a four-speed manual gearbox, as well as optional power-assisted front disc brakes. Also included was a dual exhaust system, deep-tone mufflers, special front and rear suspensions, a heavy-duty radiator, a temp-controlled de-clutching fan, quick-ratio steering, with 15 x 6-inch wheel rims, E70 x 15 white-letter tires and special body striping.

Below its hood, the Z/28 featured the same hot 302-cid Chevy small-block V-8 that had been used in 1967. This engine had an easy-to-remember 4.0 x 3.0-inch bore and stroke. It carried a single 800-cfm Holley four-barrel carburetor on top of a special intake manifold and had 11.0:1 compression pistons. Maxium horsepower was 290 at 5800 rpm and it generated 290 lbs.-ft. of torque at 4200 rpm.

The callouts on in the front stripe gave away what was under the hood of the SS.

The 1968 SS package was marketed as a "husky" option for buyers who wanted more in their Camaro.

1968 CAMARO BY THE NUMBERS

Year	Body Code	Body Type	Engine Type	W.B. (Inches)	O.L. (Inches)	Wt. (Lbs.)	HP (Gross)	Disp CID	MSP Price	Model Yr. Prod.
STANDARD CAMARO SIX										
68	STD37	2HT	6	108.0	184.7	2,810	140	230	$2,588	37,263
68	STD67	2CV	6	108.0	184.7	3,110	140	230	$2,802	2,756
TOTAL										40,019
STANDARD CAMARO V-8										
68	STD37	2HT	8	108.0	184.7	2,955	210	327	$2,694	131,373
68	STD67	2CV	8	108.0	184.7	3,245	210	327	$2,908	13,294
TOTAL										144,667
STANDARD CAMARO GRAND TOTAL										184,686
DELUXE CAMARO SIX										
68	DLX37	2HT	6	108.0	184.7	2,810	140	230	$2,693	10,193
68	DLX67	2CV	6	108.0	184.7	3,110	140	230	$2,907	757
TOTAL										10,950
DELUXE CAMARO V-8										
68	DLX37	2HT	8	108.0	184.7	2,955	210	327	$2,799	35,878
68	DLX67	2CV	8	108.0	184.7	3,245	210	327	$3,013	3,633
TOTAL										39,511
DELUXE CAMARO GRAND TOTAL										50,461
ALL CAMARO TOTAL										235,147

Gen I: The Original Camaro (1967-68)

The three-spoke steering wheel and low-back bucket seats were calling cards of the 1968 interior. This car is an SS 396.

1968 Engine Spec's

Engine	B x S	C.R.	CID	BHP
I6	3.875 x 3.25	8.50	230	140 @ 4400*
V-8	4.001 x 3.25	8.75	327	210 @ 4600+

* Optional 250 CID, C.R. 8.50, BHP 155 @ 4200
+ Optional 327 CID, C.R. 10.00, BHP 275 @ 4800 up to 396 CID, C.R. 11.00, BHP 375 @ 5600
Z/28 Coupe only: 302 CID, C.R. 11.00, BHP 290 @ 4400
COPO: 427 CID, C.R. 11.25, BHP 435 @ 5800

1968 Collector Pricing

1968 Camaro, V-8	6	5	4	3	2	1
2d Cpe	980	2,940	4,900	11,030	17,150	24,500
2d Conv	1,140	3,420	5,700	12,830	19,950	28,500
2d Z28	1,700	5,100	8,500	19,130	29,750	42,500

NOTE: Deduct 5 percent for Six (when available). Add 10 percent for A/C. Add 15 percent for Rally Sport Package (when available). Add 25 percent for SS package. Add 15 percent for SS-350 (when available).

This car was the only 1968 Z/28 convertible made. It sported a white convertible top.

In addition to the standard Muncie four-speed, a Muncie close-ratio four-speed gearbox was the only option. A 3.73:1 rear axle was standard and six other ratios were optional: 3.07:1, 3.31:1, 3.55:1, 4.10:1, 4.56:1 and 4.88:1.

The 1968 Camaro Z/28 was road tested by three major magazines. It was written up in the June issue of *Road & Track*, which recorded a 0-to-60 time of 6.9 seconds and a 14.9-second quarter-mile at 100 mph. *Car Life* did its test in July '68 recording a 7.4-second 0-to-60 run and a 14.85-second quarter-mile at 101.4 mph. *Car and Driver* really caught the attention of enthusiasts, in June, with its 5.3-second 0-to-60 and a 13.77-second quarter-mile at 107.39 mph!

No wonder Z/28 sales started to take off this year. Chevrolet put together 7,199 examples of its Camaro road racer.

The white seats and door panels of this one-of-a-kind car made for a stunning interior combination.

Gen I: The Original Camaro (1967-68)

Most talked about car on the road

That's because its excitement is contagious. Sports-styling. Instant obedience: You don't just drive a Camaro. You command it.

The fact is, you buy as much Camaro as you can handle. Twenty-four different exterior-interior selections for the ordering. A big choice of big-car V8's you specify, plus a spirited Six that snaps to when you give the order.

On the inside, the bucket seats come specially color-striped, if you like. You can also pamper yourself with other additions such as stereo tape and/or AM-FM stereo multiplex radio, air conditioning, adjustable tilt steering wheel and just about every power assist you could ask for.

On the safety side: features ranging from the new GM-developed energy-absorbing steering column, the energy-absorbing steering wheel and instrument panel to a four-way hazard-warning flasher and lane-change signal in direction-signal control.

Camaro. Most talked about car on the road. Listen real hard at your Chevrolet dealer's. Hear?

Big-car stance, almost as wide as the full-size Chevrolet, gives Camaro the cornering stability and responsive handling of a sports car. Try it!

Big-car V8 power, ranging from a 210 hp you specify on up to a 295-hp 350 cubic-incher. Plus a quick Six.

Dual master cylinder brake system with warning light and corrosion-resistant brake lines.

Fold-down rear seat is yours for the ordering. With seat-back up there's roomy traveling comfort. Just pull, and there's a spacious carpeted cargo floor for golf clubs or groceries.

Now you see them, now you don't. Headlights are concealed behind remote-controlled panels in the sporty black grille of the Camaro Rally Sport.

Lower, wider, roomier inside than any other car in with standard safety features never all built into

Camaro
as it comes, comes mighty sporty in sleek convertible or hardtop. Lively Six or V8 depending on model choice. Bucket seats up front, deep-twist carpeting underfoot, rich vinyl all round in four color choices. Select from 15 Magic-Mirror finishes.

Rally Sport
is the Camaro you ask for when you can't r hideaway headlights behind a bold black-g grille, extra touches of gleaming chrome a "RS" sports emblems all round and distin horizontal taillights framed in black.

This 1967 SS 350 sport coupe was all dressed for success in Bolero Red with a black vinyl roof.

Order your Camaro as a Rally Sport or an SS. Here are the details.

Rally Sport Rally Sport features in brief: • Concealed headlights • Special full-width grille • Parking and direction signal lights mounted below front bumper • "RS" emblem on grille • Back-up lights below bumper • "RS" emblem on gas filler cap • Lower body side molding • "Rally Sport" script on front fender • Roof drip molding on sport coupe • Wheel opening moldings • Belt molding.

Camaro SS Camaro SS features in brief: • Raised simulated air intake on special hood (stack-type with 396-cu.-in. V8) • "SS" grille emblem • Special hood insulation and chassis components • 350- or 396-cubic-inch V8 engine • Color-keyed front accent band (black with light colors; white with darker colors) • "SS" identification on front fender and fuel filler cap • Red (or white) stripe wide-oval tires • Black rear panel with 396-cubic-inch engine • Multi-leaf rear springs.

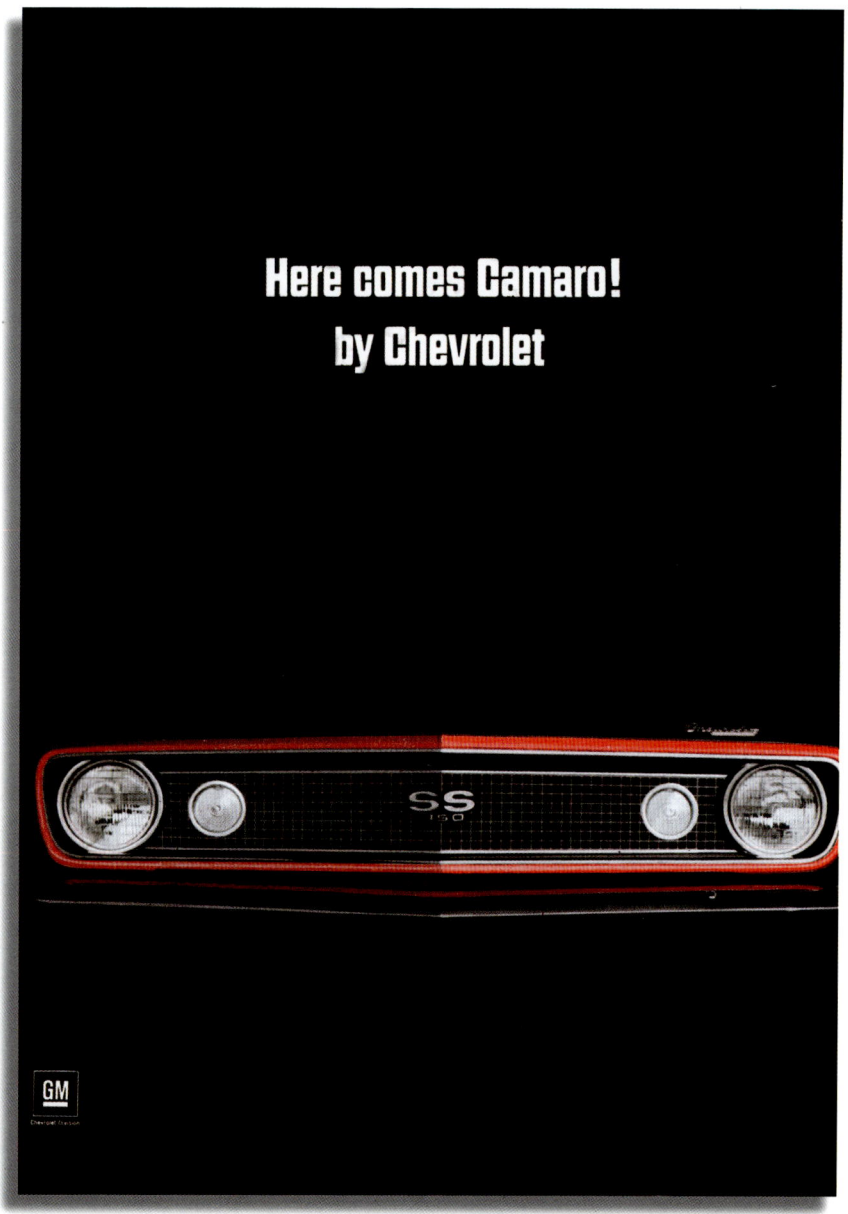

The 1968 RS and SS, at left, were compared together in this 1968 brochure.

Gen I: The Original Camaro (1967-68) 43

CHAPTER Four

In a Class of Its Own (1969)

The third Camaro was definitely in a class of its own. It was—and still is—a very distinctive car, which may explain why it is probably the most popular Camaro of all among collectors. No other Camaro has quite the same husky, ground-hugging look. No wonder they nicknamed the '69 "The Hugger."

With a beefed-up suspension, power disc brakes, dual exhausts, great looks and a big motor under the hood, the Z/28 was everything a muscle car fan could want in 1969.

Was there ever a better-looking Camaro than the wonderful '69 Z/28? Some fans would argue the model hit its styling peak in only its third year.

Single headlights, dark grille, "Camaro" script above the headlights and wide hood stripes were part of the 1969 Z/28 package.

This Z/28 carried a base 302.

Rally wheels were standard on the Z/28s of 1969.

In a Class of its Own (1969) 45

The awesome Super Yenko Camaros were sold through Don Yenko Chevrolet in Cannonsburg, Pennsylvania, in the late 1960s. The cars were equipped with a 427-cid/425 hp L72 engine. Production records are sketchy, so it's not clear how many were built and sold. Yenko company records say 201 '69s were sold, while Don Yenko himself said the figure was more like 500.

Three different Turbo-Fire 396 options were available on the 1969 Camaro SS. The L34 option was rated at 350 hp.

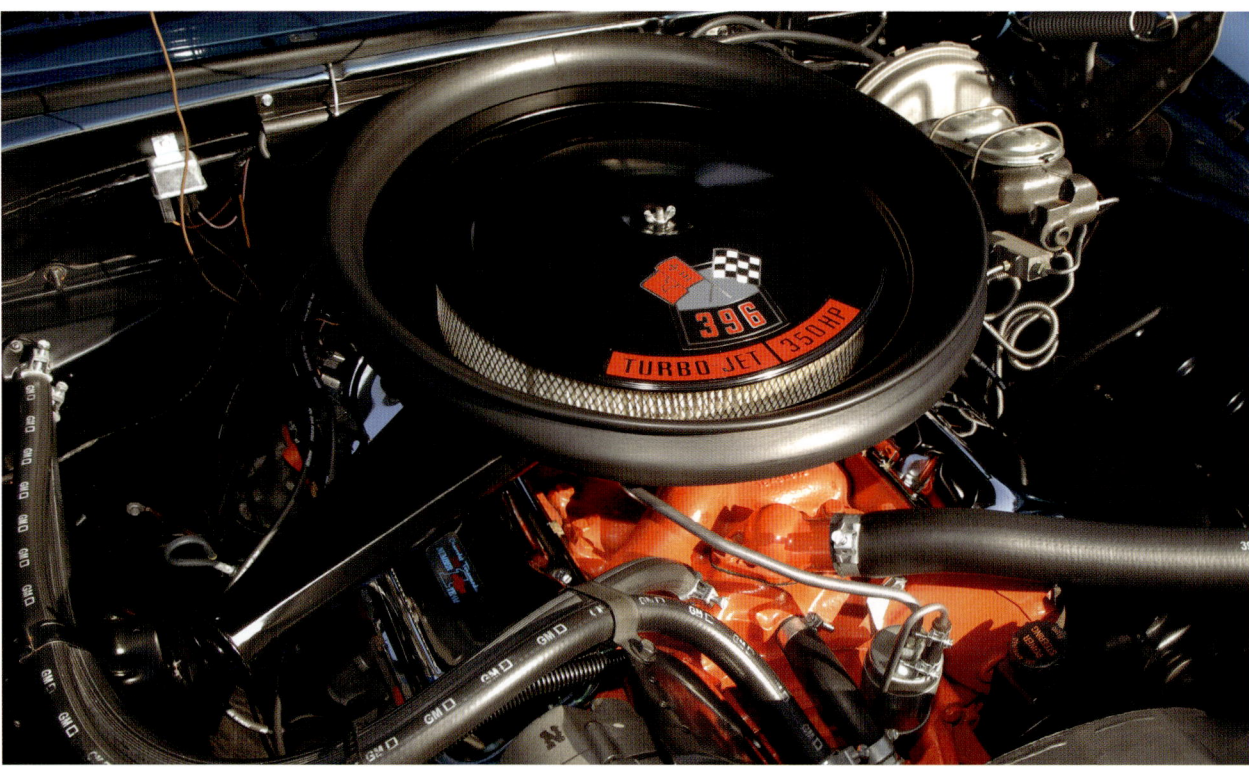

The new car arrived at a time when "The General" could do absolutely nothing wrong. GM was the "big kahuna" among the world's automakers and its biggest branch—Chevrolet—was really on the ball with its new "box car" '69 Camaro. It had squarer-looking lines than any F-car made before it or after it. This is what makes it stand out as a unique design and one of the most eye-catching Camaros ever built.

Although directly related to the first-generation '67-'68 Camaros, the '69's muscular-looking new sheet metal made the new car a killer as far as cosmetics went. The angular body had a longer, lower and wider look with flattened wheel housings and sculptured side panels. The header panel, the front valance, all four fenders, both doors, both rear quarter panels and the rear beauty panel were all completely redesigned to look lower, wider and more aggressive. The grille also had more angular contours and the tail lights were wider-than-ever-before units with three lenses in place of two. The back-up lights were moved from under the bumper into the center tail light lens.

The Camaro's underlying body structure and mechanical contents were virtually unchanged from the two previous

The base Camaro for '69 had the Chevy bowtie in the front grille. This Burgundy example carried the STD Turbo-Fire 327.

In a Class of its Own (1969)

The front fender badging on the SS models again signified the cubic inches under the hood.

The blacked-out grille became a symbol of the '69 SS Camaros.

models, but much was revised outside—as well as inside—the car. A redesigned dashboard and more passenger-friendly seats made Chevy's sports-personal compact easier to get comfortable in. A staggering array of extra-cost equipment aimed at the high-performance enthusiast set the '69 apart as the best of the '60s Camaros for the true automotive aficionado. If you wanted to go fast, without sliding off the road or burning up the binders—with the right options—this was the Camaro for you!

Styling details and equipment features varied according to which Camaro "model option" was ordered. The Rally Sport package included headlights hidden behind tri-slotted "grilles" and big "RS" letters in the center of the grille. The grille, of course, had a trendy blackout treatment. There was a variety of different body striping patterns, depending on whether you ordered your RS package as a stand-alone extra or teamed it up with other options. For instance, if the car also carried the Z/28 package, you got Z/28 striping in place of the standard RS striping. Numerous different combinations were possible according to the array of options. In fact, the minute variations can be confusing. For example, the body sills were finished in Black on most cars, but not on those painted Dusk Blue, Fathom Green, Burnished Brown or Burgundy.

The performance-oriented SS package featured a hood with a racing-car look thanks to its two rows of square, chrome-plated dummy intake ports. "Hockey-stick" body striping ran from just ahead of the door handles forward to the fender where the hockey stick's "paddle" extended down to about bottom-of-the-grille level. Naturally, there were fat tires and wheels to go with the Super Sport performance image. "SS" grille letters and body badges, a standard 350-cid/300-hp V-8 and other extras gave it a "hot" SS 350 identity. You could also tap into the engine options to build yourself an SS 396.

As mentioned, the RS and SS packages could be blended together to create an RS/SS-equipped model. With this combination, the grille read "SS," but you got the RS-type hidden headlights flanked by the tri-slotted headlight grilles and other RS features. Teaming the various options up was very common among buyers, and added a lot to Chevy's profits. Salesmen of the day were quite happy to help customers "personalize" their cars with as many extra-cost items as possible.

The base power plant was a six-cylinder engine—Chevrolet's traditional 230-cid/140-hp six-in-a-row job. One step up the ladder was a 250-cid/155-hp "big six" (which checkmated the Mustang's new-for-'69 250-cid/155-hp six). Only 15 percent of Camaro buyers were content to drive a

The Cortez Silver and black color combination gave a stunning look to the 1969 SS 396.

six-cylinder-powered car, but that represented nearly 36,500 sales and was nothing to sneeze at. With the '69's handsome lines, you didn't need a V-8 to make Ford fans envious.

The base V-8 started out as the same 327-cid/210-hp two-barrel-carburetor engine used in the two previous years, but a new 307-cid/200-hp small-block V-8 with a two-barrel carburetor was soon substituted. The 307 used a 327 crank in the old 283 block. Nearly 46 percent of all Camaros carried the base V-8, but there's no breakout of how many cars had the lower-output 327 and how many had the 307.

A new 255-hp two-barrel 350 replaced the hotter 275-hp/327 offered in '67-'68 and a higher-compression 350 with a four-barrel carburetor and 300 hp was standard (and exclusive) in the Camaro SS 350. Late in the year, a third 350 V-8 with a two-barrel carburetor and 250 hp was added to the options list.

In March 1969, *Motor Trend* published a road test of five pony cars and included the Camaro SS 350. They called the story "Five Card Stud." The Camaro tested was a sport coupe with both SS and RS equipment, including the 300-hp/350 engine. It had a base retail price of $3,153.50 and carried 18 options, including head restraints, air conditioning, an AM/FM push-button radio and mag-spoke wheel covers. The car had a four-speed Hurst shifter, which tester Bill Sanders saw as a positive change. A Muncie shifter had been used in '67-'68. Together, the options added $1,161 to the total showroom price of $4,314 (not counting dealer prep, tax, title and license). We'd say that was a little more in options than the average Camaro carried, but most still had a longer list of extras than most cars of the era.

In a Class of its Own (1969)

It wasn't always clear what "Hugger" meant, but Chevy liked the sound of it and the handle has stuck with the 1969 Camaros.

50   THE STORY OF CAMARO

1969 CAMARO BY THE NUMBERS

Year	Body Code	Body Type	Engine Type	W.B. (Inches)	O.L. (Inches)	Wt. (Lbs.)	HP (Gross)	Disp CID	MSP Price	Model Yr. Prod.
CAMARO SIX										
69	STD37	2HT	6	108.0	186.0	3,005	140	230	$2,621	See notes
69	STD67	2CV	6	108.0	186.0	3,255	140	230	$2,835	See notes
CAMARO V-8										
69	STD37	2HT	8	108.0	186.0	3,135	200	307	$2,727	See notes
69	STD67	2CV	8	108.0	186.0	3,385	200	307	$2,940	See notes
ALL CAMARO TOTAL										243,085

PRODUCTION NOTES

165,2267 base Camaro hardtops were built.
17,573 base Camaro convertibles were built.
37,773 cars had Rally Sport equipment.
36,309 cars had Super Sport equipment.
20,302 cars had the Z/28 option.
3,675 Indy Pace Car convertibles were built.
Approximately 200-300 cars had the Indy Sport Coupe option.
Numbers do not total 243,085 because some cars had multiple options.

More than 20,000 Z/28s rolled off assembly lines and onto U.S. highways in 1969.

Motor Trend's Sanders didn't exactly seem to be a Camaro fan, complaining in one photo caption that the factory custom wheel covers stuck out further than the tires. He said that the custom covers tended to get scraped and dented on curbs. Maybe that explains why a set costs so much today—or maybe it's just that they're great-looking hubcaps.

Sanders also noted the fact that the 350 V-8 was tightly packaged under the hood and hard to service. Maybe, but enthusiasts know that the small-block Chevy V-8 is one of the easiest engines to work on overall. As far as performance went, Sanders noted that the 350 was "almost as fast as the 396 we tested last year." It spun off a 0-to-60 blast in 8.3 seconds and ran a 15.9-second quarter-mile at 88 mph. Unfortunately, that was slower than the magazine registered for pair of FoMoCo competitors—the 351-powered Mustang and Cougar, as well as a Javelin SST 343.

As for track manners, Sanders was not impressed by the SS 350. "With lots of tire squeal from every low gear start, big wide tires, quick ratio steering and the special suspension that comes with the SS/RS package—we thought sure the Camaro was going to chew up all those mean corners on the race course," he said. "But it bit off more than it could chew. Handling response was quite unpredictable. It had a considerable amount of understeer, and when that rear end decided to leave the parade, there was no stopping it. It would go right on around like the last man in crack-the-whip."

The writer made a point of explaining that the SS 350's handling surprised him, because it did much better on the highway over the rugged mountain roads in the Angeles National Forest. "On that trip it took the curves flat, with only minor understeer," he acknowledged. "In fact, it was difficult to break the rear end loose, even when the steering wheel was jerked purposely."

Perhaps Sanders should have tested the Z/28 if he wanted a road course car. This race-oriented option for the Camaro was also back for the third year. The Z/28 package could be ordered only for sport coupes and only as long as they had power front disc brakes and a four-speed manual gearbox. A positraction rear axle was also a recommended Z/28 option.

The content of the early-in-the-year version of the package, priced at $458.15, included a dual exhaust system

The 1969 COPO Camaro dressed in black.

It was hard to find something wilder and faster on American roads in the late 1960s than a ZL1 Camaro.

with deep-tone mufflers, a heavy-duty front suspension, a special rear suspension, rear bumper guards, a heavy-duty radiator, a temperature-controlled de-clutching fan, quick-ratio steering, 15 x 7-in. Rally wheels, special E70-15 white-letter tires, a 3.73:1 rear axle and special Rally stripes on the hood and rear deck lid.

In October 1968, Chevrolet added bright engine accents along with two new options—a chambered exhaust system and four-wheel disc brakes. In January 1969, the chambered exhaust setup was discontinued after Chevy had problems meeting federal noise-level regulations with that system. Also, a tachometer became a required option. The package

The Super Yenko Camaro of 1969 was clocked at 114.5 mph in the quarter-mile.

1969 Engine Spec's

Engine	B x S	C.R.	CID	BHP
I6	3.875 x 3.25	8.50	230	140 @ 4400 *
V-8	3.87 x 3.25	9.00	307	200 @ 4600+

* Optional 250 CID, C.R. 8.50, BHP 155 @ 4200
+ Optional 350 CID, C.R. 9.00, BHP 255 @ 4800 up to 396 CID, C.R. 10.25, BHP 325 @ 4800.
Z/28 Coupe only: 302 CID, C.R. 11.00, BHP 290 @ 5800
COPO: 427 CID, C.R. 11.25, BHP 435 @ 5800
ZL1: 427 CID, C.R. 12.50, BHP 430 @ 5800

1969 Collector Pricing

	6	5	4	3	2	1
2d Spt Cpe	1,040	3,120	5,200	11,700	18,200	26,000
2d Conv	1,240	3,720	6,200	13,950	21,700	31,000
2d Z28	2,040	6,120	10,200	22,950	35,700	51,000
2d IPC	2,200	6,600	11,000	24,750	38,500	55,000
2d ZL-1*	5,200	15,600	26,000	58,500	91,000	130,000
2d Yenko	3,200	9,600	16,000	36,000	56,000	80,000

NOTE: Deduct 5 percent for Six, (when available). Add 10 percent for A/C. Add 10 percent for Rally Sport and 25 percent for SS-350 (except Indy Pace Car).

In a Class of its Own (1969)

price then rose by $15.80. On April 1, 1969, a front valance panel and rear spoiler became mandatory options and a $32.65 price increase was put into effect. In May, chrome exhaust tips were added to the list of standard features. In September 1969, the price went up another $15.80.

Powering all Z/28s was a special 302-cid Turbo-Fire V-8 that cranked up an amazing 290 hp at 5800 rpm. It had an 11.1:1 compression ratio, a Holley four-barrel carburetor and solid valve lifters. The Z/28 engine also featured new four-bolt main bearings with nodular iron caps, a high-rise aluminum intake manifold, a special 30/30 lash cam, aluminum impact-extruded pistons and a pair of large-port cylinder heads. This engine was designed to slide under the Sports Car Club of America's 5.0-liter limit so it could be used in Trans-Am competition. However, it delivered performance in the same neighborhood as a 350 V-8. Due to its high exposure on racetracks—especially as part of Roger Penske's "Sunoco" race team—the Z/28 drew a strong 20,302 orders.

As far as big-block options, there were no less than four versions of the 396-cid Turbo-Jet V-8 offered. All were optional in the Camaro SS, and all were not available in other models. The L35 version with 325 hp and the L34 version with 350 hp were both "cast iron" engines sharing such features as a 10.25:1 compression ratio and a single four-barrel carburetor. The L78 and L78/L89 versions both had 11.0:1 compression ratios, Holley four-barrel carbs, solid valve lifters and aluminum high-rise intakes. The L78/L89 also used aluminum heads. These engines were both rated for 375 hp. The L78/L89 went into just 311 cars, while 4,889 Camaros got the regular L78.

You could order Ram induction for the Camaro and two setups were sold. One used a big, long "power bubble" hood with the air inlet on the cowl end. On the bottom of this hood were soft rubber gaskets that sealed against the carburetor(s), creating a vacuum to suck in dense, cold air.

The dealer-installed cold-air kit offered the two previous years was also optional again. This system did not require a special hood. You got a different air cleaner and an adaptor that allowed a rubber sleeve to carry cold air from the firewall to the air cleaner.

In 1969, Chevy produced its second Camaro Indianapolis 500 Official Pace Car and offered replicas of the white RS/SS convertible with orange stripes and orange houndstooth upholstery to the public. It was the second time in three years that a Camaro served as the Official Pace Car for the classic race. Chevy had not sold pace car replicas to the public in 1967, but 1969 was a different story. Replicas were sold in both ragtop and hardtop versions.

The actual pace car was powered by a 396 connected to a Turbo Hydra-Matic transmission. Veteran green flagger Harlan Fengler led the racecars around the Brickyard on Memorial Day. Most of the replicas sold to the public had 350 V-8s. Experts say 3,675 of the Z11 Indy pace Car convertibles were made, along with a few hundred hardtops that featured a somewhat similar (and very rare) Z10 Indy Sport Coupe package. Both the Z11 and the Z10 are among the most desirable Camaros to own today.

Chevrolet introduced the "Hugger" nickname for the Camaro in 1968 and used it to promote the '69s. One advertisement showed a Frost Green SS coupe wearing a Hugger license plate. Chevy even had a Hugger Orange paint color for those who really wanted to turn heads.

Two batches of super-high-performance Camaros with 427-cid big-block V-8s were produced in extremely limited numbers under special Central Office Production Orders (COPO) No. 9560 and No. 9561. The factory COPO system had really been set up to allow dealers to order large fleets of cars with special equipment such as taxicabs, police squad cars and salesman cars. In 1968, a number of Chevrolet dealers that played to the performance market had started to shoehorn Chevrolet's biggest V-8 into the

A Camaro pickup? The 1969 Caribe Concept Car had a box instead of a trunk. Note the "roll bar" and funky dotted-line tires.

Camaro. They knew the 427 would fit fine, since the engine had the same external dimensions as the factory-installed 396 big-block.

Dealers like Fred Gibb, of Illinois, were doing quite a few big-block engine swaps into Camaros and found that it was expensive. Gibb talked to Chevrolet's performance guru Vince Piggins and discovered that he could utilize the COPO system to order a batch of 50 cars with factory-installed aluminum-block 427s. These Camaros were designated COPO 9560 ZL1s, and Gibbs planned to sell them as drag racing cars. By the time the order was finished, other dealers had ordered 19 additional cars. Because of their rarity, tremendous horsepower output and relatively low weight, the COPO 9560 Camaros are today considered the quickest and most valuable Camaros ever built.

There was also a plan to produce a batch of 100 COPO No. 9567 ZL-1 Camaros for street use. This "ZL-1 Special Camaro" (as GM paperwork called it) was dreamed up by Chevy engineer Vince Piggins. Its content was supposed to include Tuxedo Black paint with special gold striping, a de-tuned 427 with an 11.0:1 compression ratio and a list of other equipment. Piggins and his staff hand-built two prototypes—one four-speed and one THM—to show executives and to do some street racing.

Other cars made under COPO No. 9561 were basic Camaro sport coupes stuffed with 427 cubic inches of cast-iron big-block making 425 hp. Most of the 1,015 COPO 9561s built were delivered to Pennsylvania's Yenko Chevrolet for conversion into that dealership's SYC Camaro. SYC stood for "Yenko Sport Cars." The Yenko cars had special graphics to make them stand out.

By the end of 1969, Chevrolet racked up its third year in a row of climbing sales for Camaros. Model-year production peaked at 243,085 cars. The Camaro hadn't quite overtaken the Mustang in popularity, but it was getting closer to that goal each year. Sales of the 1969 models continued into the winter of 1969 and early 1970. Some of the late-year '69s may have been titled as 1970 models, leading to some confusion. The second-generation Camaro, introduced in 1970 1/2 is the only Camaro actually constructed as a 1970 model.

CHAPTER *Five*

Gen II: Bright New Beginnings (1970-1977)

Design-wise, the 1970 1/2 Camaro was a bright new beginning for Chevrolet's scrappy Mustang fighter. In terms of sales, however, things didn't look too rosy for the all-new Gen II model, which languished from mid-1970 until 1974. Like a young family dealing with kids, credit cards and consumer debt while struggling to find the road to success, the totally redesigned F-Car needed a few years to get traction. But, it did have those shiny chrome bumpers, front and rear, to help keep its outlook bright during the "dim" years.

The changes on the new 1970 Camaro Z28, and all its siblings for that matter, were easy to spot. The car was wider, more rounded and resembled a European sports car more than its predecessors.

A totally revamped grille was part of the Camaro's new look for 1970, and the unique split bumper became a desirable option. The split bumper was part of the RS package. You could get a Z28 with or without the split bumper.

The four circular tail lights were a clear departure from previous models.

Gen II: Bright New Beginnings (1970-1977) **57**

The Z/28 had a pair of optional Turbo-Fire 396 V-8s available to go with its standard 350.

If the Gen I Camaro was a "better mousetrap" alternative to the Mustang, the Gen II edition was the perfect expression of the art of automotive design. The cars of the first three years had their image and engineering dictated by Ford's pony car. They were essentially GM versions of the Mustang.

We know that GM's goal was to build a *better* Mustang, but that didn't mean the cars had to be *different* in character. From an automotive "architecture" standpoint, the early Mustang and the Gen I Camaro were really very similar. The Camaro was a good "clone job."

That was not the case with the '70 1/2 Camaro. If anything, it took its thematic influence from sleek and sophisticated European GT coupes, rather than the all-American roll-up-your-sleeves-and-kick-some-butt Mustang. The Mustang of the '70s still looked "Mustang," despite "Bunkie" Knudson's efforts to have Larry Shinoda change it. It was bigger, lower and rounder, but it had the same Mustang motifs. The Camaro of the '70s had a completely different image than its '60s counterparts, even though it was only modestly changed below its skin.

As Mike Lamm noted in *The Camaro Book*, "William

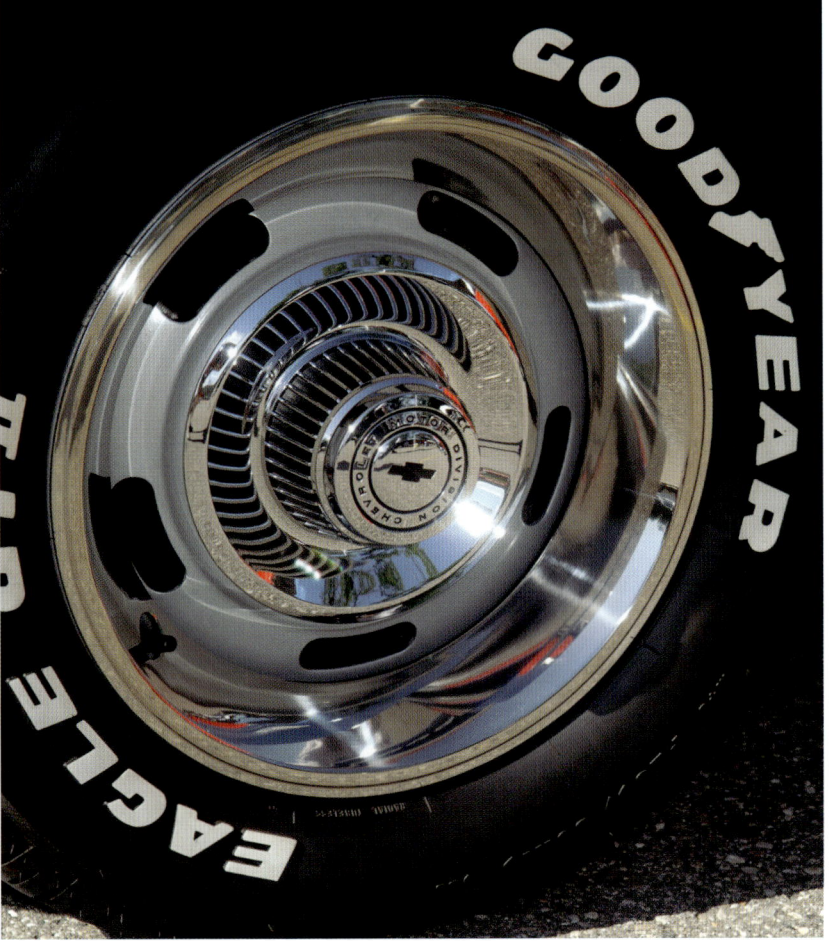

This is the base wheel on the 1970 Camaros. A wire wheel cover and Rally wheels were also available.

The RS and Z28 packages could again be combined for 1970. This car was painted Astro Blue.

L. Mitchell liked to say that the first-generation Camaro ended up being designed by committee, while the second became a designer's design. That statement might be an oversimplification, but it's basically accurate." Bill Mitchell was in charge of GM design when the Gen II Camaro and Firebird were at the "styling studio" stage.

Both new GM F-cars sat in the styling studios longer than expected. Chevrolet Studio Three had responsibility for the Camaro's design, and the all-new nature of the body created lots of "inter-office" problems. The product engineers asked for changes that would have changed the shape of the car to fit in carryover mechanical components. Mitchell told them "no way." If changes were going to be made, they were *not* going to be appearance changes made just to keep some engineer smiling. Mitchell wanted the styling to be "pure."

With the constant give and take between styling and engineering, the new Camaro—as well as the Firebird—didn't get done on time. Deadline after deadline fell by the wayside. It was February 1970 before the new GM F-cars hit the market. This put a damper on sales right from the beginning and made some higher-ups at GM wonder if the new Camaro wasn't just a big mistake.

Between the Camaro's winter 1970 introduction and 1974, things continued to look bleak. A combination of bungled GM marketing, a move away from muscle cars, government meddling and rising insurance rates on sporty cars left the Camaro spinning its wheels for almost three and a half years. At one point, the end of the nameplate seemed to be in sight. Then things turned around. The Gen II F-car became a GM hero and lasted 12 profitable years.

The styling of the Gen II F-cars certainly leaned towards that of the exotic coupes making headlines on the other side of the pond in the early '70s. America was on the verge of a period that was pretty much devoid of exciting domestic cars. The styling big shots at GM made all the European new-car shows, and there was lots happening over there. People say the Camaro's styling was inspired by the Ferrari, but the Firebird was often compared to the Maserati. Since both F-cars are clones, you could take your pick of muses, but the main message was that the "Euro" look was the hot ticket at GM.

The 1970 Camaros debuted with a body style that wouldn't change for 12 years.

1970 1/2

The 1970 1/2 Camaro was a bigger, heavier car and came only as a sport coupe. Dropping the convertible was a smart move, because it cut costs and was in line with the industry trend. Following the popularization of air conditioning and vinyl tops, you could get a coupe that was cool inside and looked like a ragtop. The passionless car buyers of the era were getting way too logical and could see no reason to put up with the hassles of a folding roof. The Mustang would offer a ragtop for several more years, but it sold poorly.

Mechanically, the Camaro was hardly as changed as it was in terms of outward image. The Gen II edition continued to share Nova underpinnings. That meant from the cowl back it was a unit-body car. The engine was mounted in line and cradled in a bolted-on front sub-frame. The sub-frame incorporated the A arms for the front suspension. Leaf springs were used at the rear. The steering gear was moved from behind the front axle to in front of it, but most other features were carryover items from the first three years of production.

Eight engines were offered—one six-cylinder and the rest V-8s. The 250-cid "big six" became the standard engine. It again carried a 155-hp rating. The base V-8 was the 307-cid/200-hp job with a two-barrel carburetor. The 350 was also offered with a two-barrel carburetor. This 250-hp V-8 took the place of the last 327. With the SS package the 350 got a four-barrel carburetor and 10.25:1 compression to reach 300 hp. Other options included a 360-hp version of the 350 with a four-barrel carburetor and an 11.0:1 compression ratio for the Z/28.

Camaro SS buyers could add 350- or 375-hp versions of

60 THE STORY OF CAMARO

The fat deck lid stripes remained on the 1970 Z28s, but almost everything else was new.

1970 CAMARO BY THE NUMBERS

Year	Body Code	Body Type	Engine Type	W.B. (Inches)	O.L. (Inches)	Wt. (Lbs.)	HP (Gross)	Disp CID	MSP Price	Model Yr. Prod.
CAMARO SIX										
70	STD87	2HT	6	108.0	186.0	3,058	155	250	$2,749	See notes
CAMARO V-8										
70	STD87	2HT	8	108.0	186.0	3,172	200	307	$2,839	See notes
ALL CAMARO TOTAL										124,901

PRODUCTION NOTES
100,967 base Camaro hardtops were built.
27,136 cars had Rally Sport equipment.
15,201 cars had Super Sport equipment.
8,733 cars had the Z/28 option.
Numbers do not total 124,901 because some cars had multiple options.

Gen II: Bright New Beginnings (1970-1977)

Sports Car Club of America (SCCA) racing rules changed in 1970, and as a result the Z28 received a new 350-cid standard power plant to replace the 302 from previous years.

the 396-cid V-8. The actual displacement of this engine was 402 cid, but it was promoted as the "396." The first version, called the L-34, used an 11.0:1 compression ratio, while the hotter L-78 had 11.0:1 compression. Both carried different single four-barrel carburetors, a Rochester on the L-34 and a Holley on the L-78. The L-78 had mechanical valve lifters, permitting higher-rpm operation.

Chevy continued to sell the Camaro with Rally Sport or Super Sport equipment separately or combined. A full-width one-piece blade-style bumper was standard. The RS featured a unique front-end appearance with a small, thin front bumperette on either side of a snout-like grille cavity. The grille sported a bright metal inner surround and crosshatched vertical and horizontal bars. The entire ensemble was surrounded by dent-resistant Endura rubber. The SS again had a beefier suspension and "SS" logos in various places.

The flagship of the Camaro line was again the Z/28, now powered by the 360-hp LT-1 version of the 350. Unlike the race-bred 302 used in the '67-'69 Z/28s, the LT-1 was a smooth-running "street-performance" engine equally capable of trips to the Seven-Eleven or the dragstrip. With this motor, the Camaro could be fitted with Turbo-Hydra-Matic transmission, as well as a stick shift.

Car and Driver tested the '70 and zipped to 60 mph in 5.8 seconds. The quarter-mile took 14.2 seconds at a brisk 100.3 mph. The magazine noted it had less bottom-end power than the earlier Z/28s.

1970 Engine Spec's

Engine	B x S	C.R.	CID	BHP
I6	3.875 x 3.53	8.50	250	155 @ 4200
V-8	3.87 x 3.25	8.50	307	200 @ 4600+

+ Optional 350 CID, C.R. 9.00, BHP 250 @ 4800 up to 402 CID, C.R. 10.25, BHP 350 @ 5200.
Z/28 only: 350 CID, C.R. 11.00, BHP 360 @ 6000

1970 Collector Pricing

	6	5	4	3	2	1
2d Cpe	760	2,280	3,800	8,550	13,300	19,000
2d Z28	920	2,760	4,600	10,350	16,100	23,000

NOTE: Deduct 5 percent for Six. Add 35 percent for the 375 hp 396, (L78 option). Add 35 percent for Rally Sport and/or Super Sport options.

Interior styling on the Z28s was radically different in 1970. The new two-spoke steering wheels was joined by all new gauges and updated styling in this Z28 with the RS package.

GM designers were clearly going in a new direction with the 1970 Camaro, with curvy styling that wasn't a huge hit initially.

The funky Rally Sport split bumper will forever be associated with the all-new second-generation Camaro that debuted in 1970.

1971

The '71 Camaro got Vega bucket seats with high-back styling, a three-piece Z/28 spoiler and not a lot more. With Uncle Sam tightening the noose on polluters, GM lowered compression ratios across the board. GM adopted net horsepower ratings, though both the gross power ratings and lower net ratings were put in sales literature. For the base six, the numbers were 145 gross (ghp) and 110 net (nhp); for the Z/28's LT-1 they were 330 ghp and 275 nhp.

Despite the minimal changes, prices jumped about $400, which was big bucks in an era when a lot of people earned about that for working a week. A total of five V-8 engines were offered, including just one big-block option (the 402-cid 300-hp LS3) for the Camaro SS.

Model-year production came to 114,643. That seemed bad compared to 149,678 Mustangs, but things would get worse.

The Z/28 got a few tweaks for 1971, but Chevy execs didn't want to mess too much with a good thing.

The base 1971 sport coupe was a beautiful car in its own right, and came with either a standard inline six or an optional 350-cid V-8.

1971 CAMARO BY THE NUMBERS

Year	Body Code	Body Type	Engine Type	W.B. (Inches)	O.L. (Inches)	Wt. (Lbs.)	HP (Gross)	Disp CID	MSP Price	Model Yr. Prod.
CAMARO SIX										
71	STD87	2HT	6	108.0	188.0	3,016	145	250	$2,758	See notes
CAMARO V-8										
71	STD87	2HT	8	108.0	188.0	3,218	200	307	$2,848	See notes
ALL CAMARO TOTAL										114,630

PRODUCTION NOTES
91,481 base Camaro hardtops were built.
18,404 cars had Rally Sport equipment.
18,287 cars had Super Sport equipment.
4,862 cars had the Z/28 option.
Numbers do not total 114,630 because some cars had multiple options.

1971 Engine Spec's

Engine	B x S	C.R.	CID	BHP
I6	3.875 x 3.53	8.50	250	145 @ 4200
V-8	3.87 x 3.25	8.50	307	200 @ 4600 +

+ Optional 350 CID, C.R. 8.50, BHP 245 @ 4800 up to 402 CID, C.R. 8.50, BHP 300 @ 4800.
Z/28 only: 350 CID, C.R. 9.00, BHP 330 @ 4000.

1971 Collector Pricing

	6	5	4	3	2	1
2d Cpe	760	2,280	3,800	8,550	13,300	19,000
2d Z28	920	2,760	4,600	10,350	16,100	23,000

NOTE: Subtract 5 percent for Six. Add 35 percent for Rally Sport and/or Super Sport options. Add 25 percent for 402 ("396") engine option.

The Z/28 remained largely unchanged for 1972, still retaining the new rounded look of the '71s and familiar wide stripes and deck lid spoiler.

1972

The '72 Camaro was promoted as "the closest thing to a Vette yet!" The problem with that was that car magazines of the day were printing stories about the Pontiac Trans Am being faster than the '72 Vette. So, Chevy's hyperbole didn't exactly ring true with the public and the Camaro's model-year production dropped off by more than 50 percent—to just 68,651 units.

Changes in the '72 model were mostly under the hood. Chevy continued offering a six and five V-8s, all rated with lower net horsepower numbers. Even the hot LT-1 could now muster just 255 nhp. The only big-block was the 402-cid LS3 V-8 (still called a "396"), which churned up all of 240 nhp. An anemic 110 nhp was again the rating for the 250-cid inline six-cylinder engine.

Government regulations and rising insurance rates were making it very hard to own a performance car and the Camaro was losing much of its market appeal. Contributing to the Camaro's drop in factory output was a United Auto Workers strike that lasted from mid-September to November 22. In all, labor disputes shut down production at the Ohio factory for a total of 117 days. Due to changing federal regulations, cars left on the assembly line at the start of the strike could not be legally sold by the time it had ended. Neither could they be updated to satisfy the new rules. As a result of the strike, more than 1,000 Camaros and Firebirds were simply scrapped. (No, we don't know the name of the junkyard they dragged them to!)

This travesty gave the bigshots at GM a severe case of aggitta and left them ready to swing the axe at the Camaro and Firebird. Co-existing with the bean counters in each of the GM branches were a bunch of guys who had poured their hearts and souls into creating the F-cars. These guys worked through their lunch hours, took work home at night (often to Woodward Avenue) and dragged Camaros and Firebirds out to racetracks on weekends. They lobbied long and hard to keep the cars breathing. In the end they won the battle by pooling their talents and finding cheaper ways to get the cars federally certified. But '72 was a low point.

The white interior was a rare choice on Z/28s.

1972 CAMARO BY THE NUMBERS

Year	Body Code	Body Type	Engine Type	W.B. (Inches)	O.L. (Inches)	Wt. (Lbs.)	HP (Gross)	Disp CID	MSP Price	Model Yr. Prod.
CAMARO SIX										
72	STD87	2HT	6	108.0	188.0	3,121	145	250	$2,730	See notes
CAMARO V-8										
72	STD87	2HT	8	108.0	188.0	3,248	200	307	$2,820	See notes
ALL CAMARO TOTAL										68,651

PRODUCTION NOTES
58,544 base Camaro hardtops were built.
11,364 cars had Rally Sport equipment.
7,532 cars had Super Sport equipment.
2,575 cars had the Z/28 option.
Numbers do not total 68,651 because some cars had multiple options.

1972 Engine Spec's

Engine	B x S	C.R.	CID	BHP
I6	3.875 x 3.53	8.50	250	110 @ 3800
V-8	3.87 x 3.25	8.50	307	130 @ 4000 +

+ Optional 350 CID, C.R. 8.50, NHP 165 @ 4000 up to 402 CID, C.R. 8.50, NHP 240 @ 4400.
Z/28 only: 350 CID, C.R. 9.00, NHP 255 @ 5600

1972 Collector Pricing

	6	5	4	3	2	1
2d Cpe	760	2,280	3,800	8,550	13,300	19,000
2d Z28	920	2,760	4,600	10,350	16,100	23,000

NOTE: Subtract 5 percent for Six. Add 35 percent for Rally Sport and/or Super Sport options.

The vinyl roof cover was an $87 option in 1973.

The Luxury Touring "LT" model was a new offering from Chevy in 1973. It was a separate model, rather than an option package, and featured a host of trim changes and styling cues that separated it from its siblings. The Type LT was available with the one-piece bumper or the RS-type two-piece bumper.

1973

September 21, 1972 brought the introduction of the '73 Camaros. All models had new impact-resistant front bumpers. Chevy claimed that they were "substantially improved in roadability, comfort and styling. Fifteen new exterior colors were offered, along with seven new vinyl roof covers. A Space-Saver spare tire was one added option.

The horsepower decline continued, with the base inline six pushing out a mere 100 nhp. The optional L82 served up only 245 nhp. Big-block V-8s were off the option sheet altogether. Only 26 percent of Camaros now carried factory dual exhaust.

Instead of offering the hot SS package, Chevy merchandised a new Type LT Camaro for the luxury-car set. Its content was comprised of several luxury options "bundled" into one everything-included package. Hide-A-Way windshield wipers, rocker panel accents and Rally wheel rims were standard.

Gen II: Bright New Beginnings (1970-1977)

The familiar Rally Sport split front bumper was still featured on so-equipped 1973 Camaros.

Horsepower fell to 245 on the 1973 Z/28, but that was still respectable as the muscle car era was winding down.

Model-year production at the Lordstown, Ohio, factory was 96,752 and included 3,614 sixes and 93,138 V-8s. This was a dramatic increase over strike-plagued 1972. Over 51 percent had air conditioning and more than 32 percent had a vinyl roof, but only 11 percent had a four-speed manual gearbox.

Camaro buyers were definitely getting more interested in "fancy" than "fast."

1973 CAMARO BY THE NUMBERS

Year	Body Code	Body Type	Engine Type	W.B. (Inches)	O.L. (Inches)	Wt. (Lbs.)	HP (Net)	Disp CID	MSP Price	Model Yr. Prod.
CAMARO SIX										
73	STD87	2HT	6	108.0	188.5	3,119	100	250	$2,781	See notes
CAMARO V-8										
73	STD87	2HT	8	108.0	188.5	3,238	115	307	$2,872	See notes
ALL CAMARO TOTAL										96,752

PRODUCTION NOTES
52,850 base Camaro hardtops were built.
32,327 Type LT Camaros were built.
16,133 cars had Rally Sport equipment.
11,574 cars had the Z/28 option.
Numbers do not total 96,751 because some cars had multiple options.

1973 Engine Spec's

Engine	B x S	C.R.	CID	BHP
I6	3.875 x 3.53	8.25	250	100 @ 3600
V-8	4.00 x 3.480	8.50	350	145 @ 4000 +

+ Optional 350 CID, C.R. 8.50, NHP 145 @ 3600 and 350 CID, C.R. 8.50, NHP 175 @ 4400.
Z/28 only: 350 CID, C.R. 9.00, NHP 245 @ 5200

1973 Collector Pricing

	6	5	4	3	2	1
2d Cpe	760	2,280	3,800	8,550	13,300	19,000
2d Z28	920	2,760	4,600	10,350	16,100	23,000

NOTE: Subtract 5 percent for Six. Add 35 percent for Rally Sport and/or Super Sport options.

The Z28 was back for another year in 1974, but the following year it went on temporary hiatus from the Camaro lineup.

1974

With fresh front and rear styling—designed to meet new federal bumper regulations—the '74 Camaro was redesigned with thick extruded-aluminum bumpers front and rear. There was only one shovel-nose grille with a lattice work insert and no RS option was available. The rear tail lights now wrapped into the fenders and doubled as side marker lights. Kelsey-Hayes wheel spiders made of high strength-low alloy steel was a '74 Camaro innovation. These wheels were 10 percent lighter than conventional styles.

But the government's meddling into the car industry was not entirely without its comic relief. One new seat belt-interlock regulation was designed to keep the car from starting unless the operator's seat belt was on. Driver's of

Either the base sport coupe or Type LT could be turned into a Z28. The LT featured, among other things, an emblem in the center of the grille.

the day were a lot less willing to accept "Big Brotherism" and wrote their congressmen so many letters on this one that the regulation was cancelled by year's end. The EPA also admitted that the newly reguired, first-generation catalytic converter was a "potential polluter."

Chevrolet promoted sales of economy axle ratios and fuel-ecoomy gauges, but neither option sold very well, especially after the first Arab oil embargo was lifted on March 1, 1974. The '74 Camaro started to gain in sales, however, as the Mustang transitioned into the smaller, more economical Mustang II. Ford's smaller new Mustang had less to offer enthusiasts who were still interested in sporty performance. In fact, the only domestic cars remaining for such buyers were the Corvette, Camaro and Firebird. Of the three, the Camaro was the high-volume model.

The Camaro's standard V-8 was a 350-cid/145-nhp job with a two-barrel carburetor that replaced last year's 307. The 350 came in three four-barrel versions: the LM1 with 160 nhp, the L48 with 185 nhp and the 245-hp Z28-only engine.

According to *Car and Driver*, the Z28 could do 0 to 60 mph in 6.7 seconds and or a 15.2-second quarter-mile at 94.6 mph. That was about as good as it got in the high-performance bracket in the middle '70s.

1974 CAMARO BY THE NUMBERS

Year	Body Code	Body Type	Engine Type	W.B. (Inches)	O.L. (Inches)	Wt. (Lbs.)	HP (Net)	Disp CID	MSP Price	Model Yr. Prod.
CAMARO SIX										
74	STD87	2HT	6	108.0	195.4	3,119	100	250	$2,828	See notes
CAMARO V-8										
74	STD87	2HT	8	108.0	195.4	3,238	145	350	$3,040	See notes
ALL CAMARO TOTAL										151,008

PRODUCTION NOTES
88,243 base Camaro hardtops were built.
48.963 Type LT Camaros were built.
13,802 cars had the Z/28 option.
Numbers do not total 151,008 because some cars had multiple options.

This original, unrestored survivor provides a good look at a vintage '74 Z28 interior, complete with a manual four-speed and an 8-track player. The steering wheel cover is not a factory item.

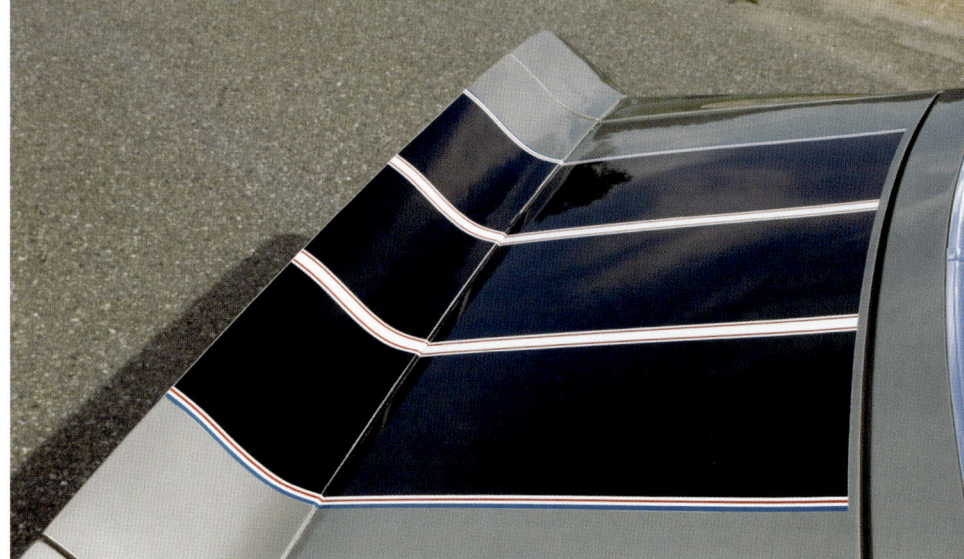

The D80 spoiler and deck striping package was a popular option on the 1974 Z28.

The sloping front grille and recessed headlights were among the biggest changes to the 1974 Camaros.

1974 Engine Spec's

Engine	B x S	C.R.	CID	BHP
I6	3.875 x 3.53	8.25	250	100 @ 3600
V-8	4.00 x 3.480	8.50	350	145 @ 3800 +

+ Optional 350 CID, C.R. 8.50, NHP 160 @ 3800 and 350 CID, C.R. 8.50, NHP 185 @ 4000.
Z/28 only: 350 CID, C.R. 9.00, NHP 245 @ 5200

1974 Collector Pricing

	6	5	4	3	2	1
2d Cpe	740	2,220	3,700	8,330	12,950	18,500
2d LT Cpe	760	2,280	3,800	8,550	13,300	19,000

NOTE: Subtract 5 percent for Six. Add 10 percent for Z28 option.

The Z28's Rally wheels were color keyed to match the body paint.

1975

The sporty Camaro had an even sportier appearance. A new "wraparound" rear window extended down into the roof sail panels, widening the driver's field of vision to the rear. Also new for '75 were more luxurious appointments and a new sport décor package. The Rally Sport package consisted of two-tone paint and some tape stripes.

With utter disregard for enthusiasts, Chevy killed the Camaro Z28 and pared the engine selection down to just three catalyst-choked "boat anchors"—the 250-cid/105-nhp six, the L65 350 with a two-barrel carb and 145 nhp, and the LM1 350 with a four-barrel carb and 155 nhp. A new technical touch was a High Energy Ignition (HEI) system, which was part of a GM Efficiency System that also included the catalytic converter.

By this time Camaro model-year assemblies were up to 145,770 units, of which 29,749 were sixes and 116,021 were V-8s. All were produced at the Lordstown facility. Model-year sales by U.S. dealers stood at 135,102, consistent with the 135,780 of 1974.

The big-collar, leisure suit-wearing 1975 Camaro customers had a long list of options to pick from, including power windows and locks, hidden windshield wipers and leather interior. The nice styling, however, couldn't hide the fact that the horsepower ratings had fallen to 155 for the Z28 and a paltry 105 for the base inline six-cylinder.

1975 CAMARO BY THE NUMBERS

Year	Body Code	Body Type	Engine Type	W.B. (Inches)	O.L. (Inches)	Wt. (Lbs.)	HP (Net)	Disp CID	MSP Price	Model Yr. Prod.
CAMARO SIX										
75	STD87	2HT	6	108.0	195.4	3,421	105	250	$3,553	See notes
CAMARO V-8										
75	STD87	2HT	8	108.0	195.4	3,532	145	350	$3,698	See notes
ALL CAMARO TOTAL										145,770

PRODUCTION NOTES
105,927 base Camaro hardtops were built.
7,000 Camaros had the new Rally Sport package
39,843 Type LT Rally Sport Camaros were built.
Numbers do not total 145,770 because some cars had multiple options.

Gen II: Bright New Beginnings (1970-1977)

The Type LT Camaro was marketed as a more upscale sport coupe in 1975.

1975 Engine Spec's

Engine	B x S	C.R.	CID	BHP
I6	3.875 x 3.53	8.25	250	105 @ 3800
V-8	4.00 x 3.480	8.50	350	145 @ 3800 +

+ Optional 350 CID, C.R. 8.50, NHP 155 @ 3800.

1975 Collector Pricing

	6	5	4	3	2	1
Cpe	680	2,040	3,400	7,650	11,900	17,000
Type LT	720	2,160	3,600	8,100	12,600	18,000

NOTE: Subtract 5 percent for Six. Add 30 percent for Camaro R/S.

The Lime Green Metallic paint option on this '76 Type LT was pure 1970s.

In its 10th year of existence, the Camaro was still a hit with the buying public, and more than 186,000 of the cars were produced.

The Type LT Rally Sport could be had with a hard-to-miss Bright Yellow and black paint scheme. The tri-color striping and matching rims only added to the high-visibility package.

1976

After the Mustang changed into the Mustang II, the Camaro and Firebird had the pony car niche more or less to themselves. The F cars were also much smaller than full-sized cars of the era, so some buyers actually bought them to try to get better gas mileage. Though they may have been disappointed with the cars' economy in the long run, such buyers also helped to generate a substantial sales increase over the early '70s numbers. The Mustang still outsold the Camaro, but that would soon change.

Gen II: Bright New Beginnings (1970-1977)

There were few changes to the '76 model, but a new spear-type molding seemed like a major styling move. An aluminum panel between the tail lights was now used on the Type LT.

Vacuum power brakes were now standard on Camaros with a V-8. An improved brake lining system and larger rear wheel cylinders were also adopted. Cruise control was a new option.

The standard engine in LT coupe and sport coupe models was now a 305-cid V-8. A 350 with a four-barrel carburetor was optional.

This was a good year for the Camaro. Its model-year number production rose to 182,959 units, of which 38,047 had six-cylinder power. While the bulk of production continued at the Lordstown factory, the Camaro's soaring popularity required Chevrolet to add manufacturing capacity and 41,280 Camaros were built in Van Nuys, California.

The shovel-nose Camaro was on a roll.

1976 CAMARO BY THE NUMBERS

Year	Body Code	Body Type	Engine Type	W.B. (Inches)	O.L. (Inches)	Wt. (Lbs.)	HP (Net)	Disp CID	MSP Price	Model Yr. Prod.
CAMARO SIX										
76	STD87	2HT	6	108.0	195.4	3,421	105	250	$3,762	See notes
CAMARO V-8										
76	STD87	2HT	8	108.0	195.4	3,511	140	350	$3,927	See notes
ALL CAMARO TOTAL										182,959

PRODUCTION NOTES
130,538 base Camaro hardtops were built.
15,855 Canaros had the Rally Sport package
52,421 Type LT Rally Sport Camaros were built.
Numbers do not total 182,959 because some cars had multiple options.

1976 Engine Spec's

Engine	B x S	C.R.	CID	BHP
I6	3.875 x 3.53	8.25	250	105 @ 3800
V-8	3.736 x 3.480	8.50	305	140 @ 3800 +

+ Optional 350 CID, C.R. 8.50, NHP 165 @ 3800.

1976 Collector Pricing

	6	5	4	3	2	1
2d Cpe	640	1,920	3,200	7,200	11,200	16,000
2d Cpe LT	680	2,040	3,400	7,650	11,900	17,000

NOTE: Subtract 5 percent for Six. Add 30 percent for RS.

1977

The '77 Camaro continued virtually unchanged. The 250-cid inline six was the standard power plant in the base sport coupe and the Type LT sport coupe. Intermittent windshield wipers were a new feature. A new puffed-texture vinyl and knit-cloth combo was used in the Type LT. Interior refinements included a new style of cloth upholstery in base models.

For '77, Camaro engine options included 305- and 350-cid V-8s with three- ands four-speed manual transmissions and three-speed automatic transmissions. A lower 2.56:1 axle ratio was used in cars with V-8 engines and automatic transmission to improve fuel economy. A 2.73:1 rear had been used previously.

After a two-year absence from the lineup, the performance-oriented Z28 model was reintroduced at the Chicago Auto Show in the middle of the year. Its standard equipment included a special 350-cid/185-nhp V-8, 15 x 7-in. mag-type wheels and special wide-profile radial tires.

Chevrolet closed the '77 model year with an eight percent sales gain over '76 and the Camaro played a role in the success. It was the first time in history that more Camaros (218,854) were built than Mustangs (153,173).

The Type LT was again a fancied-up Camaro that filled a niche in the market. More than 72,000 LTs were built for 1977.

The Z28 package for 1977 included a special tri-color hood design, striping around the wheel openings and front fender decals.

The 1977 Z28 was available in seven different body colors, including white with a white interior.

1977 CAMARO BY THE NUMBERS

Year	Body Code	Body Type	Engine Type	W.B. (Inches)	O.L. (Inches)	Wt. (Lbs.)	HP (Net)	Disp CID	MSP Price	Model Yr. Prod.
CAMARO SIX										
77	STD87	2HT	6	108.0	195.4	3,369	110	250	$4,113	See notes
CAMARO V-8										
77	STD87	2HT	8	108.0	195.4	3,476	145	305	$4,223	See notes
ALL CAMARO TOTAL										218,853

PRODUCTION NOTES
131,717 base Camaro hardtops were built.
17,026 Canaros had the Rally Sport package
72,787 Type LT Rally Sport Camaros were built.
Numbers do not total 218,853 because some cars had multiple options.

1977 Engine Spec's

Engine	B x S	C.R.	CID	BHP
I6	3.875 x 3.53	8.25	250	110 @ 3800
V-8	3.736 x 3.480	8.50	305	145 @ 3800 +

+ Optional 350 CID, C.R. 8.20, NHP 170 @ 3800 and 350 CID, C.R. 8.20, NHP 185 @ 4000.

1977 Collector Pricing

	6	5	4	3	2	1
2d Spt Cpe	520	1,560	2,600	5,850	9,100	13,000
2d Spt Cpe LT	540	1,620	2,700	6,080	9,450	13,500
2d Spt Cpe Z28	640	1,920	3,200	7,200	11,200	16,000

Gen II: Bright New Beginnings (1970-1977)

CHAPTER Six

Gen II Soft Nose (1978-1981)

A new front end design, introduced in 1978, cast the Camaro image for the final years of the Gen II models. On these cars the front end was made of a cushiony, resilient plastic that was finished in the same color as the body of the car. Enthusiasts called it the "Soft Nose" look and the last four years of the second generation became the Soft Nose era. Other new features of these cars included a plastic-wrapped body-colored rear bumper and new tail lights that wrapped around the corners of the body to function as safety side markers.

The great-looking 1978 Z28s proved popular with the buying public and continued to make up for in style and driver comforts what it lacked in horsepower compared to previous editions in the late 1960s and early '70s. This example is wearing aftermarket rims.

This same basic Soft Nose appearance characterized all Camaros until a new Gen III style arrived in the middle of 1982. There was some shuffling of different models and all-in-one packages during this time period. In addition, a major revision in power train offerings came on stream in 1980, when a V-6 engine replaced the traditional straight six in the standard Camaro. A smaller 4.4-liter (267-cid) base V-8 was also introduced to provide better fuel economy.

While some people blamed product changes for a continued tapering off of the Camaro's sales after 1978, other factors were also at play. "Old age" was probably the main cause of falling Camaro sales. The Gen II car lasted

The 1978 Z28s got new pointed hood scoop designs.

The new wraparound tail lights became a Camaro trademark, replacing the previous round lights.

The fender louvers were slanted and functional in 1978.

for more than a dozen years. It more than made up for its feeble launch during the 1974-76 period, when specialty compacts came on very strong and held a 9.5-percent market share. Sales were purring along and profit margins were high because there were barely any product updates. The continued selling of the same basic car for so many years helped GM keep tooling costs low.

As the old adage says, "all good things must come to an end" and the Gen II Camaro's success eventually started to wane. The car itself was a fine machine—good looking and easy to drive—but it was big, big-engined and thirsty. After 1977, market segmentation took on new significance in the American automobile sales race. With gas prices on the rise, "downsizing" became a buzzword among new car buyers. The Camaro and other "compact specialty" models suffered as a shift to smaller, more economical cars took place. Camaro-type cars went from an 8-percent market share in 1978 to 3.1 percent in 1981.

The downtrend in compact specialty car sales was irreversible and there was no chance of saving the classic Gen II Camaro from extinction after 1979. A totally new car, blending sportiness with higher efficiency, was what Chevy really needed. The new car had to offer up-to-date high-tech performance for those willing to spend to go faster.

Chevy needed an F-car with guts, but one that wasn't a gas guzzler. It arrived in mid-1982 when the Gen III model bowed. We'll get to Gen III soon, but the late Gen II's deserve a closer look.

1978

By 1978, the eight-year-old Camaro and its Firebird cousin were starting to compete for sales with modern "sporty" cars like the Ford Granada, Mercury Monarch and AMC Eagle. GM had not given the Camaro a major updating because it had been selling extremely well. That was soon going to change, but, in 1978, the market hadn't yet shifted towards smaller, lighter, more fuel-efficient cars. Its new body-colored "soft-nose" front-end design was a noticeable change, although it did not alter the basic character of the car.

The new body-colored soft nose was part of the Camaro's new look.

Percent of U.S. Sales For All Compact Specialty Cars 1978-1981

	Jan.	Feb.	Mar.	Apr.	May	Jun.	Jul.	Aug.	Sept.	Oct.	Nov.	Dec.	Avg.
1978	8.8	8.8	8.9	8.6	8.0	8.1	7.9	7.6	6.6	6.9	8.3	8.1	8.0
1979	7.5	8.0	7.7	7.2	7.5	6.7	5.9	5.3	5.7	6.4	6.9	5.9	6.8
1980	5.6	4.8	4.6	5.3	5.7	6.2	5.6	5.5	5.3	2.8	3.0	3.0	4.8
1981	3.1	3.4	3.7	3.5	3.8	3.2	3.4	3.2	2.6	1.9	1.9	2.2	3.1

Note: Cars in this segment included the Camaro, Firebird, Granada, Monarch and Eagle.

They wouldn't win many races against real muscle cars, but the 1978 Z28s were all dressed up and certainly had the flash, if not the dash.

1978 CAMARO BY THE NUMBERS

Year	Body Code	Body Type	Engine Type	W.B. (Inches)	O.L. (Inches)	Wt. (Lbs.)	HP (Net)	Disp CID	MSP Price	Model Yr. Prod.
CAMARO SIX										
78	STD87	2HT	6	108.0	197.6	3,300	110	250	$4,414	See notes
CAMARO V-8										
78	STD87	2HT	8	108.0	197.6	3,425	145	305	$4,599	See notes
ALL CAMARO TOTAL										272,631

PRODUCTION NOTES
134,491 base Camaro hardtops without the RS option were built.
11,902 base Camaro hardtops with the RS option were built.
65,635 Camaro Type LT models without the RS option were built.
5,696 Camaro Type LT models with the RS option were built.
54,907 Camaro Z28 models were built.

Factory literature for '78 highlighted "Camaro efficiency . . . and other standards." Fuel economy was becoming a major factor in U.S. automobile sales—cars that went further on a gallon of gas were in demand by buyers. An engine data sheet inserted in the catalog showed buyers the estimated EPA mileage ratings of all Camaros. The six was promoted as the engine that "delivers the balance of performance and economy you need for today's kind of driving." Other features that the sales catalog pushed were the HEI (High-Energy Ignition) system, the carburetor outside air intake system, the use of a catalytic converter and the use of radial-ply tires with less rolling resistance.

Model offerings remained at one body style that came in five flavors: sport coupe, Rally Sport, Type LT, Type LT Rally Sport and Z28. The inline 250-cid (or "4.1-liter" if you preferred the newer and more contemporary displacement description) six was in its next-to-last year and got a new aluminum intake manifold that reduced its weight. Other power options were based on the 305-cid (5.0-liter) V-8 and the 350-cid (5.7-liter) V-8.

Chevy knew the Gen II Camaro, though slightly dated, was still one of the best-looking cars on the market. A photo of the base sport coupe in the sales catalog stressed its "exciting, youthful image" and its "exciting, sporty, streamlined appearance." It retained a cockpit-type interior with seating for four adults. No wonder used Camaros of the day maintained a high resale value.

The Z28 remained a popular model in 1978 with almost 55,000 cars produced.

1978 Engine Spec's

Engine	B x S	C.R.	CID	BHP
I6	3.875 x 3.53	8.10	250	110 @ 3800
V-8	3.736 x 3.480	8.40	305	145 @ 3800 +

+ Optional 350 CID, C.R. 8.20, NHP 170 @ 3800 and 350 CID, C.R. 8.20, NHP 185 @ 4000.

1978 Collector Pricing

	6	5	4	3	2	1
2d Cpe	240	720	1,200	2,700	4,200	6,000
2d LT Cpe	260	780	1,300	2,930	4,550	6,500
2d Z28 Cpe	360	1,080	1,800	4,050	6,300	9,000

NOTE: Subtract 5 percent for Six-cylinder.

Gen II Soft Nose (1978-1981)

The Camaro Rally Sport edition flaunted a distinctive new two-tone paint scheme that used Black Metallic finish on the forward section of the roof, the hood and the nose. This gave it a pure '70s "wild-and-crazy-guy" look that fit right in with the era's leisure suits and burnt-orange plaid sport coats. The hub section of the Rally wheel rims came painted in body colors, which, in the case of the Rally Sport, included White, Silver, Light Blue Metallic, Bright Yellow, Camel Metallic and Red. (Eight other colors completed the Camaro spectrum).

"The 'LT' stands for luxury touring," said the '78 Camaro sales catalog. This version of the Camaro had "LT" lettering on its sail panels and included special deep-contoured bucket seats, special door trim, standard all-vinyl interiors (or optional Custom cloth), other unique interior appointments, a special instrumentation package, color-keyed Rally wheels, black body sill trim and dual sport mirrors. Buyers who wanted more could order the Type LT with the Rally Sport equipment package and combine the features of both.

"It'll put butterflies in your stomach, a lump in your throat and a smile on your face," said the '78 Camaro sales catalog about the hot new Z28. New functional front fender air louvers, a body-colored rear spoiler and an air-scooped hood panel gave the high-performance-oriented Z28 the look it needed to go with a special 185-nhp version of the biggest and hottest V-8.

Model-year sales (not production) of Camaros by new-car dealers in the United States totaled 247,437 units, up from 198,755 the previous season. That represented a strong gain of nearly 25 percent. The week of September 15-23 was promoted as "Chevy Week" and helped in setting record company sales—including deliveries of the Camaro—during that particular month.

1979

All '79 Camaros featured a redesigned instrument panel, a new anti-theft steering column and new sound system options. "The Hugger" nickname returned to the sales catalog this year, with the copywriters suggesting that a refined suspension, with a standard front stabilizer bar and steel-belted radial tires, helped the '79 models hug the road better. "A new Chevrolet Camaro and a favorite road of yours," they said. "Why not get them together?"

The 1979 Z28 had its identifying decal moved from the front fender to the door. A rear spoiler was standard equipment.

It would be the last year the standard Camaro came with an inline six-cylinder engine, as 1980 would bring a switch to a V-6 type. With 250 cubic inches, the inline six produced just 115 nhp (except in California cars, where 90 nhp was standard). It was teamed with a lowered-ratio rear axle to boost fuel economy. Other engines used in Camaros were 5.0- and 5.7-liter V-8s. Cars with an optional V-8 got a new improved Exhaust Gas Recirculation system and cold-trapped spark control system.

The base Camaro sport coupe—which was the best-selling model by far—was promoted as "where the Camaro fun begins." The sport coupe stressed affordability combined with fun and found over 111,000 buyers.

With its hard-to-miss black grille, two-tone paint accents and a rear spoiler as standard equipment, the Rally Sport version of the Camaro emphasized sportiness. Like the base sport coupe, it was available with both six-cylinder and V-8 engines. Bright moldings set off the headlights and parking lights. Color-keyed Rally wheels capped the image of a youthful-looking car. Body color choices for this model were limited to six selections, each with specific second tones. A color-coordinated Custom interior was part of the Rally Sport group.

A bright new Camaro personality to choose from was the "Berlinetta." This gussied-up F-car took the place of the Type LT. It was advertised as the "new way to take your pulse." Designer touches made it seem special, but at not much extra cost to Chevy. Based on the sport coupe body shell, it featured pinstriping on the body and black-finished rocker panels.

The big news on the 1979 Z28s was the flared front fenders and three-piece front air dam.

The Berlinetta replaced the Type LT in the 1979 Camaro lineup.

The Berlinetta name spelled out in chrome script appeared on the sail panels, the driver's side of the hood and the opposite side of the rear deck lid. Like the Type LT, the Berlinetta had special interior appointments and special instrumentation. Dual pinstripes decorated the body and white-stripe tires were standard.

Chevrolet developed the first chrome-coated flexible plastic grilles and installed them in the lower front sections of its '79 Berlinetta. They were believed to be the first major flexible plastic component applications for chrome coatings anywhere in the world. Previously, carmakers felt that the chrome plating used on soft plastic parts was not suited for production because the chrome on the flexible plastic substrate tended to chip away upon impacts. Chevy used a new process called "sputtering" that applied a coating that was thin enough to flex with the plastic base without cracking.

The Z28 got flared front wheel openings and a three-piece front air dam. In March of 1979, *Motor Trend* did an interesting comparison road test that pitted the Z28 against the 5.0-liter Mustang Cobra. The magazine described both cars as "surprisingly exciting automobiles." Writer Fred Stafford remarked, "These two take you back nearly 10 years in terms of performance." He traced the history of both cars, noting how Ford had used the Cobra label, in 1977, on "a poor imitation of what the name once stood for." But he said that the '79 versions did "justice to their heritage."

Stafford described the Z28 as a "very sleek and low-slung in the style of a European GT" and said that its cleanliness of line "makes the Mustang look cluttered by comparison." He also credited the Camaro interior with having a "richer, well-made air about it." At $6,116 as tested, the Camaro cost a bunch more in 1979 "Jimmy Carter" dollars than a $4,436 Mustang. However, the Cobra kit equalized things a bit by upping the window sticker to $5,609.

Chevrolet built its 100-millionth vehicle of all time in 1979 and boosted model-year output of the Camaro by 3.6 percent. However, dealer sales of Camaros did not keep up with the assembly line's ability to crank our vehicles and dropped to 233,802 cars.

1979 CAMARO BY THE NUMBERS

Year	Body Code	Body Type	Engine Type	W.B. (Inches)	O.L. (Inches)	Wt. (Lbs.)	HP (Net)	Disp CID	MSP Price	Model Yr. Prod.
CAMARO SIX										
79	STD87	2HT	6	108.0	197.6	3,305	110	250	$4,677	See notes
CAMARO V-8										
79	STD87	2HT	8	108.0	197.6	3,435	135	305	$4,912	See notes
ALL CAMARO TOTAL									282,582 (*)	

PRODUCTION NOTES
111,357 base Camaro hardtops were built.
19,101 Camaro RS hardtops were built.
67,236 Camaro Berlinettas were built.
84,877 Camaro Z28 models were built.
(*) Most historical sources show total production as 282,571, but industry trade journals say 282,582.

1979 Engine Spec's

Engine	B x S	C.R.	CID	BHP
I6	3.875 x 3.53	8.00	250	115 @ 3800
V-8	3.736 x 3.480	8.40	305	135 @ 3200 +

+ Optional 350 CID, C.R. 8.20, NHP 175 @ 3800 rpm

1979 Collector Pricing

	6	5	4	3	2	1
2d Spt Cpe	232	696	1,160	2,610	4,060	5,800
2d Rally Cpe	256	768	1,280	2,880	4,480	6,400
2d Berlinetta Cpe	264	792	1,320	2,970	4,620	6,600
2d Z28 Cpe	276	828	1,380	3,110	4,830	6,900

NOTE: Deduct 20 percent for Six-cylinder.

The Z28 came with white-letter tires and body-color wheels for 1980.

1980

A new "face" with revised grille treatments headlined the exterior changes to '80 Camaros. The horizontal moldings in the grille looked more prominent. The Sport Coupe carried a red-white-and-blue Camaro emblem in the center of the grille. The Rally Sport had an all-black grille with RS lettering at the upper left-hand corner. The fancy Berlinetta got bright grille work. The performance version had Z28 badges on the left-hand side in the center.

There were big changes under the hood with a

Gen II Soft Nose (1978-1981)

A new grille with a tighter crosshatch pattern was among the changes on the 1980 Z28.

completely revamped engine lineup that started with a Chevy-made 3.8-liter V-6. This lighter-weight engine produced 115 nhp (except in California cars, which had a Buick-built 3.8-liter V-6 with 110-nhp). It was available in all models except the Z28.

At the bottom of the V-8 offerings was a new 4.4-liter (267-cid) V-8 aimed at quenching the V-8 Camaro's thirst for fuel. It was available in all states except California. A 5.0-liter V-8 served up 155 nhp. Standard in the Z28, except California-built ones, was a 5.7-liter V-8 that cranked out 190 hp. The "Left Coast" Z's used a 5.0-liter V-8 rated at 165-nhp.

The Rally Sport was pretty much unchanged from the past two years in its basic concept and appearance.

However, there was a new three-tone striping package, just in case two colors weren't enough to draw attention. A few color selections were modified. Of course, the new engine choices were offered, too, including the V-6 and the smaller V-8 in so-called "federal" (states other than California) cars. The chrome badges on the front fenders now said "Rally Sport" instead of "Rally Sport" lettering above the word "Camaro." It looked a bit neater than the past two years.

Aimed largely at female buyers, the Berlinetta was continued in 1980, but didn't sell as well as in 1979. It was once again a car characterized by its sophisticated exterior appointments, lush interior and deluxe insulation package that made the interior quieter. Wire wheel covers were a new option for Chevy's "elegant and comfortable" version of the Camaro. The Berlinetta interior was also the same as the Custom interior option for other '80 Camaro models.

Chevy said that the '80 Camaro Z28 delivered a "full, high-voltage charge." It was revamped with a new grille and the addition of a hood air-intake. Functional new fender ports extracted hot engine air from below the hood and were said to enhance performance. Camaro features included the 5.7-liter V-8 in federal cars (5.0-liter V-8 in California cars), a dual resonators/tailpipes exhaust system, 15 x 7-inch body-color wheels, special coil springs, special front and rear shocks, a rear stabilizer bar, fat white-lettered tires, special instrumentation, power front disc brakes, a 3.08:1 rear axle (3.42:1 with automatic transmission and in California cars) and a four-speed manual gearbox (automatic required in California).

This was a recession year and Chevrolet built 130,000 fewer Camaros than it did the year before, registering a 46 percent tumble. Dealer sales for the model-year came in at 131,0666 – down 43.9 percent and almost 100,000 lower than the previous season.

Black headlight bezels were new on the 1980 Z28 front end.

Gen II Soft Nose (1978-1981)

1980 CAMARO BY THE NUMBERS

Year	Body Code	Body Type	Engine Type	W.B. (Inches)	O.L. (Inches)	Wt. (Lbs.)	HP (Net)	Disp CID	MSP Price	Model Yr. Prod.
CAMARO V-6										
80	STD87	2HT	6	108.0	197.6	3,218	110	231	$5,499	Below
CAMARO V-8										
80	STD87	2HT	8	108.0	197.6	3,346	120	267	$5,679	Below
ALL CAMARO TOTAL										152,005

PRODUCTION NOTES
68,174 base Camaro Sport Coupes were built.
12,015 Camaro Sport Coupes with the RS option were built.
26,679 Camaro Berlinettas were built.
45,137 Camaro Z28 models were built.

1980 Engine Spec's

Engine	B x S	C.R.	CID	BHP
V-6	3.74 x 3.48	8.60	229	115 @ 4000 *
V-8	3.50 x 3.48	8.30	267	120 @ 3600 +

California: 231-CID V-6, C.R. 8.00, NHP 110 @ 4200.
+ Optional 305 CID, C.R. 8.60, NHP 155 @ 4000 up to 350 CID, C.R. 8.20, NHP 190 @ 4000 (standard in Z/28).

1980 Collector Pricing

	6	5	4	3	2	1
2d Cpe Spt	260	780	1,300	2,930	4,550	6,500
2d Cpe	268	804	1,340	3,020	4,690	6,700
2d Cpe Berlinetta	272	816	1,360	3,060	4,760	6,800
2d Cpe Z28	360	1,080	1,800	4,050	6,300	9,000

NOTE: Subtract 10 percent for Six-cylinder.

This all-original car was one of 43,271 Z28s produced for model year 1981.

1981

The sporty specialty compact Camaro was virtually unchanged for 1981. Power brakes—discs in front—became standard equipment throughout the line and new options included halogen headlights. Another new feature was an improved maintenance-free Delco Freedom II battery with sealed side terminals to help resist corrosion. Computer Command Control became standard.

At the heart of the new CCC system was a thoroughly tested, sophisticated on-board computer that managed engine functions and gave all Chevrolets the cleanest-

Chevrolet continued to invent new ways to dress up an aging body style with its flashy wrapping on the 1981 Z28.

The base coupe was the most popular model in the 1981 Camaro lineup.

Gen II Soft Nose (1978-1981)

V-6 engines like this one outsold the V-8 options by more than a 2 to 1 margin on the base coupes in 1981.

burning gasoline engines in the company's history. The computer constantly adjusted the air-fuel mixture under a variety of different driving conditions. The system included a self-diagnostic feature to diagnose engine problems. It came with a 5-year/50,000-mile emission system warranty.

The 3.8-liter V-6 continued as standard equipment for the sport coupe and Berlinetta. On the options list for the same models were the 4.4- and 5.0-liter V-8s. Z28 engine combinations were expanded to include both 5.0-liter and 5.7-liter power plants in all 50 states. The torque converter clutch used in cars with the Z28 option and automatic transmission was computer controlled in both second and third gears.

Removable glass roof panels were a $695 option in 1981.

Styling changed slightly over the years for the "Soft Nose" generation Camaros, but the same basic shape could be traced all the way back to 1970.

Gen II Soft Nose (1978-1981) 97

The styling of the base wheels was unchanged for 1981.

Black was one of six interior color choices on the 1981 Camaro coupe.

The 1981 Z28 again had distinctive hood styling and a body-colored grille.

1981 CAMARO BY THE NUMBERS

Year	Body Code	Body Type	Engine Type	W.B. (Inches)	O.L. (Inches)	Wt. (Lbs.)	HP (Net)	Disp CID	MSP Price	Model Yr. Prod.
CAMARO V-6										
81	STD87	2HT	6	108.0	197.6	3,222	110	231	$6,780	See notes
CAMARO V-8										
81	STD87	2HT	8	108.0	197.6	3,392	115	267	$6,830	See notes
ALL CAMARO TOTAL										126,138

PRODUCTION NOTES
62,614 base Camaro Sport coupes were built.
20,253 Camaro Berlinettas were built.
43,271 Camaro Z28 models were built.

1981 Engine Spec

Engine	B x S	C.R.	CID	BHP
V-6	3.74 x 3.48	8.60	229	110 @ 4200
V-8	3.50 x 3.48	8.30	267	120 @ 3600

California: 231-CID V-6, C.R. 8.00, NHP 110 @ 4200.
+ Optional 305 CID, C.R. 8.60, NHP 150 @ 3800 up to 350 CID, C.R.

1981 Collector Pricing

	6	5	4	3	2	1
2d Cpe Spt	264	792	1,320	2,970	4,620	6,600
2d Cpe Berlinetta	272	816	1,360	3,060	4,760	6,800
2d Cpe Z28	368	1,104	1,840	4,140	6,440	9,200

NOTE: Subtract 10 percent for Six-cylinder.

CHAPTER *Seven*

Gen III: Back to the Future (1982-1992)

Chevrolet went "back to the future" with the Gen III Camaro. The car's styling and engineering seemed futuristic when it first arrived in '82. At the same time, in terms of its overall character and "fit" in the marketplace, the all-new car was very '60s-ish. There was a revived emphasis on gutsy performance and new option packages with genuine "muscle car" tendencies.

All of the Indy Pace Car replicas sold to the public had a Silver Blue Metallic paint scheme, red-accented sliver aluminum wheels and Goodyear Eagle GT white-letter tires. Buyers could go with or without the Indy 500 logos.

The interior amenities in the Indy Pace Cars included a Lear Siegler Conteur driver's seat.

The 1982 Camaros were different cars all the way around, with new bolt-on sheet metal, less rounded styling and new underpinnings.

The Z28 badging was found on the rocker panel behind the front wheel.

Gen III: Back to the Future (1982-1992) 103

Hood seals were a problem on some early production cars and at least one engine was ruined by water leaks.

The flush-mounted 62-degree windshield helped give the new Camaro a very low drag coefficient. This Z28 was one of 64,882 non-Indy Pace Cars built.

The Indy Pace Cars carried the LU5 305-cid/165-hp V-8.

There was nothing old-fashioned about the Gen III's technology and appearance. It was the first Camaro without a front sub-frame or leaf-spring rear suspension. It was a shorter car with a shorter wheelbase and weighed 500 lbs. less than an '81 model. Was it just coincidence that the size and weight of the new Camaro were in the same ballpark as the classic '69 model?

The Gen III was a car that could be merchandised to a broad spectrum of buyers. Those interested in economy could get sexy Camaro looks with a gas-sipping engine – Camaro's first four banger. Purists would have cringed, but Chevy was careful to offer them a high-tech go-power alternative in the Z28. This 165-nhp V-8 arrived with heavy indications that more was coming soon.

Gen III: Back to the Future (1982-1992)

A total of 6,360 Indy Pace Cars were sold for model year 1982.

The 1982 front end had no upper grille opening.

Model-year *sales* of Camaros immediately jumped from almost 110,000 in '81 to about 150,000 for the short '82 selling season. By '83, the total was over 175,000 and the next year it topped 207,000! Even though Chevy did a good job of keeping the excitement level high with annual improvements, model-year sales dipped to around 206,000 in '85 and dropped back to 173,000-and-change in '86. Over the next six years, the numbers tapered off from about 123,000 in '87 to around 64,500 in '92, but there were increases in '89 and '92, just to make life interesting.

While the loss of popularity was to be expected from an aging design, the total number of Camaros made over the course of the Gen III model's 11-year life cycle was pretty impressive.

1982

Gen III Camaros arrived a little late, bowing in January 1982. The low, angular body had a glass hatchback. To reduce weight, a MacPherson strut suspension was used in place of a front stub frame. Instead of leaf springs, the rear featured coils and a torque tube.

The base sport coupe came with a 2.5-liter 90-hp two-barrel four. A V-6 and V-8s were optional. It was a modern-looking car with a stark appearance. The 2.8-liter 102-hp two-barrel V-6 was standard in the one-step-up Berlinetta, which added more body insulation, a softer suspension, full instrumentation and special finish, badges and stripes. The optional 5.0-liter four-barrel V-8 (also offered in sport coupes) made 145 nhp.

This LG4 V-8 was the base Z28 engine, but buyers could substitute a 165-nhp LU5 "Cross-Fire Injection" V-8—the first factory-fuel-injected Camaro V-8. The Crossfire concept was similar to Chrysler's old ram-tuned V-8, except with *throttle bodies* on criss-crossing intake manifolds instead of carburetors. The CFI engine came with automatic transmission only.

A Camaro paced the Indy 500. Silver and Blue replicas became the most collectible '82s. The actual pace cars carried a special 5.7-liter V-8. *Motor Trend* named the '82 Camaro "Car of the Year."

1982 CAMARO BY THE NUMBERS

Year	Body Code	Body Type	Engine Type	W.B. (Inches)	O.L. (Inches)	Wt. (Lbs.)	HP (Net)	Disp CID	MSP Price	Model Yr. Prod.
CAMARO FOUR										
82	P87	2CPE	4	101.0	187.8	2,798	90	151	$7,631	See notes
CAMARO V-6										
82	P87	2CPE	V-6	101.0	187.8	2,846	102	173	$7,755	See notes
CAMARO V-8										
82	P87	2CPE	V-8	101.0	187.8	3,025	145	305	$7,925	See notes
ALL CAMARO TOTAL										189,735

MODEL-YEAR PRODUCTION NOTES
802 base Camaro fours were built.
45,820 base Camaro V-6s were built.
11,127 base Camaro V-8s were built.
23,945 Camaro Berlinetta V-6s were built.
15,799 Camaro Berlinetta V-8s were built.
58,522 regular Camaro Z28s were built.
6,360 Camaro Z28 Indy Pace Car replicas were built.
1,300 export Camaro Z28s were built.

1982 Engine Spec's

Engine	B x S	C.R.	CID	BHP
L-4	4.00 x 3.00	8.20	151	90 @ 4000
V-6	3.50 x 2.99	8.50	173	102 @ 5100
V-8	3.74 x 3.48	8.60	305	145 @ 4000 +

+ Optional 305 CID, C.R. 8.60, NHP 145 @ 4000 up to 305 CID, C.R. 8.60, NHP 165 @ 4200 (Optional in Z/28 only).

1982 Collector Pricing

	6	5	4	3	2	1
2d Cpe (6-cyl)	252	756	1,260	2,840	4,410	6,300
2d Cpe Berlinetta (6-cyl)	260	780	1,300	2,930	4,550	6,500
2d Cpe (V-8)	268	804	1,340	3,020	4,690	6,700
2d Cpe Berlinetta (V-8)	276	828	1,380	3,110	4,830	6,900
2d Cpe Z28 (V-8)	376	1,128	1,880	4,230	6,580	9,400

NOTE: Deduct 10 percent from Six price for inline Four.

1983

The Camaro sport coupe, Berlinetta and Z28 continued into 1983 with the same appearances. On most Z28's the SMC (sheet molded compound) hood changed to steel, but the LU5 air-induction hood was made of SMC. Z28s with a new midyear engine got "5.0 Liter H.O." badges. Sport coupe/Berlinetta engines were similar, but both the V-6 and the optional carbureted V-8 gained five horsepower. The 150-hp four-barrel V-8 was standard in Z28s, which also offered the 175-hp CFI V-8.

As hinted at in '82, the Z28 got a new 5.0-liter H.O. V-8 option in mid-'83. Sporting a Corvette-spec cam, special exhausts and a healthy four-barrel carb, the L69 engine was rated at 190 nhp. It could be backed by a new five-speed manual transmission. Also new was the 700R4 automatic used in all V-8 cars.

The 5.0-liter H.O. V-8 kick started the modern muscle era and played an important role in making American cars seem exciting again. It proved that those with a passion for performance could once again find what they desired in a domestic product and it showed the powers that be in Detroit that a big market for acceleration and power still existed in the United States.

The 1983 Camaros changed very little in the looks department from the previous year.

The Camaro may have it a high point (or a low point, depending on your point of view) when it came to gawdy interior styling with its upholstery on the 1983 Z28.

1983 CAMARO BY THE NUMBERS

Year	Body Code	Body Type	Engine Type	W.B. (Inches)	O.L. (Inches)	Wt. (Lbs.)	HP (Net)	Disp CID	MSP Price	Model Yr. Prod.
CAMARO FOUR										
83	P87	2CPE	4	101.0	187.8	2,798	92	151	$7,845	See notes
CAMARO V-6										
83	P87	2CPE	V-6	101.0	187.8	2,878	107	173	$8,186	See notes
CAMARO V-8										
83	P87	2CPE	V-8	101.0	187.8	3,035	150	305	$8,386	See notes
ALL CAMARO TOTAL										154,381

MODEL-YEAR PRODUCTION NOTES
9,926 base Camaro fours were built.
39,859 base Camaro V-6s were built.
14,571 base Camaro V-8s were built.
14,473 Camaro Berlinetta V-6s were built.
13,452 Camaro Berlinetta V-8s were built.
62,100 Camaro Z28s were built.
550 export Camaro Z28s were built.

1983 Engine Spec's

Engine	B x S	C.R.	CID	BHP
L-4	4.00 x 3.00	9.00	151	92 @ 4000
V-6	3.50 x 2.99	8.50	173	107 @ 4800
V-8	3.74 x 3.48	8.60	305	150 @ 4000 +

+ Optional 305 CID, C.R. 8.60, NHP 175 @ 4800 up to 305 CID, C.R. 9.50, NHP 190 @ 4800 (Optional in Z/28 only.)

1983 Collector Pricing

	6	5	4	3	2	1
2d Cpe Spt (V-6)	256	768	1,280	2,880	4,480	6,400
2d Cpe Berlinetta (V-6)	264	792	1,320	2,970	4,620	6,600
2d Cpe Spt (V-8)	272	816	1,360	3,060	4,760	6,800
2d Cpe Berlinetta (V-8)	360	1,080	1,800	4,050	6,300	9,000
2d Cpe Z28 (V-8)	380	1,140	1,900	4,280	6,650	9,500

NOTE: Deduct 10 percent from Six price for inline Four-cylinder.

Gen III: Back to the Future (1982-1992)

1984

1984 was a not-many-changes year for the Chevy pony car. The sport coupe switched from a carb to TBI. Berlinettas got a digital speedo, bar-graph tach and redundant-controls steering wheel. The dash was more exciting than the engine.

Other '84 changes included dropping the three-speed automatic and the SMC hood. All Camaros had steel hoods (a flap-type functional induction hood was available for Z28s). *Road & Track* named the Camaro one of the world's top 12 cars.

I owned an '84 Z28. My wife called it my "male menopause" car. It was. Even with the four-barrel V-8 it was fun, but the build quality was poor. The crooked inside door handle bothered me.

My daughter Suzy bought the car in Colorado and took it for service. The dealer's computer said the mileage was wrong. The previous owner—a dentist—had spun the clock back. The DA got a settlement from the tooth doc, but his check bounced! I bought the car to bail Suzy out. It had lived a rough life and needed a ring job, but it went fast. I traded it in on a '91 Camry and smiled. Now, I wish I had it back. I can't believe I let it go for $1,200!

The Z28 production soared to a record 100,416 cars for model year 1984.

1984 CAMARO BY THE NUMBERS

Year	Body Code	Body Type	Engine Type	W.B. (Inches)	O.L. (Inches)	Wt. (Lbs.)	HP (Net)	Disp CID	MSP Price	Model Yr. Prod.
CAMARO FOUR										
84	P87	2CPE	4	101.0	187.8	2,813	92	151	$7,995	See notes
CAMARO V-6										
84	P87	2CPE	V-6	101.0	187.8	2,907	107	173	$8,245	See notes
CAMARO V-8										
84	P87	2CPE	V-8	101.0	187.8	3,091	150	305	$8,545	See notes
ALL CAMARO TOTAL										261,591

MODEL-YEAR PRODUCTION NOTES
10,687 base Camaro fours were built.
86,447 base Camaro V-6s were built.
30,611 base Camaro V-8s were built.
11,994 Camaro Berlinetta V-6s were built.
21,406 Camaro Berlinetta V-8s were built.
100,416 Camaro Z28s were built.
478 export Camaro Z28s were built.

A special Camaro Sarajevo Winter Olympics Package was offered in November and December of 1984. This was SEO (Special Equipment Option) 1A3. The cars were white with red/white/blue striping and winter Olympics insignias with "Sarajevo '84."

By its third year of existence, the Gen II Camaro was a full-fledged hit with buyers and a design that would last right through the decade.

1984 Engine Spec's

Engine	B x S	C.R.	CID	BHP
L-4	4.00 x 3.00	9.00	151	92 @ 4000
V-6	3.50 x 2.99	8.50	173	107 @ 4800
V-8	3.74 x 3.48	8.80	305	150 @ 4000 +

+ Optional 305 CID, C.R. 9.50, NHP 190 @ 4800 (Optional in Z/28 only).

1984 Collector Pricing

	6	5	4	3	2	1
2d Cpe (V-8)	264	792	1,320	2,970	4,620	6,600
2d Cpe Berlinetta (V-8)	272	816	1,360	3,060	4,760	6,800
2d Cpe Z28 (V-8)	364	1,092	1,820	4,100	6,370	9,100

NOTE: Deduct 10 percent for V-6. Deduct 20 percent for Four.

1985

Camaro styling went the facelift route in '85 with new front fascias. The sport coupe and the Berlinetta used a new multi-port fuel-injected version of the 2.8-liter V-6 that pushed 28 more ponies (135 nhp) than the previous two-barrel version. The Berlinetta's aluminum wheels became an extra-cost option. The optional four-barrel V-8 now had 155 nhp in both models.

A quantum leap in Gen III Camaro power came with the 1985 introduction of the IROC-Z. The letters IROC stood for "International Race of Champions," the name of a series of televised races for drivers of identically prepped Camaros. "Z" stood for Z28. IROC features included big 16-inch spoke wheels, fat Gatorback tires, special underpinnings and specific body graphics.

Engines available in the Z28 included the 155-nhp four-barrel V-8 that was optional in sport coupes and Berlinettas, the 190-nhp 5.0-liter H.O. (also running a four-barrel carburetor) and a hot new Tuned Port Injection (TPI) V-8 that produced 215 nhp. The latter engine could only be had with the four-speed automatic transmission, but it could be had in either the Z28 or the IROC-Z.

Performancewise, enthusiasts were beginning to think they were back in the '60s, though the Camaro looked thoroughly modern.

Fog lights, a ground-hugging front air dam and twin hood louvers were part of the new IROC-Z package for 1985.

The 1985 Z28s sported silver or gold lower body accents.

Silver Metallic was one of 12 color choices on the 1985 paint chart. This original car is a Z28.

The IROC-Zs arrived in 1985 and were patterned after the Camaros that raced in the International Race of Champions. More than 21,000 of the new Z cars rolled off assembly lines for the model year.

The twin foglamps in the grille openings were one of the most obvious differences between the IROC-Z (left) and the standard 1985 Z28.

The 1985 Camaro GTZ Concept car was a customized Z28 with a performance look that included smoked glass, a special finned hood, hood hold-down pins, whale tail spoiler and other cool add-ons.

Gen III: Back to the Future (1982-1992)   115

V-8s were slightly more popular among Berlinetta buyers than V-6s in 1985.

1985 CAMARO BY THE NUMBERS

Year	Body Code	Body Type	Engine Type	W.B. (Inches)	O.L. (Inches)	Wt. (Lbs.)	HP (Net)	Disp CID	MSP Price	Model Yr. Prod.
CAMARO FOUR										
85	P87	2CPE	4	101.0	187.8	2,813	88	151	$8,363	See notes
CAMARO V-6										
85	P87	2CPE	V-6	101.0	187.8	2,907	135	173	$8,698	See notes
CAMARO V-8										
85	P87	2CPE	V-8	101.0	187.8	3,091	155	305	$8,998	See notes
ALL CAMARO TOTAL										180,018

MODEL-YEAR PRODUCTION NOTES
3,318 base Camaro fours were built.
72,652 base Camaro V-6s were built.
21,996 base Camaro V-8s were built.
5,663 Camaro Berlinetta V-6s were built.
7,986 Camaro Berlinetta V-8s were built.
47,226 Camaro Z28s were built.
21,177 Camaro IROC-Zs were built.
204 export Camaro Z28s were built.

The Berlinetta was a distant fourth in popularity in the Camaro lineup behind the base coupe, Z28 and IROC-Z, and the model would be gone after the 1986 model year.

The IROC-Z could be had with three different 305-cid engines.

1985 Engine Spec's

Engine	B x S	C.R.	CID	BHP
L-4	4.00 x 3.00	9.00	151	88 @ 4400
V-6	3.50 x 2.99	8.50	173	135 @ 5100
V-8	3.74 x 3.48	9.50	305	155 @ 4200 +

+ Optional 305 CID, C.R. 9.50, NHP 190 @ 4800 up to 305 CID, C.R. 9.50, NHP 215 @ 4400 (Optional in Z/28)

1985 Price Guide

	6	5	4	3	2	1
2d Cpe	268	804	1,340	3,020	4,690	6,700
2d Cpe Berlinetta	276	828	1,380	3,110	4,830	6,900
2d Cpe Z28	368	1,104	1,840	4,140	6,440	9,200
2d Cpe IROC-Z	384	1,152	1,920	4,320	6,720	9,600

NOTE: Deduct 30 percent for 4-cyl. Deduct 20 percent for V-6.

Gen III: Back to the Future (1982-1992)

1986

A high-mounted stoplight on the center of the rear deck lid and new looks for the base model characterized Camaroland '86. A new type of base coat/clearcoat paint was introduced.

The sport coupe could now be made to resemble the Z28 if the right options were added. You could even add the Z28-style fog lamps. When the sport coupe was ordered with a MFI V-6 or four-barrel V-8 you got a sport suspension, fat tires, styled wheels and a cool-sounding sport-tone exhaust system. Engine choices and horsepower ratings for the non-Z28 models were unchanged from '85.

Base engine in both Z28s and IROC-Zs was a 5.0-liter four-barrel job, but no longer the same one that was optional in other models. This "base" Z28 engine cranked up 165 nhp. An H.O. version, also offered in both Zs, was rated at 190 nhp. The rare 5.0-liter TPI V-8 was also available in both Zs. It lost a few ponies (190 nhp at 4400 rpm) and gained a few foot-pounds of torque (285 ft.-lbs.). A IROC-Z with the 5.7-liter TPI "Corvette" engine was another rarity. It was probably made for test purposes only and pushed out 220 nhp and 320 lbs.-ft.

The 1986 Camaro coupes continued to sell well, but total new-car registration figures fell to 165,883 from 200,091 in 1985.

The Z28 was an option package on the base 1986 Camaro. Factory list price for the standard Z car was $11,902.

1986 CAMARO BY THE NUMBERS

Year	Body Code	Body Type	Engine Type	W.B. (Inches)	O.L. (Inches)	Wt. (Lbs.)	HP (Net)	Disp CID	MSP Price	Model Yr. Prod.
CAMARO FOUR										
86	F/P	2CPE	4	101.0	187.8	2,871	88	151	$8,363	See notes
CAMARO V-6										
86	F/P	2CPE	V-6	101.0	187.8	2,912	135	173	$8,698	See notes
CAMARO V-8										
86	F/P	2CPE	V-8	101.0	187.8	3,071	155	305	$8,998	See notes
ALL CAMARO TOTAL										192,219

MODEL-YEAR PRODUCTION NOTES
99,608 base Camaros were built.
99,608 Camaro Berlinettas were built.
88,132 Z28s and IROC-Zs (combined) were built.

The IROC-Z decals were forward on the door in the 1985-87 IROC-Zs. The same 16-inch wheel style was also used in those years.

1986 Engine Spec's

Engine	B x S	C.R.	CID	BHP
L-4	4.00 x 3.00	9.00	151	88 @ 4400
V-6	3.50 x 2.99	8.50	173	135 @ 5100
V-8	3.74 x 3.48	9.50	305	165 @ 4400 +

+ Optional 305 CID, C.R. 9.50, NHP 190 @ 4800 up to 305 CID, C.R. 9.50, NHP 190 @ 4000 (Optional in IROC-Z only).

1986 Collector Pricing

	6	5	4	3	2	1
2d Cpe (V-8)	272	816	1,360	3,060	4,760	6,800
2d Cpe Berlinetta (V-8)	360	1,080	1,800	4,050	6,300	9,000
2d Cpe Z28 (V-8)	380	1,140	1,900	4,280	6,650	9,500
2d Cpe IROC-Z (V-8)	400	1,200	2,000	4,500	7,000	10,000

NOTE: Deduct 30 percent for 4-cyl. Deduct 20 percent for V-6.

1987

It was the Camaro's 20th birthday in 1987. A new convertible carried a special "20th Anniversary Commemorative Edition" dash badge. American Sunroof Corporation made the ragtop from a coupe. Chevy dealers sold it.

It was also a year for horsepower junkies to rejoice as Chevy ditched the four-cylinder engine for ever-evolving Camaro.

The sport coupe got new Rally wheels, lower body stripes and Argent headlight recesses. A new LT option replaced the Berlinetta and included most of its features, except electronic instrumentation. Late in '87, a V-6-only RS that shared some Z28 motifs was sold in California. The same 135-hp V-6 was base engine in sport coupes. A 170-hp four-barrel 5.0-liter V-8 was optional in sport coupes and standard in Z-cars.

The 215-hp 5.0-liter TPI motor was offered only for Z-cars with a five-speed. Those with the 305-cid TPI V-8 and automatic got a milder cam and 190-nhp rating. A 350 was available in the IROC-Z with automatic. These cars had "5.7 Tuned Port Injection" badges. All 5.7-liter TPI Camaros had a yellow-at-5000-and-red-at-5500 tach.

V-8s had roller lifters and heads with a new raised-lip design that sealed better with valve covers. Delco-Bose sound systems and leather interiors were introduced and available in all Camaros. A 7.75:1 axle and four-wheel disc brakes were available for IROC-Z convertibles.

The 1987 IROC-Z was hotter than ever with the new 225-hp L98 engine option.

The IROC-Z coupe came with a $13,488 window sticker in 1987.

1987 CAMARO BY THE NUMBERS

Year	Body Code	Body Type	Engine Type	W.B. (Inches)	O.L. (Inches)	Wt. (Lbs.)	HP (Net)	Disp CID	MSP Price	Model Yr. Prod.
CAMARO SPORT COUPE V-6										
87	F/P	2CPE	V-6	101.0	187.8	2,912	135	173	$9,995	See notes
CAMARO SPORT COUPE V-8										
87	F/P	2CPE	V-8	101.0	187.8	3,071	165	305	$10,395	See notes
CAMARO CONVERTIBLE V-8										
87	F/P	2CPE	V-8	101.0	187.8	3,071	165	305	$14,794	See notes
ALL CAMARO TOTAL										137,760

MODEL-YEAR PRODUCTION NOTES
60,439 Camaro V-6 Sport Coupes were built.
23,451 Camaro V-8 Sport Coupes were built.
263 (base) Camaro convertibles were built.
52,863 Camaro Z-28 and IROC-Z coupes were built (*).
744 Z-28 and IROC-Z convertibles were built (*).
* Combined production of all IROC-Z models was 38,889 (included above)

A leather interior, automatic transmission, four-wheel disc brakes, positraction and a new engine were part of IROC-Z package.

1987 Engine Spec's

Engine	B x S	C.R.	CID	BHP
1987 (COUPE)				
V-6	3.50 x 2.99	8.50	173	135 @ 5100
V-8	3.74 x 3.48	9.50	305	165 @ 4400 +
1987 (CONVERTIBLE)				
V-8	3.74 x 3.48	9.50	305	165 @ 4400 +

+ Optional 305 CID, C.R. 9.50, NHP 190 @ 4800 and 350 CID, C.R. 9.00, NHP 225 @ 4000 (Optional in IROC-Z only).

1987 Collector Pricing

	6	5	4	3	2	1
2d Cpe, V-6	276	828	1,380	3,110	4,830	6,900
2d Cpe LT, V-6	360	1,080	1,800	4,050	6,300	9,000
2d Cpe, V-8	368	1,104	1,840	4,140	6,440	9,200
2d Cpe LT, V-8	372	1,116	1,860	4,190	6,510	9,300
2d Cpe Z28, V-8	388	1,164	1,940	4,370	6,790	9,700
2d Cpe IROC-Z, V-8	410	1,220	2,040	4,590	7,140	10,200
2d Conv IROC-Z, V-8	800	2,400	4,000	9,000	14,000	20,000

NOTE: Add 20 percent for 350 V-8 where available. Add 10 percent for Anniversary Edition.

Gen III: Back to the Future (1982-1992)

1988

Chevy cut to the chase in '88, offering only base Camaros and IROC-Zs. The sport coupe came in V-6 and V-8 flavors and a base convertible was available. A coupe and convertible made up the IROC-Z line.

Base models were upgraded with Silver or Gold 15-inch five-spoke wheels, Z28 body skirting, body-color mirrors and a new spoiler that integrated the high-mounted stoplight. An improved version of the 5.0-liter V-8, previously standard in Z28s, was optional on base Camaros. A throttle body injection system upped horsepower to 170.

The IROC-Z had restyled 16-inch wheels as standard equipment. For the sake of change—or because someone thought it looked better—the IROC-Z lower-door lettering was moved rearward. The pinstriping now had a black stripe on top and a body-color stripe in the middle. Two MFI V-8s were offered for the IROC-Z. The 5.0-liter H.O. produced 195 hp with automatic and 220-hp with a five-speed manual transmission. The 5.7-liter 230-hp came only with a four-speed automatic transmission.

The rarest option was the 1LE road racing package for IROCs with TPI V-8s. It featured oversize brakes, an aluminum driveshaft and a well-tweaked suspension and was built for showroom stock racing.

The lower door lettering was moved forward on the 1988 IROC-Zs—one of the few ways they were noticeably different from the 1987 versions.

The only cars in the Camaro lineup for 1988 were the IROC-Z (left) and the sport coupe.

1988 CAMARO BY THE NUMBERS

Year	Body Code	Body Type	Engine Type	W.B. (Inches)	O.L. (Inches)	Wt. (Lbs.)	HP (Net)	Disp CID	MSP Price	Model Yr. Prod.
CAMARO SPORT COUPE V-6										
88	F/P	2CPE	V-6	101.0	192.0	3,054	135	173	$10,995	See Notes
CAMARO SPORT COUPE V-8										
88	F/P	2CPE	V-8	101.0	192.0	3,228	170	305	$11,395	See Notes
CAMARO CONVERTIBLE V-8										
88	F/P	2CPE	V-8	101.0	192.0	3,350	170	305	$16,255	See Notes
ALL CAMARO TOTAL										96,275

MODEL-YEAR PRODUCTION NOTES
66,605 Camaro Sport Coupes were built.
1,859 base Camaro convertibles were built.
24,050 Camaro IROC-Z coupes were built.
3,761 Camaro IROC-Z convertibles were built

The IROC-Z package for 1988 included body-colored ground effects panels, specific body striping and matching door decals.

The IROC-Z was still on the Chevy menu in 1988, but the car it was based on, the Z28, was strangely absent.

More than 66,000 of the base Camaro coupes rolled out of assembly lines for 1988.

1988 Engine Spec's

Engine	B x S	C.R.	CID	BHP
1988 (COUPE)				
V-6	3.50 x 2.99	8.90	173	135 @ 4900
V-8	3.74 x 3.48	9.30	305	170 @ 4400 +
1988 (CONVERTIBLE)				
V-8	3.74 x 3.48	9.30	305	170 @ 4400 +

+ Optional 305 CID, C.R. 9.30, NHP 220 @ 4400 and 350 CID, C.R. 9.30, NHP 230 @ 4400 (TPI option for IROC)

1988 Collector Pricing

	6	5	4	3	2	1
2d Cpe (V-6)	220	660	1,100	2,480	3,850	5,500
2d Cpe (V-8)	240	720	1,200	2,700	4,200	6,000
2d Conv (V-8)	560	1,680	2,800	6,300	9,800	14,000
2d IROC-Z Cpe (V-8)	420	1,260	2,100	4,730	7,350	10,500
2d IROC-Z Conv (V-8)	700	2,150	3,600	8,100	12,600	18,000

Gen III: Back to the Future (1982-1992)

1989

The base 1989 Camaro sport coupes and convertibles were replaced by new Camaro RS models of the same body styles. The RS sport coupe was reminiscent of the 1985 Z28. Available power plants included a 2.8-liter 135-hp MFI V-6, or an optional 5.0-liter 170-hp TBI V-8. The 15-inch wheels used on these cars were restyled to look like the optional 16-inchers.

The same 170-hp TBI V-8 was standard in the IROC-Z coupe and convertible, which rode on new P245/50VR-16 tires. Cars with optional four-wheel disc brakes got bigger brake rotors. Optional engines included the 5.0-liter TPI V-8, which churned up 220-hp, and the 5.7-liter TPI V-8 that produced 230 hp (240 hp with the G92 exhaust kit). The TPI "mills" were fitted with improved Multec injectors that noticeably increased performance.

GM's "PASS-Key" theft-deterrent system was standard in all '88 Camaros. The G92 option package for stick-shift IROC coupes included a performance exhaust system with dual catalytic converters. To get this extra you had to also order the B2L V-8 (or LB9 V-8 with five-speed), 16-inch wheels, a no-spin rear axle, four-wheel disc brakes and P45/50ZR-16 "Gatorback" tires. The racing-oriented 1LE package not only returned, but sold better, too.

The third-generation Camaro body style may have been getting a little long in the tooth by 1989, but it would soldier on for three more years and there was no denying that a Dark Red Metallic IROC-Z convertible like this one was still a very attractive ride.

T-tops remained a strong selling point for the IROC-Z.

The RS returned to the Camaro lineup in 1989 as a replacement for the base coupe.

Gen III: Back to the Future (1982–1992)

The 1989 Concept California Camaro hinted at the next body style that would finally become a reality in 1993.

1989 CAMARO BY THE NUMBERS

Year	Body Code	Body Type	Engine Type	W.B. (Inches)	O.L. (Inches)	Wt. (Lbs.)	HP (Net)	Disp CID	MSP Price	Model Yr. Prod.
CAMARO RS COUPE V-6										
89	F/P	2CPE	V-6	101.0	192.0	3,082	135	173	$11,495	See notes
CAMARO RS COUPE V-8										
89	F/P	2CPE	V-8	101.0	192.0	3,285	170	305	$11,895	See notes
CAMARO CONVERTIBLE V-8										
89	F/P	2CPE	V-8	101.0	192.0	3,350	170	305	$16,995	See notes
ALL CAMARO TOTAL										96,275

MODEL-YEAR PRODUCTION NOTES
83,487 Camaro RS Coupes were built.
3,245 base Camaro convertibles were built.
20,067 Camaro IROC-Z coupes were built.
3,940 Camaro IROC-Z convertibles were built

Chevy unveiled the XT-2 Pace Truck concept based on the Camaro in 1989. The car was really a futuristic IROC with a sculpted pickup box and a rocking 360-hp V-6 under the hood.

The IROC-Z continued in 1989 and was the lone muscle car in the Camaro lineup with the loss of the Z28 from the menu.

1989 Engine Spec's

Engine	B x S	C.R.	CID	BHP
1989 (COUPE)				
V-6	3.50 x 2.99	8.90	173	135 @ 4900
V-8	3.74 x 3.48	9.30	305	170 @ 4000 +
1989 (CONVERTIBLE)				
V-8	3.74 x 3.48	9.30	305	170 @ 4000 +

+ Optional 305 CID, C.R. 9.30, NHP 220 @ 4400 and 350 CID, C.R. 9.30, NHP 240 @ 4400 (TPI option for IROC)

Gen III: Back to the Future (1982-1992)

Black-painted headlight bezels and halogen headlights were seen on the mildly tweaked 1990 IROC's.

1990

With a face-lifted '91 Camaro coming, the '90 models lasted only half a year. Due to the termination of Chevrolet's sponsorship of IROC series races (Dodge took it over), no IROC-Z models were built after December 31, 1989.

Despite their short production life, '90 Camaros are easy to spot. It was the first year for an interior featuring a redesigned instrument panel, a driver's airbag, yellow dashboard lettering and rounded controls. You can't get another RS or IROC Camaro with this interior and the '90 RS is the only one with the new interior and older-style body skirting.

A larger 3.1-liter/144-hp V-6 was the standard engine. The base 5.0-liter/170-hp TBI V-8 remained available in base Camaros. This engine was no longer used in IROC-Zs, which had a standard 5.0-liter/220-hp TPI V-8. To get a 230-hp hot-cammed 5.0-liter V-8 with a five-speed, the G92 kit was mandatory. Previously, *all* five-speed IROC-Zs got the hotter engine. The '90 5.7-liter V-8 had lighter pistons and 245 hp.

New standard equipment included halogen headlights, tinted glass, intermittent windshield wipers and tilt steering. The G80 limited-slip axle became standard on IROC-Zs. P245/50ZR-16 tires and 16-in. wheels were standard for IROC-Z convertibles.

The IROC-Z models were only temporary offerings in 1990. Production of the cars halted after Dec. 31, 1989.

The convertible IROC-Zs were much scarcer than the coupe versions. Only 1,294 ragtops were reportedly built.

Gen III: Back to the Future (1982-1992)

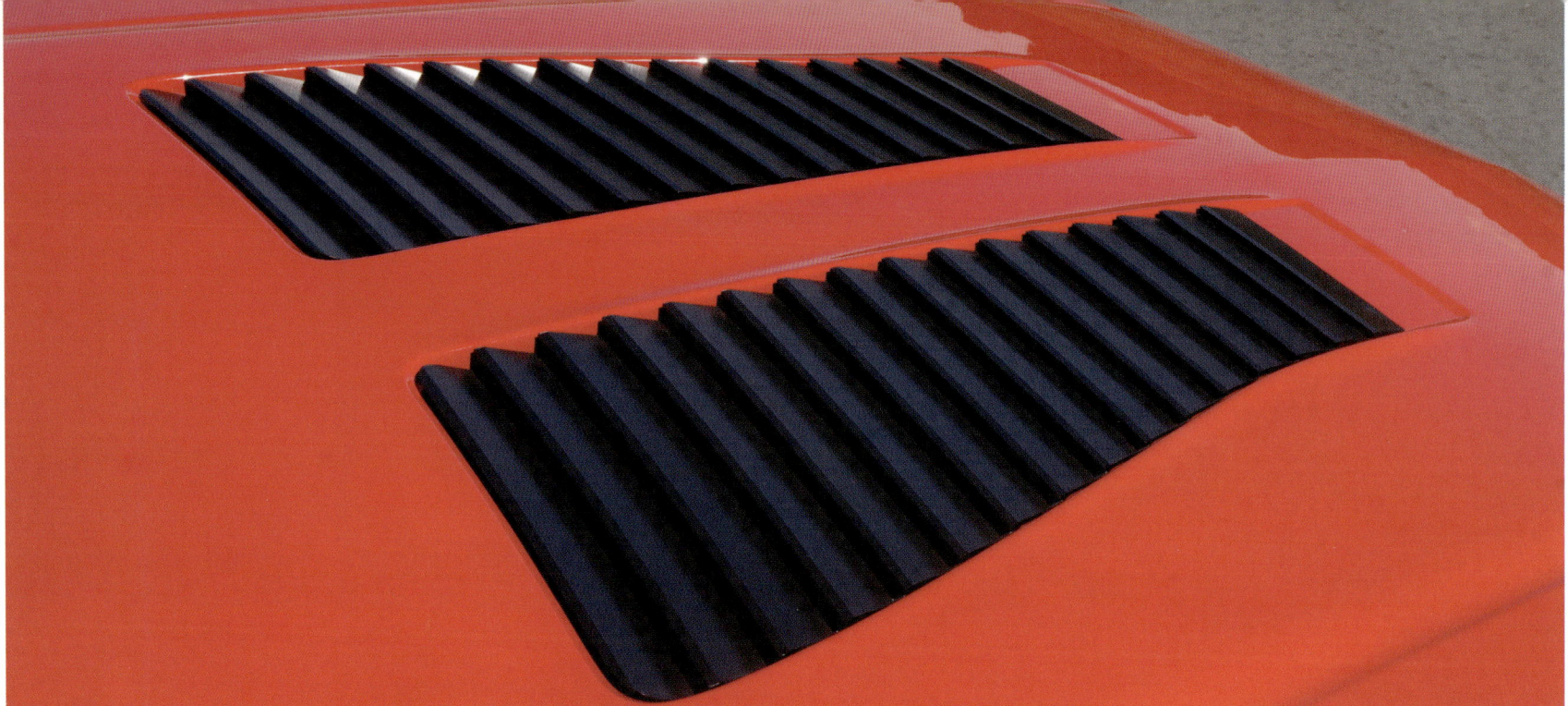

The 1990 simulated hood louvers were strictly for looks.

The 16-inch alloy wheels were upgraded to standard equipment on the IROC-Z convertible.

The 1990 IROC was equipped with a 5.0-liter electronically fuel-injected V-8 that produced 230 hp.

The compartmented, horizontal banks of tail lights continued in 1990.

The Z28 badging was omnipresent on the IROC-Z.

Cloth interiors were still standard in 1990, but leather was on the options list.

This 1990 convertible IROC had a black ragtop to go with its Bright Red paint job.

This IROC-Z had a red interior to match its paint.

1990 CAMARO BY THE NUMBERS

Year	Body Code	Body Type	Engine Type	W.B. (Inches)	O.L. (Inches)	Wt. (Lbs.)	HP (Net)	Disp CID	MSP Price	Model Yr. Prod.
CAMARO RS COUPE V-8										
90	F/P	2CPE	V-6	101.0	192.6	2,975	144	191	$10,995	28,750
CAMARO RS CONVERTIBLE V-8										
90	F/P	2CPE	V-8	101.0	192.0	3,270	170	305	$16,880	729
CAMARO IROC-Z COUPE V-8										
90	F/P	2CPE	V-8	101.0	192.6	3,264	170	305	$14,145	4,213
CAMARO IROC-Z CONVERTIBLE V-8										
90	F/P	2CPE	V-8	101.0	192.0	3,272	170	305	$18,945	1,294
ALL CAMARO TOTAL										34,986

1990 Engine Spec's

Engine	B x S	C.R.	CID	BHP
1990 (COUPE)				
V-6	3.50 x 3.31	8.80	191	144 @ 4400
V-8	3.74 x 3.48	9.30	305	170 @ 4000 +
1990 (CONVERTIBLE)				
V-8	3.74 x 3.48	9.30	305	170 @ 4000 +

+ Optional 305 CID, C.R. 9.30, NHP 220 @ 4400 and 350 CID, C.R. 9.30, NHP 230 @ 4400 (TPI option for IROC-Z only).

1990 Collector Pricing

2d RS Cpe (V-6)	240	720	1,200	2,700	4,200	6,000
2d RS Cpe (V-8)	264	792	1,320	2,970	4,620	6,600
2d RS Conv (V-8)	600	1,800	3,000	6,750	10,500	15,000
2d IROC-Z Cpe (V-8)	520	1,560	2,600	5,850	9,100	13,000
2d IROC-Z Conv (V-8)	680	2,040	3,400	7,650	11,900	17,000

1991

With Dodge backing IROC, Chevy could no longer use the initials. When the restyled '91 Camaro took an early bow in spring 1990, the RS returned as the base series. The high-performance Camaro was again dubbed the Z28.

Camaros had revised body skirting. The RS got Z28-type grid tail lights. Available for the first time on the RS were 16-inch wheels. The center high-mounted stop lamp moved under the glass hatch, so a plain spoiler was used.

The Z28 got a tall Ferrari F40-style rear wing, a power blister hood and new five-spoke wheels. The hot engine was the 5.7-liter/245-hp TPI V-8.

Law enforcement agencies got an even hotter '91 Camaro with the introduction of the Camaro B4C "Special Service" package. The cop cars were all RS sport coupes with the Z28 engines. Chevy offered a choice of the 5.0- or 5.7-liter TPI V-8. Also included were Z28 drive line and suspension upgrades, 16-inch wheels, P245/50-ZR16 tires, an engine oil cooler, four-wheel disc brakes and a limited-slip rear end. Heavier-duty brakes became a police car option during the year. These were the only Camaros to offer the big brakes teamed with A/C. Very few B4Cs were built by Chevrolet.

The '91 and '92 Z28 coupes are recognizable by their taller rear spoiler.

The RS convertible was back for 1991 and came with a standard V-8, although buyers could order the V-6 that was standard in the coupe.

The Z28 returned after a brief hiatus in 1991. It replaced the IROC-Z.

The new rocker panels and front fascia were part of the updates on 1991 Z28s.

1991 CAMARO BY THE NUMBERS

Year	Body Code	Body Type	Engine Type	W.B. (Inches)	O.L. (Inches)	Wt. (Lbs.)	HP (Net)	Disp CID	MSP Price	Model Yr. Prod.
CAMARO RS COUPE V-6										
91	F/P	2CPE	V-6	101.0	192.6	3,103	140	191	$12,180	79,854
CAMARO RS CONVERTIBLE V-8										
91	F/P	2CPE	V-8	101.0	192.6	3,484	170	305	$12,530	5,329
CAMARO COUPE V-8										
91	F/P	2CPE	V-8	101.0	192.6	3,319	170	305	$15,455	12,452
CAMARO CONVERTIBLE V-8										
91	F/P	2CPE	V-8	101.0	192.6	3,400	170	305	$20,815	3,203
ALL CAMARO TOTAL										100,838

Gen III: Back to the Future (1982-1992)

Among the changes on the 1991 Z28s were new colors and new alloy wheels. The convertibles retained the smaller spoiler, while the coupes got the new, more prominent rear wing.

1991 Engine Spec's

Engine	B x S	C.R.	CID	BHP
1991 (COUPE)				
V-6	3.50 x 3.31	8.80	191	140 @ 4400
V-8	3.74 x 3.48	9.30	305	170 @ 4000 +
1991 (CONVERTIBLE)				
V-6	3.50 x 3.31	8.80	191	140 @ 4400
V-8	3.74 x 3.48	9.30	305	170 @ 4000 +

+ Optional 305 CID, C.R. 9.30, NHP 230 @ 4400 and 350 CID, C.R. 9.30, NHP 245 @ 4400 (TPI option for IROC-Z).

1991 Collector Pricing

	6	5	4	3	2	1
2d Cpe (V-6)	240	720	1,200	2,700	4,200	6,000
2d Conv (V-6)	560	1,680	2,800	6,300	9,800	14,000
2d RS Cpe (V-8)	260	780	1,300	2,930	4,550	6,500
2d RS Conv (V-8)	580	1,740	2,900	6,530	10,150	14,500
2d Z28 Cpe (V-8)	420	1,260	2,100	4,730	7,350	10,500
2d Z28 Conv (V-8)	660	1,980	3,300	7,430	11,550	16,500

1992

This was a milestone year for the Camaro. In addition to the nameplate turning 25 years old, a generation was ending. The next Camaro would be an all-new car. In addition, it was the final year for production in Van Nuys, California. A new factory in Canada would turn out the F-cars from model year 1993 on.

Camaros had a "25th Anniversary" instrument panel badge. For $175, any Camaro could have a "Heritage Edition" package and 8,197 of these were sold. Goodies included Gen I-style hood and rear deck stripes, a body-colored grille, black headlight housings and "25th Anniversary" badging (in different spots on each model). Early versions of the package were offered only on White, Black and Red cars, but Polo Green and Purple Haze versions came later.

Chevrolet had planned a special "Collector's Edition" Camaro to mark the 25th year of the marque, but this program was cancelled after just two prototypes were built. These cars were White RS models with the "Heritage Edition" package and the B4C police package, which meant they had 270 hp on tap. The regular engines included the 140-hp V-6 and the 170-hp V-8. Also available were the 5.0-liter/230 hp V-8 and the 5.7-liter/245-hp V-8.

Out of the 70,007 Camaros built for model year 1992, only 2,562 were RS convertibles.

The Heritage Appearance Package was available on 1992 Camaros with a choice of Red, White or Black exteriors.

Gen III: Back to the Future (1982-1992)

Both the Z28 coupe and convertible could be ordered with the 5.0-liter TPI V-8, which kept the top-end Camaro among the quickest American cars on the road in 1992.

The horsepower rating for the 5.7-liter TPI grew to 245 for 1992.

T-tops were a popular option on the 25th anniversary Camaros.

Sarah Werbelow

The 1992 RS was the last RS model until the designation reappeared in 1996.

1992 CAMARO BY THE NUMBERS

Year	Body Code	Body Type	Engine Type	W.B. (Inches)	O.L. (Inches)	Wt. (Lbs.)	HP (Net)	Disp CID	MSP Price	Model Yr. Prod.
CAMARO RS COUPE V-6										
92	F/P	2CPE	V-6	101.0	192.6	3,103	140	191	$12,075	60,994
CAMARO RS CONVERTIBLE V-8										
92	F/P	2CPE	V-8	101.0	192.6	3,484	170	305	$18,424	2,562
CAMARO COUPE V-8										
92	F/P	2CPE	V-8	101.0	192.6	3,319	170	305	$16,055	5,197
CAMARO CONVERTIBLE V-8										
92	F/P	2CPE	V-8	101.0	192.6	3,400	170	305	$21,500	1,254
ALL CAMARO TOTAL										70,007

A total of 1,254 Z28 convertibles were built for 1992.

Heritage editions—this one is dressed in Arctic White with Red stripes—were easy to spot by the tapering hood stripes.

1992 Engine Spec's

Engine	B x S	C.R.	CID	BHP
1992 (COUPE)				
V-6	3.50 x 3.31	8.80	191	140 @ 4400
V-8	3.74 x 3.48	9.30	305	170 @ 4000 +
1992 (CONVERTIBLE)				
V-6	3.50 x 3.31	8.80	191	140 @ 4400
V-8	3.74 x 3.48	9.30	305	170 @ 4000 +

+ Optional 305 CID, C.R. 9.30, NHP 230 @ 4400 and 350 CID, C.R. 9.30, NHP 245 @ 4400 (TPI option for IROC-Z only).

1992 Collector Pricing

	6	5	4	3	2	1
2d RS Cpe (V-6)	400	1,200	2,000	4,500	7,000	10,000
2d RS Conv (V-6)	600	1,800	3,000	6,750	10,500	15,000
2d Cpe (V-8)	440	1,320	2,200	4,950	7,700	11,000
2d Z28 Cpe (V-8)	540	1,620	2,700	6,080	9,450	13,500
2d Z28 Conv (V-8)	680	2,040	3,400	7,650	11,900	17,000

CHAPTER *Eight*

Gen IV: The Perfect Camaro (1993-2002)

"We blew a deadline, ticked everyone off, cost the company a bundle and we did the right thing," read Jim Perkin's handwritten scrawl in a GM advertisement that appeared in *Ward's 1994 Automotive Yearbook*. The ad copy told the story of how plans to debut "an important flagship model" were delayed "because not every car coming off the line was just right." It revealed that Chevy general manager Jim Perkins had "pulled the plug on the introduction" and quoted Perkins as saying, "When we know we got it right, we'll bring out the car." It added that Perkins got a good night's sleep.

The Z28 was back as the Indy Pace Car for 1993.

The ad doesn't mention the Camaro, but I'll give you odds it was the car in question. The new F-cars were assembled in a factory in Ste. Terese, Quebec, Canada. The plant dated to '65, but was heavily revamped to build the Gen IV cars. Workers were formed into teams, with each department functioning independently. The goal of this approach was a defect-free automobile—the perfect Camaro—no matter how long it took to achieve.

When the futuristic-looking Camaro took its showroom bow in January '93, thousands of enthusiasts agreed Perkins had "done the right thing." The car was almost—but not quite—"all new." It shared its floor pan stamping and rear suspension system with the Gen III, but the rest of it was different, from its "spaceship" styling to engines like a 3.4-liter V-6 and a 5.7-liter Corvette V-8.

In a sense, it was amazing that the Gen IV made it to market at all in a year that GM gave "pink slips" to its 44-year-old Coupe DeVille, its more youthful Allante convertible, its GEO storm, its Pontiac LeMans, the Olds Bravada and the Buick Riviera coupe. In fact, during 1993, GM's light-vehicle market share hit an all-time low of 34.2 percent. It was the year that GM offered early retirement to workers between February 1 and March 1. The 50 to 61-year-olds could collect full benefits with no cap on earnings; those 62 and older got a full pension, health "bennies" for life, a $10,000 voucher towards the purchase of a U.S.-built GM vehicle, plus $3,000 to use on top of the voucher.

Model-year sales for the '93 Camaro were 68,773 units. That was up from 56,909 in '92. True, it wasn't as good as it could have been with a full 12 months of selling, but the slow start was not due to the new Gen IV model itself. By '94, the sales figure would swell to over 116,000 units— the highest total since '87. Chevy did many things to promote the new model, including pacing the Indy 500 and competing in Trans-Am Racing with Jack Baldwin and Scott Sharp. It just took a little while for the entire program to kick in.

In 1994, Major League Baseball went on strike, but U.S. car makers hit a home run. With a presidential election under its belt, the economy seemed to be strengthening. GM netted $4.9 billion, up from $2.5 billion in '93 and slightly higher than the previous record set in 1988. GM employees were happy after depositing the first profit-sharing checks they had seen in four years.

Despite GM's bonanza, '94 was a bad year for Chevrolet, which went from being GM's most-improved division in '93 to its second-worst in '94. Chevy's market share took a .7-percent hit. Nevertheless, the Gen IV Camaro was the company's saving grace with sales up 69.5 percent (about 48,000 units). The model-year sales total was 116,592 (11.6 percent of Chevy's business), versus 68,773 (6.6 percent of business) in '93. Product news for '94 included a convertible and engine, gearbox and economy improvements.

You could tell '95 wasn't the greatest year for GM when the company announced plans to trim development costs by 25 percent and eliminate 5,000 white-collar jobs by '97. The head honchos boasted that they were going to restore market share to 35 percent, though such a result was not in the cards.

Though only two years old, the "perfect" Camaro was already doing less than perfect in the sales department. This came as no surprise, as GM and Chevy did little to make headlines with exciting innovations. The hottest new attraction was the availability of traction control starting in December 1994. As in the past, the Camaro got a major— and magnificent—revamp, and was then left to slowly sell fewer and fewer units each passing year.

Model-year sales through U.S. dealers in 1995 peaked at 97,525, which seemed putrid, but was about as good as it was going to get until the end came in 2002. During the 12 months of calendar-year 1995, the factory in Canada cranked out 110,689 cars, versus 135,234 the previous period. (By the way, sales of Camaros to Canadian buyers were going in the "right" direction with 567 sold in '92, 751 in '93, 2,350 in '94 and 2,581 in '95).

In 1996, GM decided to move its world headquarters from the historic General Motors Building to the new Ren-Cen in downtown Detroit. Amid plans for a major launch of new GM models in '97, few changes were made in the '96 products, and those the Camaro got were primarily mechanical. They included a new 3800 V-6, an anti-theft system and some V-6 performance options.

It was a year of labor strife at GM overall and Canadian output fell by 5,000 units. Early in the calendar year, GM of Canada eliminated a second shift at the F-car factory due to dwindling demand for the sports cars. Model-year sales south of the border dropped to 75,336. Up north, calendar-year production was down to 56,843—a really huge decline (nearly half) from the '95 number.

The Camaro continued to taper in its market appeal in '97 with U.S. model-year sales of 58,152 and Canadian calendar-year production of 58,010 coming in almost neck and neck. In trade magazines, GM's new vehicle programs listed a major redo of the F-cars for 2000, but it was never to happen. A 30th Anniversary option for the Z28 pumped up a bit of excitement, but overall, the Camaro story was the same old-same old one more year.

By '98, the Gen IV Camaro was ready for a trip to the beauty parlor for the latest in facial treatments, but a new hood, fenders and nose did little to stem continuing erosion of sales, which fell to 48,806 units in the model year. Canada reported calendar-year output of 47,049 Chevy-brand F-cars. The release of a modified 5.7-liter LS1 V-8 for the Z28 and a new SS performance kit added just a bit of interest for muscle car maniacs with the need for speed.

Remember the pledge by GM brass, in 1995, to get the company's market share back above 35 percent? Well, for '99, the number was below 32 percent! These were not good years for "The General" and the Camaro was beginning to be viewed as part of the problem, rather than any type of cure. It took some strenuous bargaining by Canadian autoworkers involved in labor negotiations to even secure the future of the Ste. Terese plant until 2001, when GM said it was planning to kill off the Camaro and the Firebird. Model-year sales in the U.S. came in at 41,412. Canadian

Smooth, slightly wrapped tail lights and a small integrated spoiler were part of the new Z28 look.

Gen IV: The Perfect Camaro (1993-2002)

production for the calendar year was 41,412.

By 2000, everyone knew the Camaro was nearing the end of the trail. Chevy gave it a new steering wheel with redundant radio controls and an optional performance handling package with a choice of painted or polished 16-inch wheel rims. Both the 3800 V-6 and the LS1 V-8 were revised to meet new federally mandated low-emissions vehicle requirements. Some people were starting to view the Camaro as a future collector's item, so model-year sales registered a slight bump to 41,962 units. Calendar-year output in the aging Ste. Terese plant was 44,136 cars.

When terrorists took down the World Trade Center in New York on September 11, 2001, there were shock waves felt immediately in the Canadian auto industry. As the border between the U.S. and its neighbor to the north tightened, the economic advantages of making cars in Canada began to disappear. While it was a record year for auto sales there, dark clouds hung over the horizon. GM of Canada had been the first to issue bad news, with its early-2001 announcement that it planned to cease Camaro and Firebird production in September and idle 1,700 Canadian workers. Sales fell off to 34,053 and production for the calendar year was only 27,108 vehicles.

The 2002 Camaro still managed to arrive and went out in style. Every car built carried a 35th anniversary dash plaque and a full 35th Anniversary package was optional. With a get-one-before-they're-gone mentality kicking in, the "last" Camaro generated an uptick to 35,310 model-year sales, but calendar-year production at Ste. Terese stalled at 23,012.

The Z28 coupe was one of only two Camaros offered for 1993. The base coupe was the other. Both were radically different from any previous Chevy pony cars.

1993

The '93 Camaro had many new features: plastic front fenders, a short-and-long-arm front suspension, rack-and-pinion steering and "flying saucer" styling. The base V-6-powered sport coupe took its motivation from a new 3.4-liter/160-hp V-6. A treat for Z28 buyers was a 275-hp version of the 5.7-liter "Corvette" LT1 V-8.

The 3.4-liter Code S V-6 with a five-speed transmission was the standard power train for the base Camaro in 1993.

The Camaro was no stranger to the Indy 500 bricks by the time the 1993 Z28 was named to pace the race.

The most powerful Camaro small-block since the '70 LT-1 (with a hyphen), the LT1 put awesome power into the hands of modern muscle car fans. It came hooked to a four-speed automatic or six-speed manual gearbox. Standard goodies included 16-in. wheels and tires, four-wheel anti-lock brakes and a black-colored roof. A first for Camaro and Chevy was the use of a non-ozone-depleting cfc A/C refrigerant. The 1LE Special Performance option included a beefed-up suspension and heavy-duty cooling.

For a fourth time (three of four generations) the Camaro was picked to pace the Indy 500. The Official Pace Car was a striking-looking coupe with removable roof panels. It had a Black-over-White paint job with special multi-colored stripes and interior seat covers. The LT1-powered car didn't need many modifications to stay ahead of the racing cars. Replicas were offered to the public and 663 were built.

The redesigned 1993 Z28s were a big leap forward for Chevrolet. They were, stylish, technologically advanced, popular with the public and second only to the Corvette in racecar-like performance.

The deck, roof, doors and hatch panel on the new-generation Camaros were made of a sheet-molded compound (SMC) derived from chopped glass and polyester resin.

Medium Patriot Blue Metallic was a new color choice in 1993.

152 THE STORY OF CAMARO

The Z28 interior was loaded with gauges in a very airplane-like cockpit.

Gen IV: The Perfect Camaro (1993-2002)

The 1993 LT1-powered Z28 gave police departments a very swift pursuit vehicle. At the time, the 154-mph top speed of these 275-hp cars made them the fastest police vehicles ever tested.

Phil Kunz

1993 CAMARO BY THE NUMBERS

Year	Body Code	Body Type	Engine Type	W.B. (Inches)	O.L. (Inches)	Wt. (Lbs.)	HP (Net)	Disp CID	MSP Price	Model Yr. Prod.
CAMARO V-6										
93	F/P87	2CPE	V-6	101.1	193.2	3,241	160	207	$13,339	21,253
Z28 V-8										
93	F/P87	2CPE	V-8	101.1	193.2	3,373	275	350	$16,799	17,850
ALL CAMARO TOTAL										39,103 (*)

MODEL-YEAR PRODUCTION NOTES
(*) domestic – total North American production for U.S. and Canada was 40,224
10 Camaros with 1LE included in Z28 total above.
633 Camaros with Indy Pace Car package included in Z28 total above.

1993 Engine Spec's

Engine	B x S	C.R.	CID	BHP
V-6	3.62 x 3.31	9.00	207	160 @ 4600
V-8	4.00 x 3.48	10.50	350	275 @ 5000

1993 Collector Pricing

	6	5	4	3	2	1
CAMARO (160-HP L32 V-6)						
2d Cpe	340	1,020	1,700	3,830	5,950	8,500
2d Conv	380	1,140	1,900	4,280	6,650	9,500
CAMARO Z28 (275-HP LT1 V-8)						
2d Cpe	700	2,100	3,500	7,880	12,250	17,500
2d Conv	760	2,280	3,800	8,550	13,300	19,000
CAMARO Z28 INDY PACE CAR (275-HP LT1 V-8; ONLY 633 BUILT)						
2d Cpe	920	2,760	4,600	10,350	16,100	23,000
2d Conv	1,000	3,000	5,000	11,250	17,500	25,000
CALLOWAY CAMARO C8 (383-HP LT1 V-8)						
2d Cpe	1,840	5,520	9,200	20,700	32,200	48,000
DOUG RIPPLE CAMARO C8 (383-HP LT1 V-8)						
2d Cpe	1,400	4,200	7,000	15,750	24,500	35,000

1994

A convertible returned to the Camaro lineup as a mid-season addition in 1994. Its chassis was beefed up and considerably stiffer than that of the last Camaro convertible offered in '92. The ragtop style was offered in both the base and Z28 car lines. The very cool-looking convertible included a power-operated top, a full headliner and a heated rear window.

New features for the Camaro's long list of standard equipment included a remote keyless entry system, "flood light"-style interior illumination, and a compact disc system with co-axial speakers. Leather seating surfaces in two colors—Beige and Graphite—were made available late in the production run.

The Z28's 5.7-liter LT1 V-8 received sequential fuel injection for 1994 to provide a smoother idle and lower emissions. The T56 six-speed transmission utilized Computer-Aided Gear Selection to improve fuel economy. The 4L60 automatic transmission now featured electronic controls.

Advertised power ratings for both engines remained the same. The LT1 produced its maximum 275 hp at 5200 rpm and cranked up 325 lbs.-ft. of torque. With this engine under its hood, a Z28 moved from 0 to 60 mph in 6.3 seconds and could do the quarter-mile in 14.8 seconds at 97 mph.

More than 40,000 new Z28s were produced for 1994.

GM photo

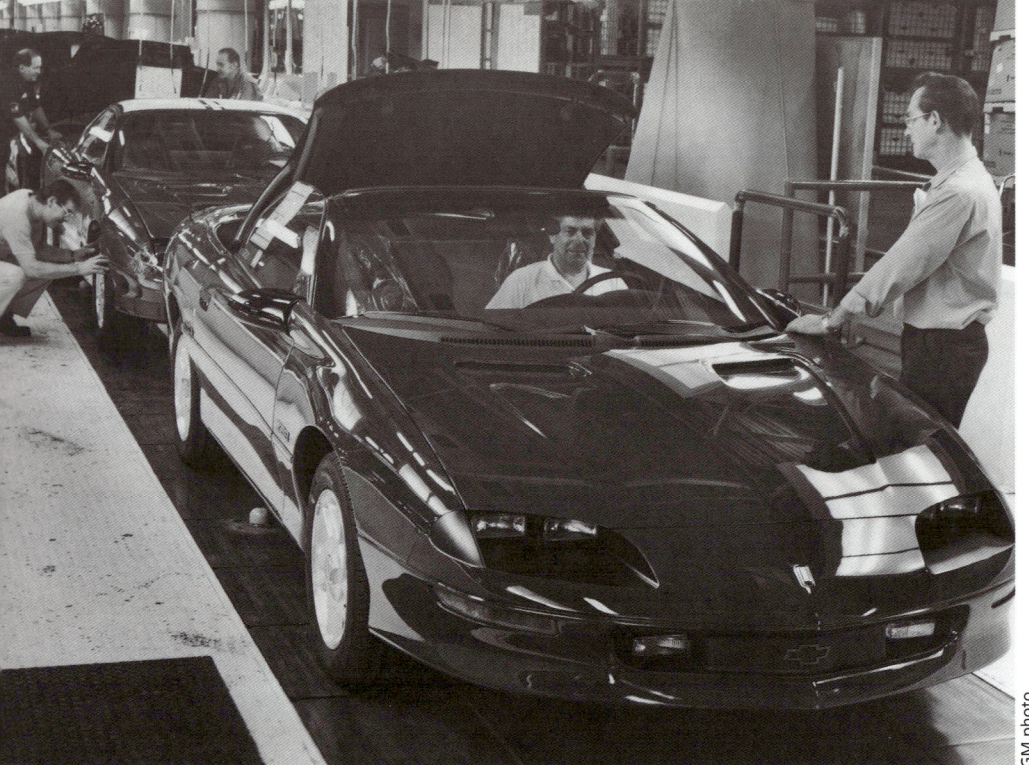

The first 1994 Z28 convertible comes off the assembly line at GM's final assembly plant in Ste. Therese, Quebec, Canada.

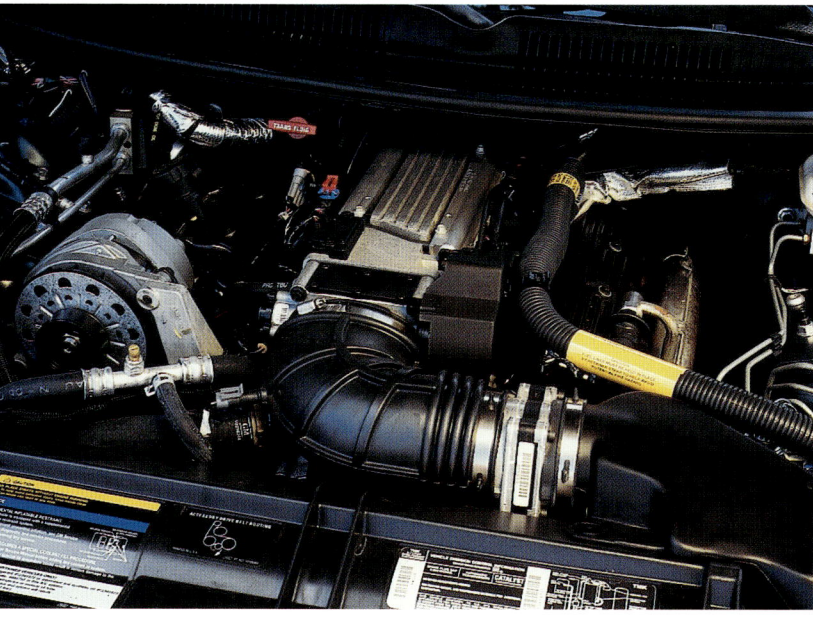

The sequential fuel injection on the LT1 V-8 was meant to provide smoother idling and better emissions.

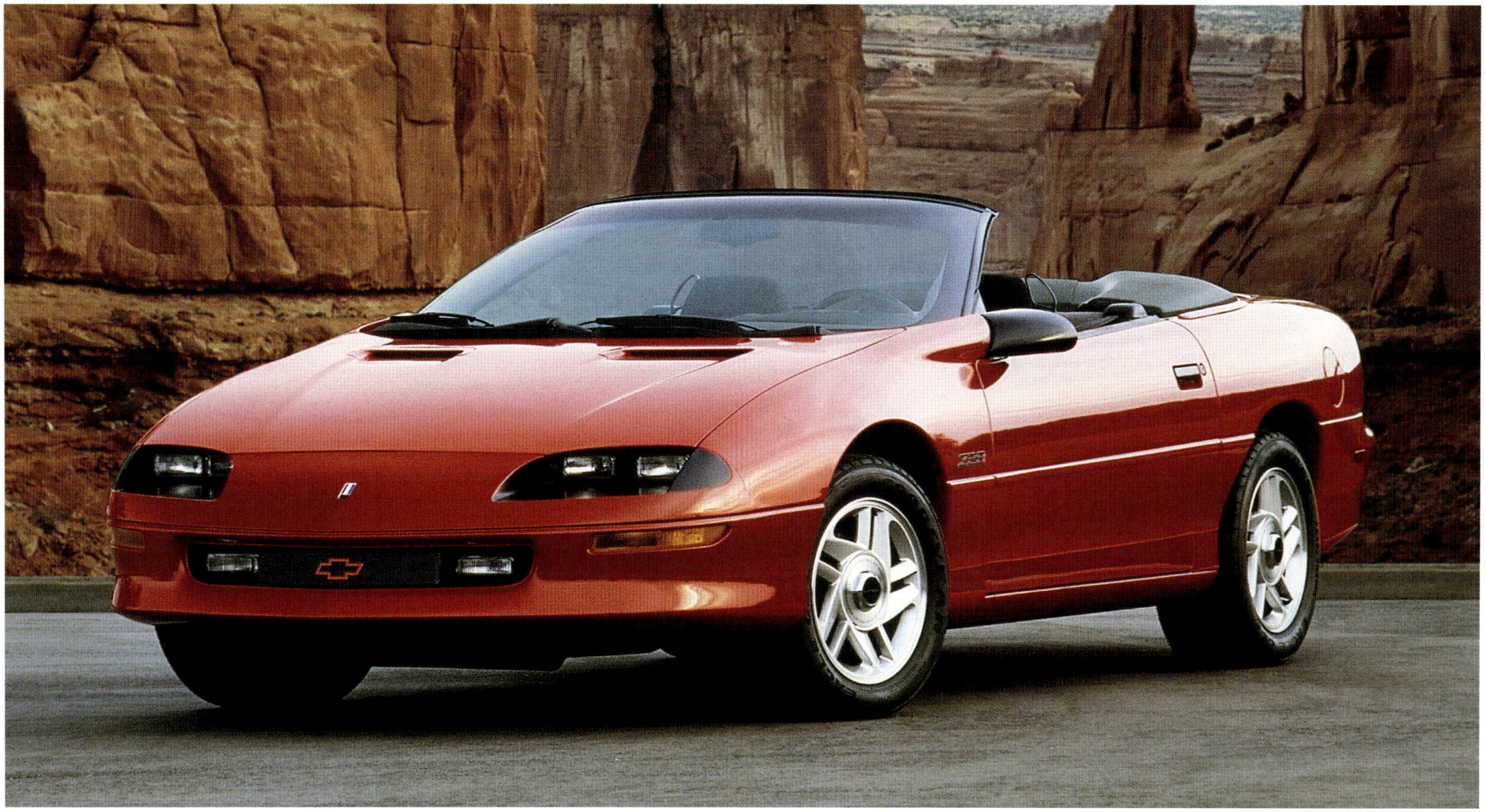

The convertible was a midseason addition to the Camaro lineup in 1994. This is the Z28 version.

Air bags, center console, full gauge package and Scotchguarded fabric were all part of the 1994 Camaro interior amenities.

1994 CAMARO BY THE NUMBERS

Year	Body Code	Body Type	Engine Type	W.B. (Inches)	O.L. (Inches)	Wt. (Lbs.)	HP (Net)	Disp CID	MSP Price	Model Yr. Prod.
CAMARO V-6										
94	F/P87	2CPE	V-6	101.1	193.2	3,247	160	207	$13,339	76,531
94	F/P87	2CONV	V-6	101.1	193.2	3,342	160	207	$18,745	2,328
Z28 V-8										
94	F/P87	2CPE	V-8	101.1	193.2	3,424	275	350	$16,799	36,008
94	F/P87	2CONV	V-8	101.1	193.2	3,524	275	350	$22,075	4,932
ALL CAMARO TOTAL										19,799 (*)

MODEL-YEAR PRODUCTION NOTES
(*) domestic – total North American production for U.S. and Canada was 125,244
135 Camaros with 1LE included in Z28 total above.

Gen IV: The Perfect Camaro (1993-2002)

The power top folded flush with the 1994 Camaro body and was covered by a three-piece tonneau cover.

1994 Engine Spec's

Engine	B x S	C.R.	CID	BHP
COUPE				
V-6	3.62 x 3.31	9.00	207	160 @ 4600
V-8	4.00 x 3.48	10.50	350	275 @ 5000
CONVERTIBLE				
V-6	3.62 x 3.31	9.00	207	160 @ 4600
V-8	4.00 x 3.48	10.50	350	275 @ 5000

1994 Collector Pricing

	6	5	4	3	2	1
CAMARO (160-HP L32 V-6)						
2d Cpe	350	1,100	1,800	4,050	6,300	9,000
2d Conv	400	1,200	2,000	4,500	7,000	10,000
CAMARO Z28 (275-HP LT1 V-8)						
2d Cpe	450	1,300	2,200	4,950	7,700	11,000
2d Conv	520	1,560	2,600	5,850	9,100	13,000
CALLOWAY CAMARO C8 (383-HP LT1 V-8)						
2d Cpe	1,900	5,750	9,600	21,600	33,600	48,000

1995

For 1995, the same four Camaro models were marketed. There were a couple of new body colors—Dark Purple, Sebring Silver and Mystic Teal. Hardcore fans can tell you that the base models now had body-color sport mirrors on both sides of the car. For the first time, buyers of coupes with removable roof panels could have the roof and outside rearview mirrors painted the same color as the car.

Many new features were limited to a specific car/drivetrain combination or sold as optional equipment. For example, a 3.8-liter 200-hp V-6 (a.k.a. "3800" engine) was optional in the base sport coupe. The Z28 was now available with traction control and all-season tires.

The base Camaros came with the 3.4-liter/160-hp V-6 mated to a five-speed manual gearbox. Z28s featured the 275-hp LT1 V-8 mated to a Borg-Warner six-speed manual transmission. A four-speed electronically controlled automatic transmission was optional.

An extra planned for '95 that failed to arrive until '98 was a package combining speed-rated performance tires, a 150-mph speedometer and an optional Acceleration Slip Regulation traction-control system.

Jim Perkins, the enthusiast who ran Chevrolet and did much to promote its performance image, was replaced as general manager by John G. Middlebrook.

The 1995 Camaro was very difficult to tell apart from the previous year's model. Nothing obvious changed on the exterior.

A buyer could pick up a 1995 Z28 coupe for less than $18,000 new. A very nice survivor sells for about half that cost today, making these cars very nice "sleeper" buys on the secondary market.

The LT1 350-cid V-8 was again rated at 275 hp in 1995.

1995 CAMARO BY THE NUMBERS

Year	Body Code	Body Type	Engine Type	W.B. (Inches)	O.L. (Inches)	Wt. (Lbs.)	HP (Net)	Disp CID	MSP Price	Model Yr. Prod.
CAMARO V-6										
95	F/P87	2CPE	V-6	101.1	193.2	3,251	160	207	$14,250	See notess
95	F/P87	2CONV	V-6	101.1	193.2	3,342	160	207	$19,495	See notess
CAMARO V-8										
95	F/P87	2CPE	V-8	101.1	193.2	3,390	275	350	$17,915	See notess
95	F/P87	2CONV	V-8	101.1	193.2	3,480	275	350	$22,075	See notess
ALL CAMARO TOTAL										122,725

MODEL-YEAR PRODUCTION NOTES
Sport coupes (base and Z28): 115,365
Convertibles (base and Z28): 7,360

The 1995 Z28 convertible had the same power top, form-fitting tonneau cover and rear-window defogger as the previous year.

1995 Engine Spec's

Engine	B x S	C.R.	CID	BHP
COUPE				
V-6	3.62 x 3.31	9.00	207	160 @ 4600
V-6	3.80 x 3.40	9.40	231	200 @ 5300
V-8	4.00 x 3.48	10.50	350	275 @ 5000
CONVERTIBLE				
V-6	3.62 x 3.31	9.00	207	160 @ 4600
V-6	3.80 x 3.40	9.40	231	200 @ 5300
V-8	4.00 x 3.48	10.50	350	275 @ 5000

1995 Collector Pricing

	6	5	4	3	2	1
CAMARO (160-HP L32V-6)						
2d Cpe	380	1,140	1,900	4,280	6,650	9,500
2d Conv	400	1,200	2,000	4,500	7,000	10,000
CAMARO (200-HP L36V-6)						
2d Cpe	380	1,140	1,900	4,280	6,650	9,500
2d Conv	400	1,200	2,000	4,500	7,000	10,000
CAMARO Z28 (275-HP LT1 V-8)						
2d Cpe	460	1,380	2,300	5,180	8,050	11,500
2d Conv	540	1,620	2,700	6,080	9,450	13,500
CALLOWAY CAMARO C8 (383-HP LT1 V-8)						
2d Cpe	1,950	5,900	9,800	22,050	34,300	49,000

1996

With sales roaring in '95, Chevy blew out the '96 Camaro with new RS (Rally Sport) versions of the coupe and convertible. An SS version of each body was added at midyear. The 3800 became the standard V-6.

A V-6 Performance Handling package was available for base Camaros. V-6s with automatic got a new second-gear-select switch that allowed second gear starting for improved "launch" on slippery surfaces. The RS featured front and rear fascia extensions, a ground effects package and a three-piece rear spoiler extension. The Z28's 5.7-liter V-8 gained 10 hp.

The big news in Camaroland for '96 was the return of an SS. Chevy teamed up with SLP Engineering, of Troy, Michigan, to bring back the SS name. SLP took the Z28, tweaked the engine and slapped on 17-inch five-spoke wheels with P245/40ZR17 BFGoodrich Comp T/A tires. The 305-hp bomb was the first Camaro to break the 300-hp barrier.

Chevrolet built a pair of special Z28/SS models to pace the Brickyard 400 stock car race in August 1996. By then, the production of '96 models had closed, but the race and the pace cars proved popular. Chevy offered a Brickyard 400 package for '97 Camaro Z28/SS models.

The wide hood stripes were back on the 1996 Z28s. This car had the ultra-cool Bright Red with Black treatment.

SLP Engineering of Red Bank, New Jersey, turned the 1996 Camaro SS into an even hotter car with a bunch of serious upgrades. The cars got a composite hood with "ant eater" air scoop, big 17-inch wheels, a performance suspension and differential, special air intake and exhaust that boosted the horsepower rating to 305.

The Z28 returned to the Brickyard as the pace car in 1996.

The SS was back after a 24-year absence in 1996. SLP Engineering turned out 2,410 of these cars, which were actually fancy, higher-performance versions of the Z28.

Styled 17-inch aluminum alloy wheels were part of the SS package.

A forced-air intake helped the SS inhale.

1996 CAMARO BY THE NUMBERS

Year	Body Code	Body Type	Engine Type	W.B. (Inches)	O.L. (Inches)	Wt. (Lbs.)	HP (Net)	Disp CID	MSP Price	Model Yr. Prod.
CAMARO V-6										
96	F/P87	2CPE	V-6	101.1	193.2	3,306	200	231	$14,990	31,528
96	F/P87	2CONV	V-6	101.1	193.2	3,440	200	231	$21,270	2,994
CAMARO RS V-6										
96	F/P87	2CPE	V-8	101.1	193.2	3,306	200	231	$17,490	8,091
96	F/P87	2CONV	V-8	101.1	193.2	3,440	200	231	$22,720	908
CAMARO Z28 V-8										
96	F/P87	2CPE	V-8	101.1	193.2	3,466	285	350	$19,390	14,906
96	F/P87	2CONV	V-8	101.1	193.2	3,593	285	350	$24,490	2,938
CAMARO SS V-8										
96	F/P87	2CPE	V-8	101.1	193.2	—	305	350	$22,999	See notes
96	F/P87	2CONV	V-8	101.1	193.2	—	305	350	$28,149	See notes
ALL CAMARO TOTAL										61,362

MODEL-YEAR PRODUCTION NOTES
Included in Z28 production were 2410 Camaro Z28s with the SS package.
Two actual Brickyard 400 Pace Cars based on the 1996 Camaro were included in Z28/SS production.
A Brickyard 400 replica package was offered for the 1997 Camaro SS/Z28.

Restyled deck lid spoilers gave the SS a different look from behind.

1996 Engine Spec's

Engine	B x S	C.R.	CID	BHP
COUPE				
V-6	3.80 x 3.40	9.40	231	200 @ 5300
V-8	4.00 x 3.48	10.50	350	285 @ 5000
CONVERTIBLE				
V-6	3.80 x 3.40	9.40	231	200 @ 5300
V-8	4.00 x 3.48	10.50	350	285 @ 5000

+ Optional 350 CID, NHP 305 @ 5500 and 350 CID, NHP 310 @ 5500 (Optional in Camaro SS only).

1996 Collector Pricing

	6	5	4	3	2	1
CAMARO (200-HP L36 V-6)						
2d Cpe	400	1,200	2,000	4,500	7,000	10,000
2d Conv	420	1,260	2,100	4,730	7,350	10,500
CAMARO Z28 (305-HP LT1 V-8)						
2d Cpe	500	1,500	2,500	5,630	8,750	12,500
2d Conv	600	1,750	2,900	6,530	10,200	14,500
CAMARO Z28 SS (305-HP LT1 V-8)						
2d Cpe	700	2,050	3,450	7,740	12,000	17,200
2d Conv	760	2,280	3,800	8,550	13,300	19,000
CAMARO Z28 SS (310-HP LT1 V-8)						
2d Cpe	700	2,100	3,500	7,880	12,250	17,500
2d Conv	800	2,400	4,000	9,000	14,000	20,000
CALLOWAY CAMARO C8 (383-HP LT1 V-8)						
2d Cpe	1,950	5,900	9,800	22,050	34,300	49,000

1997

It was the Camaro's 30th year of production. To mark this manufacturing milestone, all '97 Camaros featured a 30th Anniversary logo on the front seats. A new instrument panel and floor console featured built-in power outlets and cup holders. Coupes got a new 200-watt sound system. At the rear of the car, the tail lights were changed to an international tri-color design. New up-level five-spoke wheels were introduced and automatic transmission became standard equipment in Z28s.

To celebrate the Camaro's 30th anniversary, Chevy offered a special Z4C 30th Anniversary edition package for $575. It included a White monochromatic exterior with Hugger Orange racing stripes, White five-spoke aluminum wheels, 30th Anniversary embroided emblems on the front floor mats and headrests. With Arctic White seats with black-and-white houndstooth inserts, it paid homage to the famous '69 Indy Pace Car. You could get this package on both Z28 and Z28/SS coupes and convertibles.

Replica's of the two special '96 Camaro Z28/SS Brickyard 400 Pace Cars were offered to the public during model year 1997. This option was offered for all Z28 and SS models. SLP Engineering also produced an extremely limited run of 106 Camaro Z28s equipped with the 5.7-liter/330-hp LT4 "Corvette" V-8.

At nearly $30,000 for the convertible and more than $24,000 for the coupe (and extra for the T-tops), the 30th anniversary SS was the fanciest, highest-priced Camaro built to date, but they were probably also among the best Camaros of any era.

The 30th anniversary SS Camaros were memorable white-and-orange models that have developed their own fan clubs.

1997 CAMARO BY THE NUMBERS

Year	Body Code	Body Type	Engine Type	W.B. (Inches)	O.L. (Inches)	Wt. (Lbs.)	HP (Net)	Disp CID	MSP Price	Model Yr. Prod.
CAMARO V-6										
97	F/P87	2CPE	V-6	101.1	193.2	3,294	200	231	$16,215	See notes
97	F/P87	2CONV	V-6	101.1	193.2	3,455	200	231	$21,770	See notes
CAMARO RS V-6										
97	F/P87	2CPE	V-8	101.1	193.2	3,307	200	231	$17,970	See notes
97	F/P87	2CONV	V-8	101.1	193.2	3,455	200	231	$23,170	See notes
CAMARO Z28 V-8										
97	F/P87	2CPE	V-8	101.1	193.2	3,433	285	350	$20,115	See notes
97	F/P87	2CONV	V-8	101.1	193.2	3,589	285	350	$25,520	See notes
CAMARO SS V-8										
97	F/P87	2CPE	V-8	101.1	193.2	--	305	350	$24,114	See notes
97	F/P87	2CONV	V-8	101.1	193.2	--	305	350	$29,513	See notes
ALL CAMARO TOTAL										54,972

MODEL-YEAR PRODUCTION NOTES
Sport Coupes (all model): 48292
Convertibles (all models): 6680
Included in Z28 production were 3035 Camaro Z28s with the SS package

Colorado was among the states that employed the Camaro for State Patrol duty in 1997. The 350-cid fuel-injected V-8 was hard to outrun.

Gen IV: The Perfect Camaro (1993-2002)

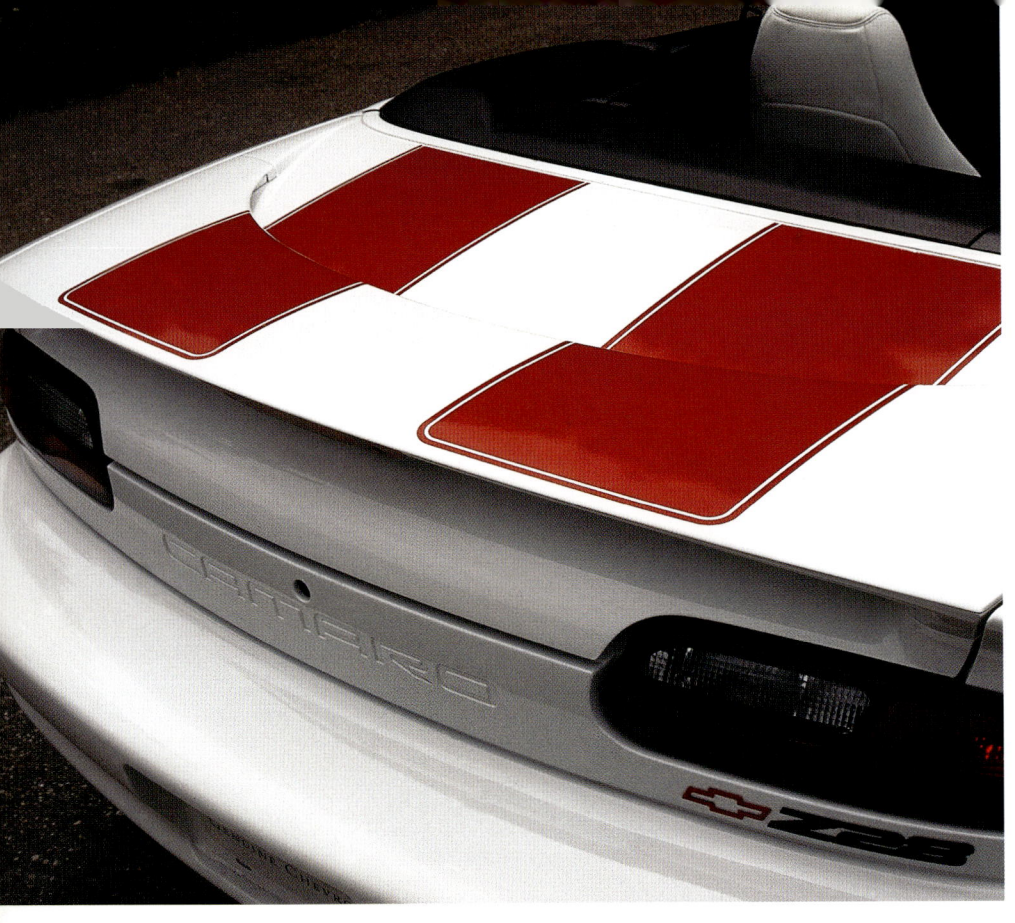

1997 Engine Spec's

Engine	B x S	C.R.	CID	BHP
COUPE				
V-6	3.80 x 3.40	9.40	231	200 @ 5300
V-8	4.00 x 3.48	10.50	350	285 @ 5000
CONVERTIBLE				
V-6	3.80 x 3.40	9.40	231	200 @ 5300
V-8	4.00 x 3.48	10.50	350	285 @ 5000

+ Optional 350 CID, NHP 305 @ 5500 and 350 CID, NHP 310 @ 5500 (Optional in Camaro SS only).

1997 Collector Pricing

	6	5	4	3	2	1
CAMARO (200-HP L36 V-6)						
2d Cpe	420	1,260	2,100	4,730	7,350	10,500
2d Conv	450	1,300	2,200	4,950	7,700	11,000
CAMARO Z28 (285-HP LT1 V-8)						
2d Cpe	500	1,500	2,500	5,630	8,750	12,500
2d Conv	600	1,750	2,900	6,530	10,200	14,500
CAMARO Z28 30TH ANNIVERSARY (285-HP LT1 V-8)						
2d Cpe	520	1,560	2,600	5,850	9,100	13,000
2d Conv	600	1,800	3,000	6,750	10,500	15,000
CAMARO Z28 BRICKYARD 400 PACE CAR (305-HP LT1 V-8)						
2d Cpe	700	2,100	3,500	7,880	12,250	17,500
2d Conv	760	2,280	3,800	8,550	13,300	19,000

Note: This 1997 Camarao paced the 1996 Brickyard 400 stock car race.

	6	5	4	3	2	1
CAMARO Z28 SS (305-HP LT1 V-8)						
2d Cpe	760	2,280	3,800	8,550	13,300	18,000
2d Conv	760	2,280	3,800	8,550	13,300	19,500
CAMARO Z28 SS (310-HP LT1 V-8)						
2d Cpe	740	2,220	3,700	8,330	12,950	18,500
2d Conv	800	2,400	4,000	9,000	14,000	20,000
BERGER CHEVROLET SS CAMARO (380 HP)						
2d Cpe	1,200	3,600	6,000	13,500	21,000	30,000
2d Conv	1,300	3,850	6,400	14,400	22,400	32,000

NOTE: Add 10 percent for Z28 30th Anniversary Package.

The paint scheme and wide hood and deck lid stripes of the 1997 SS were clearly nods to the Camaro's past.

1998

The Gen IV Camaro was "refreshed" a bit for '98. The result was a nice-looking car with a more Euro flavor. The hood had a new "double-bubble" motif with two bulges above new "gel-cap" composite headlights (with reflector optics). The bumper/grille ensemble was redone, too, with a more oblong-shaped, black-finished "mouth." The RS models were replaced with an optional Sport Appearance package.

Technically speaking, all '98s received a new Bosch four-wheel disc brakes system with integrated ABS, as well as a one-piece, all-welded exhaust system. The base engine was still the 3.8-liter 200-hp L36 V-6, which came attached to a five-speed manual gearbox. A 4L60-E electronically controlled automatic transmission was standard in Z28s and otherwise optional.

More big news was below the hood of the Z28, where there was a new Gen III 305-hp "Corvette" LS-1 small-block V-8. This 346-cid (not 350) 5.7-liter "mill" was the first all-aluminum engine used in any Camaro since the '69 ZL-1.

Chevy made the bulk of the SS models at the Canadian F-car plant, although SLP added the special air-induction hood and SS-style rear deck lid spoiler. The SS featured the LS-1 with standard Ram Air and came with a choice of 315 or 320 hp.

Only 478 SS convertibles were produced by SLP Engineeering for 1998. This car was painted Sport Gold Metallic.

There was about a $7,000 price difference between the 1998 Z28 coupe and convertible. The convertible had traction control as standard equipment, along with an upgraded sound system and a few other amenities.

The 1998 SS was undoubtedly one of the best-looking Camaros ever produced.

The 1998 Z28 convertible carried a price tag of $27,975.

Gen IV: The Perfect Camaro (1993-2002)

The 1996 limited edition Dale Earnhardt Signature Series Camaro had an abundance of NASCAR-inspired styling inside and the "Intimidator's" signature on the doors.

The Z28 was rated at 315 hp for 1998, and buyers could bump that to 320 with the optional performance exhaust system.

1998 CAMARO BY THE NUMBERS

Year	Body Code	Body Type	Engine Type	W.B. (Inches)	O.L. (Inches)	Wt. (Lbs.)	HP (Net)	Disp CID	MSP Price	Model Yr. Prod.
CAMARO V-6										
98	F/P87	2CPE	V-6	101.1	193.5	3,294	200	231	17,150	See notes
98	F/P87	2CONV	V-6	101.1	193.5	3,446	200	231	22,650	See notes
CAMARO Z28 V-8										
98	F/P87	2CPE	V-8	101.1	193.5	3,433	305	346	20,995	See notes
98	F/P87	2CONV	V-8	101.1	193.5	3,589	305	346	27,975	See notes
CAMARO SS V-8										
98	F/P87	2CPE	V-8	101.1	193.5	--	315	346	24,495	See notes
98	F/P87	2CONV	V-8	101.1	193.5	--	315	346	31,475	See notes
ALL CAMARO TOTAL										49,218

MODEL-YEAR PRODUCTION NOTES
Sport coupes (all model): 45,630
Convertibles (all models): 3,858
Included in Z28 production were 2,397 Camaro SS coupes and 478 Camaro SS convertibles

Gen IV: The Perfect Camaro (1993-2002)

Berger Chevrolet began producing "dealer" muscle cars of its own in 1960s, and the dealership was still turning out its own unique Camaros in 1998.

1998 Engine Spec's

Engine	B x S	C.R.	CID	BHP
COUPE				
V-6	3.80 x 3.40	9.40	231	200 @ 5200
V-8	3.90 x 3.62	10.10	346	305 @ 5000
CONVERTIBLE				
V-6	3.80 x 3.40	9.40	231	200 @ 5200
V-8	3.90 x 3.62	10.10	346	305 @ 5000

+ Optional 346 CID, NHP 315 (Standard in Camaro SS) and 346 CID, NHP 320 (Optional in Camaro SS only).

1998 Collector Pricing

	6	5	4	3	2	1
CAMARO (200-HP L36 V-6)						
2d Cpe	450	1,300	2,200	4,950	7,700	11,000
2d Conv	460	1,380	2,300	5,180	8,050	11,500
CAMARO Z28 (305-HP LS1 V-8)						
2d Cpe	540	1,620	2,700	6,080	9,450	13,500
2d Conv	620	1,860	3,100	6,980	10,850	15,500
CAMARO Z28 SS (315-HP LS1 V-8)						
2d Cpe	760	2,280	3,800	8,550	13,300	19,000
2d Conv	820	2,460	4,100	9,230	14,350	20,500
CAMARO Z28 SS (320-HP LS1 V-8)						
2d Cpe	760	2,280	3,800	8,550	13,300	19,500
2d Conv	840	2,520	4,200	9,450	14,700	21,000

1999

"Why settle for just any sports car, when you can get something with attitude?" asked Chevrolet Motor Division in its 1999 Camaro sales catalog. "That's what the Camaro is all about." That's true, and there was very little change in attitude—or anything else—in the 1999 models. Sport coupes and convertibles were again offered in Camaro, Z28 and SS formats. You could add the "RS-style" Y3F Sport Appearance Package to a base Camaro for a *mere* $1,755. It included rocker and fascia moldings, 16-inch aluminum wheels and P235/55R15 all-season black sidewall tires.

The most significant mechanical change of the year was a Zexel Torsen differential to replace all limited-slip rear axle applications. Traction control was now available on all Camaros, including V-6s. A Monsoon premium sound system made by a company named Monsoon Automotive Audio was added to the convertible's options list. V-6 models got a new electronic throttle control and all Camaros had a new telltale light to monitor oil life. With a larger fuel tank, Camaro owners (16.8 gallons instead of 15.5) could go further on a thankful of gas. Bright Blue Metallic, Hugger Orange and Light Pewter Metallic were the Camaro's new "Heritage" exterior colors.

A total of 4,817 cars were built with the SS option in 1999. The SS option was officially listed as the WU8 "SS Performance & Appearance" package.

Gen IV: The Perfect Camaro (1993-2002)

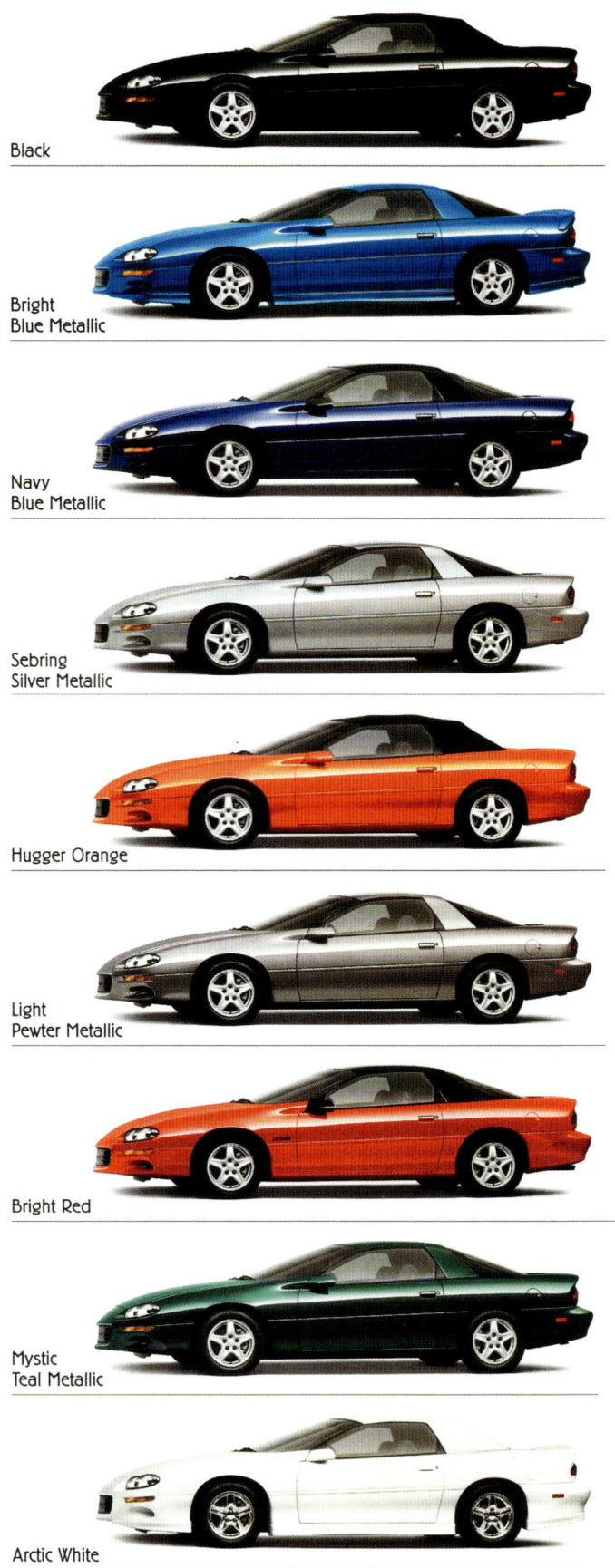

Seventeen-inch cast-aluminum wheels rode at the corners of the SS.

- Black
- Bright Blue Metallic
- Navy Blue Metallic
- Sebring Silver Metallic
- Hugger Orange
- Light Pewter Metallic
- Bright Red
- Mystic Teal Metallic
- Arctic White

The Camaro was again available in a rainbow of colors for 1999.

Flashy white bucket seats were paired with Hugger Orange paint on this SS—a combination that dates back to the 1960s on the Camaro.

1999 CAMARO BY THE NUMBERS

Year	Body Code	Body Type	Engine Type	W.B. (Inches)	O.L. (Inches)	Wt. (Lbs.)	HP (Net)	Disp CID	MSP Price	Model Yr. Prod.
CAMARO V-6										
99	F/P87	2CPE	V-6	101.1	193.2	3,308	200	231	$16,625	See notes
99	F/P87	2CONV	V-6	101.1	193.2	3,340	200	231	$22,125	See notes
CAMARO Z28 V-8										
99	F/P87	2CPE	V-8	101.1	193.2	3,446	305	346	$20,870	See notes
99	F/P87	2CONV	V-8	101.1	193.2	3,565	305	346	$27,850	See notes
CAMARO SS V-8										
99	F/P87	2CPE	V-8	101.1	193.2	3,446	320	346	$24,370	See notes
99	F/P87	2CONV	V-8	101.1	193.2	3,565	320	346	$31,350	See notes
ALL CAMARO TOTAL										42,098

MODEL-YEAR PRODUCTION NOTES
Sport coupes (all model): 38,800
Convertibles (all models): 3,298
Included in Z28 production were 810 Camaro SS coupes, 3,207 SS T-tops and 800 Camaro SS convertible.
Of the 4,817 cars that got the SS package, 222 were built for the Canadian market.

Gen IV: The Perfect Camaro (1993-2002)

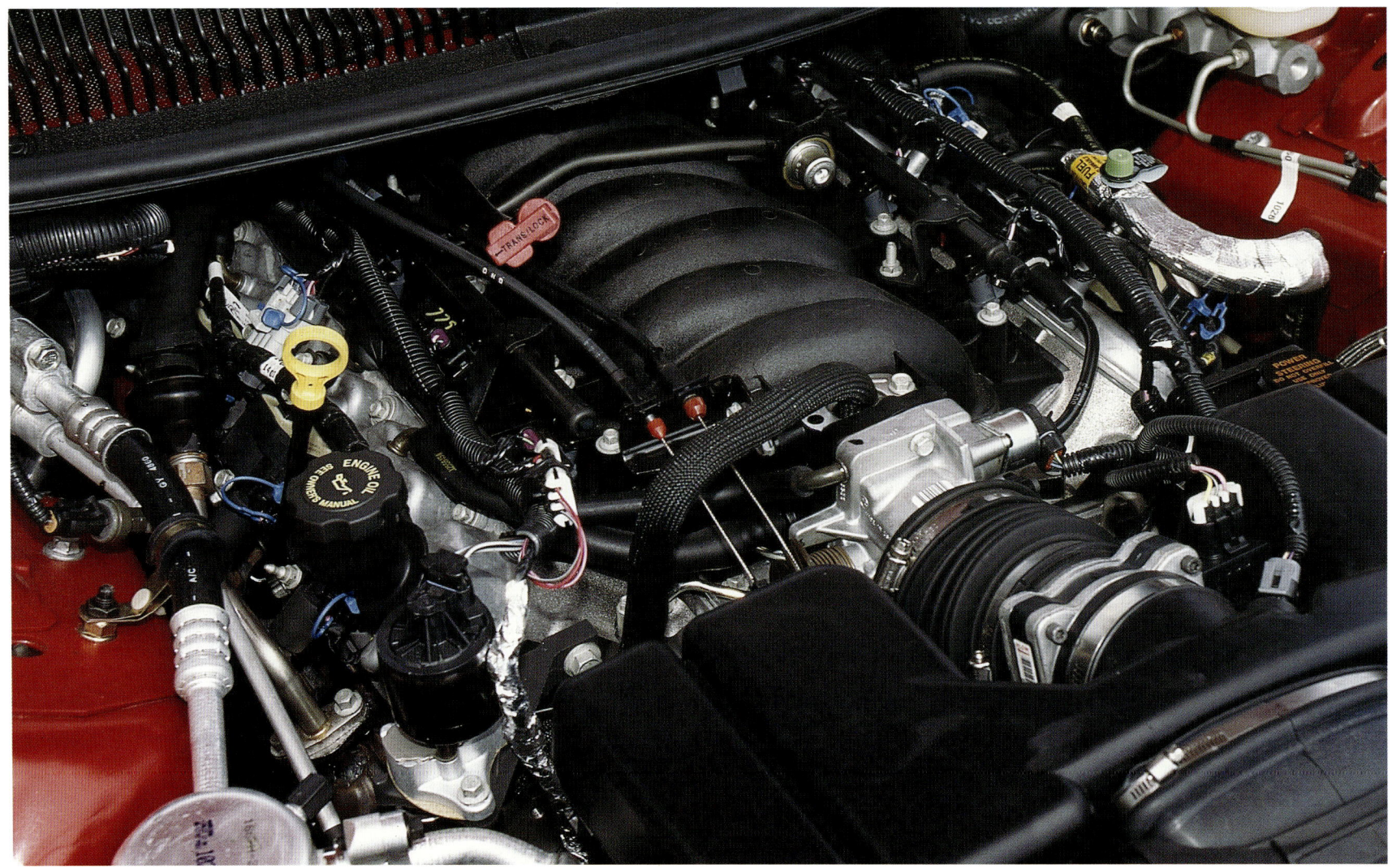

The SS package included a 320-hp version of the LS1 power train.

1999 Engine Spec's

Engine	B x S	C.R.	CID	BHP
COUPE				
V-6	3.80 x 3.40	9.40	231	200 @ 5200
V-8	3.90 x 3.62	10.10	346	305 @ 5200
CONVERTIBLE				
V-6	3.80 x 3.40	9.40	231	200 @ 5200
V-8	3.90 x 3.62	10.10	346	305 @ 5200

+ Optional 346 CID, NHP 315 (Standard in Camaro SS) and 346 CID, NHP 320 (Optional in Camaro SS only).

1999 Collector Pricing

	6	5	4	3	2	1
CAMARO (200-HP L36 V-6)						
2d Cpe	460	1,380	2,300	5,180	8,050	11,500
2d Conv	480	1,440	2,400	5,400	8,400	12,000
CAMARO Z28 (305-HP LS1 V-8)						
2d Cpe	560	1,680	2,800	6,300	9,800	14,000
2d Conv	640	1,920	3,200	7,200	11,200	16,000
CAMARO Z28 SS (320-HP LS1 V-8)						
2d Cpe	840	2,520	4,200	9,450	14,700	21,000
2d Conv	920	2,760	4,600	10,350	16,100	23,000

2000

The 2000s bowed with the Camaro getting several appearance upgrades. A new Monterey Maroon Metallic paint was added to the color spectrum. Z28s also got new dual, body-colored outside rearview mirrors. The 16- and 17-inch aluminum wheels were restyled. "Redundant" radio controls were now integrated into the leather-wrapped steering wheel.

Inside the 2000 Camaro, buyers could add a new Ebony interior color, which replaced Dark Gray. A Medium Gray cloth interior also replaced the former Arctic White leather interior. New fabrics were used to trim the seats and door panels. The premium Monsoon audio system was re-engineered to be compatible with Chevy's optional trunk-mounted 12-disc CD changer.

All Camaro motors were revised so they met Low Emission Vehicle regulations in effect in California and several other states requiring comparable emission systems. Once again, the V-6 generated 200 hp and the V-8 came in 305- and 320-hp versions.

Chevy teamed up with Westech Automotive to make a "302 Camaro" to exhibit at the Specialty Vehicle Market Association's 2000 SEMA show. Based on the LS1 V-8, the high-revving "302" was an awesome showcase of special high-performance hardware, from its SLP lightweight flywheel to its 18-inch American Racing Torq-Thrust II rims.

Only 1,085 of the lovely SS coupes were produced for the 2000 model year.

The functional hood scoop remained a distinctive feature on the SS.

The curvy, wraparound tail lights were bordered by bow tie and SS badging.

The fourth-generation Camaros were frequently dressed up with aftermarket packages. This SS covertible received black-and-red sport seats, additional striping and a 330-hp hood decal, strut tower braces, new 13-spoke alloy wheels and a few other goodies that help it stand out.

Gen IV: The Perfect Camaro (1993-2002)

This 2000 SS has been outfitted with a number of upgrades as part of a custom package from GMMC Inc., a private conversion company.

Gen IV: The Perfect Camaro (1993-2002) 187

2000 CAMARO BY THE NUMBERS

Year	Body Code	Body Type	Engine Type	W.B. (Inches)	O.L. (Inches)	Wt. (Lbs.)	HP (Net)	Disp CID	MSP Price	Model Yr. Prod.
CAMARO V-6										
00	F/P87	2CPE	V-6	101.1	193.5	3,308	200	231	$16,840	See notes
00	F/P87	2CONV	V-6	101.1	193.5	3,500	200	231	$21,140	See notes
CAMARO Z28 V-8										
00	F/P87	2CPE	V-8	101.1	193.5	3,439	305	346	$21,265	See notes
00	F/P87	2CONV	V-8	101.1	193.5	3,574	305	346	$28,365	See notes
CAMARO SS V-8										
00	F/P87	2CPE	V-8	101.1	193.5	—	320	346	$24,965	See notes
00	F/P87	2CONV	V-8	101.1	193.5	—	320	346	$32,065	See notes
ALL CAMARO TOTAL										45,461

MODEL-YEAR PRODUCTION NOTES
Sport Coupes (all model): 41,825
Convertibles (all models): 3,636
Included in Z28 production were 1,085 Camaro SS coupes, 6,255 SS T-tops and 1,572 Camaro SS convertible.
Of the 8,912 cars that got the SS package, 224 were built for the Canadian market.

2000 Engine Spec's

Engine	B x S	C.R.	CID	BHP
COUPE				
V-6	3.80 x 3.40	9.40	231	200 @ 5200
V-8	3.90 x 3.62	10.10	346	305 @ 5200
CONVERTIBLE				
V-6	3.80 x 3.40	9.40	231	200 @ 5200
V-8	3.90 x 3.62	10.10	346	305 @ 5200

2000 Collector Pricing

	6	5	4	3	2	1
CAMARO (200-HP L36 V-6)						
2d Cpe	460	1,380	2,300	5,180	8,050	11,500
2d Conv	480	1,440	2,400	5,400	8,400	12,000
CAMARO Z28 (305-HP LS1 V-8)						
2d Cpe	560	1,680	2,800	6,300	9,800	14,000
2d Conv	640	1,920	3,200	7,200	11,200	16,000
CAMARO Z28 SS (320-HP LS1 V-8)						
2d Cpe	840	2,520	4,200	9,450	14,700	21,000
2d Conv	920	2,760	4,600	10,350	16,100	23,000

2001

As the 2001 model year kicked off, things looked bleak. On September 26—the same day of the year that the '67 Camaro bowed—GM of Canada confirmed rumors that the Camaro was going out of production. "GM loses some old muscle," said the *Detroit News*. GM Officials said the F-car factory in St. Therese would be shuttered and the plant's 1,700 employees would be out of jobs.

Sporty-car sales were on the skids and the only thing keeping the Camaro assembly line rolling was a labor agreement that had been inked with Canadian autoworkers. It remained in effect until 2002. The 2001 models arrived, but due to the writing being on the wall, there was little reason to make product changes.

A new "de-contented" Z28 was introduced. A new Sunset Orange Metallic body color replaced Sebring Silver Metallic. The 16-inch wheels were restyled again. Under the hood, both versions of the LS-1 had five added horsepower (310 for the Z28 and 325 for the SS). The Z28 could do 0 to 60 in 5.5 seconds and the quarter-mile took 14 seconds at 101.3 mph. The SS blazed 5.3 seconds and 13.7 seconds at 105.6 mph.

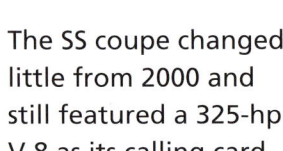

The SS coupe changed little from 2000 and still featured a 325-hp V-8 as its calling card.

Wieck Media

The 2001 Camaro SS convertible is likely to end up as a nice collectible car in the future. This Navy Blue convertible with a brown top and interior was one of only 864 ragtop SS cars produced for the model year.

Sales of the Z28 and its Camaro siblings may have been dwindling, but it wasn't because the Z28 wasn't a hot car. It still carried a 310-hp LS1 V-8, power everything, Bose premium sound system, 16-inch alloys, ABS, standard automatic transmission, and a no-cost manual six-speed for gear munchers.

Rumors persisted that the Camaro would be gone soon, but the 2001 saw "The General" still rolling out a very formidable pony car.

2001 CAMARO BY THE NUMBERS

Year	Body Code	Body Type	Engine Type	W.B. (Inches)	O.L. (Inches)	Wt. (Lbs.)	HP (Net)	Disp CID	MSP Price	Model Yr. Prod.
CAMARO V-6										
01	F/P87	2CPE	V-6	101.1	193.2	3,308	200	231	$17,880	See notes
01	F/P87	2CONV	V-6	101.1	193.2	3,500	200	231	$25,175	See notes
CAMARO Z28 V-8										
01	F/P87	2CPE	V-8	101.1	193.2	3,439	310	346	$22,450	See notes
01	F/P87	2CONV	V-8	101.1	193.2	3,574	310	346	$29,555	See notes
CAMARO SS V-8										
01	F/P87	2CPE	V-8	101.1	193.2	—	325	346	$26,400	See notes
01	F/P87	2CONV	V-8	101.1	193.2	—	325	346	$33,505	See notes
ALL CAMARO TOTAL										29,009

MODEL-YEAR PRODUCTION NOTES
Sport Coupes (all model): 23681
Convertibles (all models): 5328
The total number of Z28s built was 6320
Included in Z28 production were 5468 Camaro SS coupes and 864 Camaro SS convertible.

The Z28 interior had all the latest creature comforts, including a six-way power driver's seat and leather-wrapped steering wheel.a

2001 Engine Spec's

Engine	B x S	C.R.	CID	BHP
COUPE				
V-6	3.80 x 3.40	9.40	231	200 @ 5200
V-8	3.90 x 3.62	10.10	346	310 @ 5200
CONVERTIBLE				
V-6	3.80 x 3.40	9.40	231	200 @ 5200
V-8	3.90 x 3.62	10.10	346	310 @ 5200

2001 Collector Pricing

	6	5	4	3	2	1
CAMARO (200-HP L36 V-6)						
2d Cpe`	480	1,440	2,400	5,400	8,400	12,000
2d Conv	500	1,500	2,500	5,630	8,750	12,500
SLP CAMARO RS (205-HP L36 V-6)						
2d Cpe	560	1,680	2,800	6,300	9,800	14,000
2d Conv	640	1,920	3,200	7,200	11,200	16,000
CAMARO Z28 (305-HP LS1 V-8)						
2d Cpe`	600	1,750	2,900	6,530	10,200	14,500
2d Conv	660	1,980	3,300	7,430	11,550	16,500
CAMARO Z28 SS (320-HP LS1 V-8)						
2d Cpe`	880	2,640	4,400	9,900	15,400	22,000
2d Conv	960	2,880	4,800	10,800	16,800	24,000

Gen IV: The Perfect Camaro (1993-2002)

2002

Paradise by the dashboard lights had come to an end as the last year for the Camaro unfolded. Product changes were still made, however. The revisions included a standard eight-speaker Monsoon sound system, a standard automatic transmission for V-6 convertibles (second-gear start was dropped on all Camaros), an anti-entrapment release handle in the trunk and a new power steering cooler for Z28s. P245/55R16 tires were listed as standard fare for all Z28s, while base models got P235/55R16s.

Chevrolet did celebrate the 35th anniversary of the Camaro with a special graphics package for the Z28/SS sport coupe and convertible. Its special features included Rally Red paint, unique badging and Silver racing stripes, a unique grille, a tail panel appliqué, special 17-inch rims, embroidery on the front seat headrests and front floor mats and a luxurious Ebony leather interior. This package was priced at $2,500.

SLP Engineering, of Troy, Michigan, also whipped up the $849 RS package for 2002 V-6-powered Camaro models. It was available only on cars painted White, Pewter, Silver, Navy Blue, Black, Maroon, Orange, Teal or Rally Red. The option included a special bow-tie-logo grille, RS badging, a dual-outlet exhaust, a high-performance muffler and Black or Silver body striping.

The base V-6-powered Camaro coupe bowed out as a sleek, sophisticated aerodynamic car that could still be picked up new for less than $19,000.

The wide hood graphics, Rally Red paint, racing stripes and special grille were all part of the 35th Anniversary package.

The 2002 SS without the special anniversary package was still a very hot car. The SS could again be had in either coupe or ragtop varieties, and was actually a $3,625 upgrade package for the Z28.

The 2002 Berger Camaro was a fully loaded beast with special striping, dimpled front and rear spoilers, 17-inch chrome rims, fancy badging and decals, special springs, catback exhaust and other cool stuff.

The 35th Anniversary SS was chosen to pace the 2002 Brickyard 400.

196 THE STORY OF CAMARO

Special anniversary badging adorned the seats of the leather interior on the limited edition 35th Anniversary SS.

A 35th Anniversary SS was minted in 2002 to send the Camaro into retirement in style.

Gen IV: The Perfect Camaro (1993-2002) **197**

2002 CAMARO BY THE NUMBERS

Year	Body Code	Body Type	Engine Type	W.B. (Inches)	O.L. (Inches)	Wt. (Lbs.)	HP (Net)	Disp CID	MSP Price	Model Yr. Prod.
CAMARO V-6										
02	F/P87	2CPE	V-6	101.1	193.2	3,306	200	231	$18,655	See notes
02	F/P87	2CONV	V-6	101.1	193.2	3,500	200	231	$26,650	See notes
CAMARO Z28 V-8										
02	F/P87	2CPE	V-8	101.1	193.2	3,439	310	346	$23,070	See notes
02	F/P87	2CONV	V-8	101.1	193.2	3,574	310	346	$30,165	See notes
CAMARO SS V-8										
02	F/P87	2CPE	V-8	101.1	193.2	—	325	346	$26,695	See notes
02	F/P87	2CONV	V-8	101.1	193.2	—	325	346	$33,790	See notes
ALL CAMARO TOTAL										41,777

MODEL-YEAR PRODUCTION NOTES
A total of 41,777 Camaros were built for worldwide distribution..
8,083 were convertibles
11,191 were SS models.
13,614 were Z28 or B4C Special Service models.

2002 Engine Spec's

Engine	B x S	C.R.	CID	BHP
2002 (COUPE)				
V-6	3.80 x 3.40	9.40	231	200 @ 5200
V 8	3.90 x 3.62	10.10	346	310 @ 5200 +
2002 (CONVERTIBLE)				
V-6	3.80 x 3.40	9.40	231	200 @ 5200
V-8	3.90 x 3.62	10.10	346	310 @ 5200 +

+ Optional 346 CID, NHP 325 (Optional in Camaro SS only).

Note: Compiled from a variety of contemporary soures. Minor differences in measurements are obviously due to the way the car was measured, rather than changes in the car itself.

2002 Collector Pricing

	6	5	4	3	2	1
CAMARO (200-HP L36 V-6)						
2d Cpe	520	1,560	2,600	5,850	9,100	13,000
2d Conv	600	1,750	2,900	6,530	10,200	14,500
SLP CAMARO RS (205-HP L36 V-6)						
2d Cpe	600	1,800	3,000	6,750	10,500	15,000
2d Conv	680	2,040	3,400	7,650	11,900	17,000
CAMARO Z28 (310-HP LS1 V-8)						
2d Cpe	640	1,920	3,200	7,200	11,200	16,000
2d Conv	760	2,280	3,800	8,550	13,300	19,000
CAMARO Z28 INDY 500 FESTIVAL CAR (310-HP LS1 V-8; 55 BUILT)						
2d Conv	1,000	3,000	5,000	11,250	17,500	25,000
CAMARO Z28 FLORIDA STATE PATROL 9C1 (310-HP LS1 V-8)						
2d Cpe	760	2,280	3,800	8,550	13,300	19,000
CAMARO Z28 SS (325-HP LS1 V-8)						
2d Cpe	1,040	3,120	5,200	11,700	18,200	26,000
2d Conv	1,120	3,360	5,600	12,600	19,600	28,000
CAMARO Z28 SS 35TH ANNIVERSARY (325-HP LS1 V-8)						
2d Cpe	1,200	3,600	6,000	13,500	21,000	30,000
2d Conv	1,320	3,960	6,600	14,850	23,100	33,000

CHAPTER *Nine*

CONCEPT CAMARO

Holy Hubcaps! The Batmobile Meets Z28. Zip! Baff! Zowie!

Looking a bit like a Z28 that made the mistake of parking in front of the Bat Cave entrance just before the Caped Crusader's latest crime call, the Camaro Z28 concept car made its debut at early 2006 auto shows. Combining dramatic design and exciting performance, the car had its first curtain call in Detroit and drew predominantly rave reviews. Chevrolet said it captured "the spirit of one of the most popular Sport Coupes of all time" and insisted the car—hinted to be a 2008 production possibility—"redefines the Camaro for a new generation."

GM chose modern muscle styling (left) rather than a more retro look for the reicarnated Camaro.

Concept Camaro 199

GM designers and engineers were faced with a big challenge in trying to build an all-new car that would please Camaro fans.

Instant comparisons were made to the current "retro" Mustang, as well as the Dodge Challenger concept car that bowed at the same time. There were votes on either side of the aisle as to whether Chevy hit the nail on the head with its back-to-'69 stab. There was little debate over whether the car's architecture was gorgeous, but some questioned whether it captured the essence of a bygone muscle car era as well as its rivals did.

For those interested in my two cents, I couldn't help thinking of the motion-picture Batmobile when I saw the concept car in magazines and on the Web. The front stresses a low, wide "squished" look different from the blunt front end of the original "Hugger." Personally, I think the grille needs to be more '69-like to please real Camaro enthusiasts and the roof line needs some tweaking, too.

Details aside, the Camaro Concept embodies the performance and much of the passion that have collectors paying six figures for Camaros at Barrett-Jackson auctions.

200   THE STORY OF CAMARO

The all-new Camaro concept car: the epitome of modern muscle.

GM photo

Of course, some of the new technology that evolved since '69 makes the concept car a more fuel-efficient machine with much more sophisticated chassis engineering than existed 37 years ago. GM said that one of its goals was to make the sexy-looking sport coupe "relevant to younger enthusiasts while retaining its appeal to its current fans."

"Millions of people of all ages fell in love with the Camaro for all of the right reasons," said GM design VP Ed Welburn. "Camaros were beautiful to look at and offered performance that could rival expensive European GTs. Yet they were practical enough to drive every day and priced within the reach of many new car buyers."

GM press releases equated the long hood, short deck and wide stance of the concept car to a perception that it's "a serious performance car." Of course, some rather mundane lick-'em-stick-'em '70s cars had the muscle car look, too. The Camaro Concept is no such pretender. Its visual hints at musclecar-dom are backed up with a 400-hp

Concept Camaro 201

all-aluminum small-bock V-8, a six-speed stick and a road-gripping four-wheel independent suspension.

To make it a "street machine," the concept car incorporates "Active Fuel Management" cylinder deactivation technology. It can deliver 30 mpg. Not bad for a car of its size with a back seat two adults can squeeze into. The design is dominated by a long hood and powerful fender lines. The grille and "power-bulge" hood hint at the gustiness of the car's "Corvette" V-8. It has larger wheels and tires than a real '60s car and the brakes have the currently fashionable "exposed" look. The brakes are said to match the car's awesome power. The four-wheel vented

GM photo

GM photo

discs with 14-inch rotors provide confident stopping under all conditions.

The interior features gauges that bring back memories of the Gen I Camaros. A splash of orange interior trim is another retro touch. However, the overall look of the cockpit stresses modern, no-nonsense functionality. Power is provided by a high-tech 6.0-liter LS2 small-block V-8 linked to a six-speed manual transmission with a wide spread of ratios to allow aggressive off-the-line acceleration, power on demand for smooth passing and merging and outstanding cruising efficiency for such a powerful engine.

The totally-up-to-date rear-wheel-drive chassis combines independent front and rear suspensions with progressive-rate springs and gas-shocks. The car rides on specific 21-inch front/22-inch rear five-spoke cast-alloy wheels.

"CHEVYSPEAK"

GM design VP Ed Welburn: "The Camaro Concept is designed to have that same broad appeal (as the '69), with unmistakable style, spirit and performance."

Bob Boniface, director of Warren Advanced Design Studio: "The fact that the Camaro has been out of production for a number of years made it particularly important that the Camaro Concept honors the Camaro heritage in the right way."

GM photo

Concept Camaro Spec's

BODY STYLE:	2-door, 4-passenger rear-wheel-drive Sport Coupe
WHEELBASE:	110.5 in.
LENGTH:	186.2 in.
WIDTH:	79.6 in.
HEIGHT:	53 in.
FRONT TRACK:	63.8 in.
REAR TRACK:	63.3 in.
ENGINE:	LS-2 V-8
DISPLACEMENT:	6.0-Liter
POWER:	400 hp
TRANSMISSION:	T56 6-speed manual
SUSPENSION	
FRONT:	Independent; MacPherson strut front, gas dampers
REAR:	Progressive-rate coil springs, gas-pressurized dampers
BRAKES:	4-wheel disc, 15-in. rotors with 4-piston calipers
FRONT WHEELS:	21-in. cast aluminum
REAR WHEELS:	22-in. cast aluminum
FRONT TIRES:	275/30R21
REAR TIRES:	305/30R22

Tom Peters, GM design director: "The overall proportions, long hood and powerful fender forms say, "This is a front-engine, rear-wheel drive performance vehicle. The Camaro Concept isn't just a styled shape, the design incorporates what the vehicle needs to perform to its optimum level."

"OTHERSPEAK"

Jerry Heasley, automotive photographer/writer: "It looks a little formal with that roofline and that surprised me. The roof says 'Ford' to me. I think reaction to the design will depend on how big it really is."

Angelo Van Bogart, associate editor *OLD CARS WEEKLY*: "It reminds me of a Corvette ... like GM is trying to go back to the '80s when the Camaro was just a 'junior Corvette.'"

GM photo

Concept Camaro

APPENDIX

Year-by-Year Camaro Options

1967
AL4 Strato-Back front bench seat ($26.35). AS1 front shoulder belts ($23.20). AS2 Strato-Ease headrests ($52.70). A01 Soft-Ray all tinted glass ($30.55). A02 Soft-Ray tinted windshield only ($21.10). A31 power windows ($100.10). A39 custom deluxe front and rear belts ($6.35). A67 rear folding seat ($31.60). A85 custom deluxe front shoulder belts ($26.35). B37 color-keyed floor mats ($10.55). B93 door edge guards ($3.20). C06 power convertible top ($52.70). C08 vinyl roof cover ($73.75). C48 heater and defroster deletion ($31.65 credit). C50 rear window defroster with Sport Coupe ($21.10). C50 rear window defroster with convertible ($31.60). C60 air conditioning ($356). D33 left-hand remote-controlled outside rearview mirror ($9.50). D55 center front seat console ($47.40). D91 Front end "bumblebee" stripe ($14.75). F41 heavy-duty Sport suspension ($10.55). G80 Positraction rear axle ($42.15). Optional axle ratios 3.31:1, 3.55:1, 2.73:1, 3.07:1 and 7.73:1 ($2.15 each). J50 power brakes ($42.15). J52 front disc brakes ($79). J56 heavy-duty front disc brakes ($105.35) J65 special metallic brake facings ($36.90). K02 temperature-controlled de-clutching fan ($15.80). K19 Air Injector Reactor for California car ($44.75). K24 closed positive crankcase ventilation system ($5.25). K30 speed and cruise control ($50.05). K76 61-amp Delcotron alternator ($21.10). K79 42-amp Delcotron alternator ($10.55). L22 250-cid inline six-cylinder engine ($26.35). L30 327-cid 275-hp V-8 ($92.70). L35 396-cid 325-hp V-8 in Camaro SS only ($263.30). L48 350-cid 295-hp V-8 ($210.65). L78 396-cid 375-hp V-8 ($500.30). M11 floor-mounted gearshift lever ($10.55). M13 special three-speed manual transmission ($79). M20 wide-ratio four-speed manual transmission ($184.35). M21 close-ratio four-speed manual transmission ($184.35). M35 Powerglide automatic transmission with six-cylinder engines ($184.35). M35 Powerglide automatic transmission with small-block V-8s ($194.35). M40 Turbo-Hydra-Matic transmission ($226.45). N10 dual exhaust system ($22.10). N30 deluxe steering wheel ($7.40). N33 Comfortilt steering wheel ($42.15). N34 walnut grained steering wheel ($31.60). N40 power steering ($84.30). N44 "Quick-Response" variable-ratio steering ($15.80). N61 dual exhaust system ($21.10). N96 mag-style wheel covers ($73.75). PQ2 7.35 x 14 nylon white sidewall tires ($52). PW6 D70-14 red stripe tires ($62.50). P01 bright metal wheel covers ($21.10). P12 five 14 x 6 wheels ($5.30). P58 7.35 x 14 white sidewall tires ($31.35). T60 heavy-duty battery ($7.40). U03 tri-volume horn ($13.70). U15 speed warning indicator ($10.55). U17 special instrumentation ($79). U25 luggage compartment light ($2.65). U26 underhood light ($2.65). U27 glove compartment light ($2.65). U28 ashtray light ($2.65). U29 courtesy lights ($4.25). U35 electric clock ($15.80). U57 stereo tape player ($128.50). U63 AM radio ($57.40). U69 AM/FM radio ($133.80). U73 manual rear-mounted radio antenna ($9.50). U80 rear seat speaker ($13.90). V01 heavy-duty radiator ($10.55). V31 front bumper guard ($12.65). V32 rear bumper guard ($9.50). Z21 style trim ($40.05). Z22 Rally Sport package ($105.35). Z23 special interior group ($10.55). Z28 Special Performance package ($358.10). Z28 Special Performance package ($779.40). Z28 Special Performance package ($858.40). Z87 custom interior ($94.80).

1968
AK1 custom deluxe seat and shoulder belts ($11.10). AL4 Strato-Back front bench seat ($32.65). AS1 front shoulder belts ($23.20). AS2 Strato-Ease headrests ($52.70). AS4 custom deluxe rear shoulder belts ($26.35). AS5 standard rear shoulder belts ($23.20). A01 Soft-Ray all tinted glass ($30.55). A02 Soft-Ray tinted windshield only ($21.10). A31 power windows ($100.10). A39 custom deluxe front and rear belts ($7.90). A67 rear folding seat ($42.15). A85 custom deluxe front shoulder belts ($26.35). B37 color-keyed floor mats ($10.55). B93 door edge guards ($4.25). C06 power convertible top ($52.70). C08 vinyl roof cover ($73.75). C50 rear window defroster with Sport Coupe ($21.10). C50 rear window defroster with convertible ($31.60). C60 air conditioning ($360.20). D33 left-hand remote-controlled outside rearview mirror ($9.50). D55 center front seat console ($50.60). D80 rear deck lid spoiler ($32.65). D90 Sport striping ($25.30). D91 Front end "bumblebee" stripe ($14.75. D96 accent striping ($13.70). F41 heavy-duty Sport suspension ($10.55). G31 special heavy-duty rear springs ($20.05). G80 positraction rear axle ($42.15). Optional axle ratios ($2.15). J50 power brakes ($42.15). J52 front disc brakes ($100.10). KD5 positive crankcase ventilation ($6.35). K02 temperature-controlled de-clutching fan ($15.80). K30 speed and cruise control ($52.70). K76 61-amp Delcotron alternator ($26.35). K79 42-amp Delcotron alternator ($10.55). L30 327-cid 275-hp V-8 ($92.70). L34 396-cid 350-hp in Camaro SS only ($368.65). L35 396-cid 325-hp V-8 in Camaro SS only ($263.30). L48 350-cid 295-hp V-8 ($210.65). L78 396-cid 375-hp V-8 ($500.30). L78/L89 396-cid 375-hp V-8 with aluminum cylinder heads in Camaro SS only ($868.95). MB1 Torque drive transmission ($68.65). M11 floor-mounted gearshift lever ($10.55). M13 special three-speed manual transmission ($79). M20 wide-ratio four-speed manual transmission ($184.35). M21 close-ratio four-speed manual transmission ($184.35). M22 close-ratio heavy-duty four-speed manual transmission ($310.70). M35 Powerglide automatic transmission with six-cylinder engines ($184.35). M35 Powerglide automatic transmission with small-block V-8s ($194.35). M40 Turbo-Hydra-Matic transmission ($237.00). NF2 Deep-Tone dual exhaust system ($27.40). N10 dual exhaust system ($27.40). N33 Comfortilt steering wheel ($42.15). N34 walnut grained steering wheel ($31.60). N40 power steering ($84.30). N44 "Quick-Response" variable-ratio steering ($15.80). N65 Spacesaver spare tire ($19.35). N95 simulated wire wheel covers ($73.75). N96 mag-style wheel covers ($73.75). PA2 mag-spoke wheel covers ($73.75). PW7 F70-14 white sidewall tires ($64.75). PW8 F70-14 red stripe tires ($64.75). PY4 F70-14 fiberglass-belted tires ($26.55). PY5 fiberglass-belted red stripe tires ($26.55). P01 bright metal wheel covers ($21.10). P58 7.35 x 14 white sidewall tires ($31.35). T60 heavy-duty battery ($7.40). U03 tri-volume horn ($13.70). U15 speed warning indicator ($10.55). U17 special instrumentation ($94.80). U46 light monitoring system ($26.35). U57 stereo tape player ($133.80). U63 AM radio ($61.10). U69 AM/FM radio ($133.80). U73 manual rear-mounted radio antenna ($9.50). U79 push-button AM/FM stereo radio ($239.15). U80 rear seat speaker ($13.20). V01 heavy-duty radiator ($13.70). V31 front bumper guard ($12.65). V32 rear bumper guard ($12.65). ZJ7 Rally wheels ($31.60). ZJ9 auxiliary lighting in Sport Coupe without custom interior option ($13.70). ZJ9 auxiliary lighting in Sport Coupe with custom interior option ($11.10). ZJ9 auxiliary lighting in convertible without custom interior option ($9.50). ZJ9 auxiliary lighting in convertible with custom interior option ($6.85). Z21 style trim ($47.40). Z22 Rally Sport package ($105.35). Z23 special interior group ($17.95). Z27 Camaro Super Sport package ($210.65-$868.95). Z28 Special Performance package ($400.25-$858.40). Z87 custom interior ($110.60).

1969
AS1 front shoulder belts ($23.20). AS4 custom deluxe rear shoulder belts ($26.35). AS5 standard rear shoulder belts ($23.20). A01 Soft-Ray tinted glass ($32.65). A31 power windows ($105.35). A39 custom deluxe front and rear belts ($9). A67 rear folding seat ($42.15). A85 custom deluxe

front shoulder belts ($26.35). B37 color-keyed floor mats ($11.60). B93 door edge guards ($4.25). CE1 headlight flasher ($15.80). C06 power convertible top ($52.70). C08 vinyl roof cover ($84.30). C50 rear window defroster with Sport Coupe ($22.15). C50 rear window defroster with convertible ($32.65). C60 air conditioning ($376). DX1 front accent striping ($25.30). D33 left-hand remote-controlled outside rearview mirror ($10.55). D34 visor-vanity mirror ($3.20). D55 center front seat console ($53.75). D90 Sport striping ($25.30). D96 fender striping ($15.80). F41 heavy-duty Sport suspension ($10.55). G31 special heavy-duty rear springs ($20.05). G80 positraction rear axle ($42.15). Optional axle ratios ($2.15). JL8 power four-wheel disc brakes ($500.30). J52 power front disc brakes ($64.25). J50 power brakes ($42.15). KD5 positive crankcase ventilation ($6.35). K02 temperature-controlled de-clutching fan ($15.80). K05 engine block heater ($10.55). K79 42-amp Delcotron alternator ($10.55). K85 63-amp Delcotron alternator ($26.35). LM1 350-cid 255-hp V-8 ($52.70). L22 250-cid 155-hp six-cylinder engine ($26.35). L34 396-cid 350-hp in Camaro SS only ($184.35). L35 396-cid 325-hp V-8 in Camaro SS only ($63.20). L65 350-cid 250-hp V-8 ($21.10). L78 396-cid 375-hp V-8 ($316). L78/L89 396-cid 375-hp V-8 with aluminum cylinder heads in Camaro SS only ($710.95). MB1 Torque drive transmission ($68.65). MC1 special three-speed manual transmission ($79). MC11 floor-mounted gearshift lever ($10.55). M20 wide-ratio four-speed manual transmission ($195.40). M21 close-ratio four-speed manual transmission ($195.40). M22 close-ratio heavy-duty four-speed manual transmission ($322.10). M35 Powerglide automatic transmission with six-cylinder engines ($163.70). M35 Powerglide automatic transmission with small-block V-8s ($14.25). M40 Turbo-Hydra-Matic transmission ($190.10). NC8 chambered dual exhaust system ($15.80). N10 dual exhaust system ($30.55). N33 Comfortilt steering wheel ($45.30). N34 woodgrained steering wheel ($34.80). N40 power steering ($94.80). N44 "Quick-Response" variable-ratio steering ($15.80). N65 Spacesaver spare tire ($19). N95 simulated wire wheel covers ($73.75). N96 mag-style wheel covers ($73.75). PA2 mag-spoke wheel covers ($73.75). PK8 E78-14 white sidewall tires ($32.10). PL5 F70-14 white-letter tires ($63.05). PW7 F70-14 white sidewall tires ($62.60). PW8 F70-14 red stripe tires ($62.60). PY4 F70-14 fiberglass-belted tires ($88.60). PY4 F0-14 fiberglass-belted white sidewall tires on Camaro SS ($26.25). PY5 fiberglass-belted red stripe tires ($88.60). PY5 fiberglass-belted red stripe tires on Camaro SS ($26.25). P01 bright metal wheel covers ($21.10). P06 wheel trim rings ($21.10). T60 heavy-duty battery ($8.45). U15 speed warning indicator ($11.60). U17 special instrumentation ($94.80). U35 electric clock ($15.80). U16 tachometer ($52.70). U46 light monitoring system ($26.35). U57 stereo tape player ($133.80). U63 AM radio ($61.10). U69 AM/FM radio ($133.80). U73 manual rear-mounted radio antenna ($9.50). U79 push-button AM/FM stereo radio ($239.10). U80 rear seat speaker ($13.20). VE3 special body-color front bumper ($42.15). V01 heavy-duty radiator ($14.75). V31 front bumper guard ($12.65). V32 rear bumper guard ($12.65). ZJ9 auxiliary lighting in Sport Coupe without custom interior option ($13.70). ZJ9 auxiliary lighting in Sport Coupe with custom interior option ($11.10). ZJ9 auxiliary lighting in convertible without custom interior option ($9.50). ZJ9 auxiliary lighting in convertible with custom interior option ($6.85). ZK3 custom deluxe seat and shoulder belts ($12.15). ZL2 special cold-air-induction hood for Camaro SS or Camaro Z/28 ($79). Z11 special Indy 500 convertible package ($36.90). Z21 style trim ($47.40). Z22 Rally Sport package ($131.65). Z23 special interior group ($17.95). Z27 Camaro Super Sport package ($295.95). Z28 Special Performance package ($458.15). Z87 custom interior ($110.60). Two-tone paint ($31.60).

1970

AK1 color-keyed seat and shoulder belts ($12.15). AS4 rear shoulder belts ($26.35). A01 Soft-Ray tinted glass ($37.95). B37 color-keyed floor mats ($11.60). B93 door edge guard moldings ($5.30). C08 vinyl roof cover ($89.55). C24 Hide-A-Way windshield wipers ($19). C50 rear window defogger ($26.35). C60 Four-Season air conditioning ($380.25). D34 visor-vanity mirror ($3.20). D35 sport mirrors ($26.35). D55 center console ($59). D80 rear deck lid spoiler ($32.65). F41 Sport suspension ($30.55). G80 Positraction rear axle ($44.25). J50 power brakes ($47.30). L34 "396 Turbo-Jet" 402-cid 350-hp V-8 ($152.75). L65 350-cid 350 250-hp Turbo-Fire four-barrel V-8 ($31.60). L78 "396 Turbo-Fire" 402-cid 375-hp V-8 ($385.50). M20 four-speed wide-ratio manual transmission ($205.95). M35 Powerglide automatic transmission with six-cylinder engine ($174.25). M40 Turbo-Hydra-Matic automatic transmission with Z/28 ($290.40). M40 Turbo-Hydra-Matic automatic transmission with Camaros SS with optional L34 V-8 ($221.80). M40 Turbo-Hydra-Matic automatic transmission with other Camaros ($200.65). NA9 California emission controls ($36.90). N33 Comfortilt steering wheel ($45.30). N40 power steering ($105.35). PL3 E-78-14 white sidewall tires ($26.05). PL4 F70-14 white letter tires ($65.35). PX6 F78-14 white sidewall tires ($43.30). PY4 F70-14 white sidewall tires ($65.70). PO1 bright metal wheel trim covers ($26.35). P02 custom wheel trim covers ($79). T60 heavy-duty battery ($15.80). U14 special instrumentation ($84.30). U35 electric clock ($15.80). U63 AM radio ($61.10). U69 AM/FM radio ($133.80). U80 rear seat speaker ($14.75). VF3 deluxe front and rear bumpers ($36.90). V01 heavy-duty radiator ($14.75). YD1 trailering axle ratio ($12.65). ZJ7 Rally wheels with trim rings ($42.15). ZJ9 auxiliary lighting without custom interior option ($13.70). ZJ9 auxiliary lighting with custom interior option ($11.10). ZQ9 performance axle ratio ($12.65). Z21 style trim ($52.70). Z22 Rally Sport package ($168.55). Z23 interior accent group ($21.10). Z27 Camaro Super Sport package ($289.65). Z28 Special Performance package ($572.95). Z87 custom interior ($115.90).

1971

AK1 color-keyed seat and shoulder belts ($15.30). AN6 adjustable seatback ($19). AS4 rear shoulder belts ($26.35). A01 Soft-Ray tinted glass ($40.05). B37 color-keyed floor mats ($12.65). B93 door edge guard moldings ($6.35). C08 vinyl roof cover ($89.55). C24 Hide-A-Way windshield wipers ($21.10). C50 rear window defogger ($31.60). C60 Four-Season air conditioning ($402.35). D34 visor-vanity mirror ($3.20). D35 sport mirror ($15.80). D55 center console ($59). D80 front and rear spoilers ($79). F41 Sport suspension ($30.55). G80 Positraction rear axle ($44.25). J50 power brakes ($47.30). LS3 "396 Turbo-Jet V-8 ($99.05). L65 350-cid 350 Turbo-Fire four-barrel V-8 ($26.35). M20 four-speed wide-ratio manual transmission ($205.95). M21 four-speed close-ratio manual transmission ($205.95). M22 heavy-duty four-speed close-ratio manual transmission ($237.60). M35 Powerglide automatic transmission with six-cylinder engine ($179.55). M35 Powerglide automatic transmission with V-8 engine ($190.10). M40 Turbo-Hydra-Matic automatic transmission with Z/28 ($306.25). M40 Turbo-Hydra-Matic automatic transmission with Camaros SS with optional LS3 V-8 ($237.60). M40 Turbo-Hydra-Matic automatic transmission with other Camaros ($216.50). NK2 custom steering wheel ($15.80). NK4 sport steering wheel ($15.80). N33 Comfortilt steering wheel ($45.30). N40 power steering ($110.60). PL3 E-78-14 white sidewall tires ($26.05). PL4 F70-14 white letter tires ($81.50). PY4 F70-14 white sidewall tires ($68.05). PO1 bright metal wheel trim covers ($26.35). P02 custom wheel trim covers ($84.30). T60 heavy-duty battery ($15.80). U14 special instrumentation ($84.30). U35 electric clock ($16.90). U63 AM radio ($66.40). U69 AM/FM radio ($139.05). U80 rear seat speaker ($15.80). VF3 deluxe front and rear bumpers ($36.90). V01 heavy-duty radiator ($14.75). YD1 trailering axle ratio ($12.65). ZJ7 Rally wheels with trim rings ($45.30). ZJ9 auxiliary lighting without custom interior option ($18.45). ZJ9 auxiliary lighting with custom interior option ($15.80). ZQ9 performance axle ratio ($12.65). Z21 style trim ($57.95). Z22 Rally Sport package ($179.05). Z23 interior accent group ($21.10). Z27 Camaro Super Sport package ($313.90). Z28 Special Performance package ($786.75). Z87 custom interior ($115.90).

1972

AK1 color-keyed seat and shoulder belts ($14.50). AN6 adjustable seatback ($18). A01 Soft-Ray tinted glass ($39). 37 color-keyed floor mats

($12). B84 body side moldings ($33). B93 door edge guard moldings ($6). C08 vinyl roof cover ($87). C24 Hide-A-Way windshield wipers ($21). C50 rear window defogger ($31). C60 Four-Season air conditioning ($397). D34 visor-vanity mirror ($3). D35 sport mirror ($15). D55 center console ($57). D80 front and rear spoilers ($77). F41 sport suspension ($30). G80 positraction rear axle ($45). J50 power brakes ($46). LS3 402-cid "396 Turbo-Jet 240-hp V-8 ($96). L65 350-cid 165-hp four-barrel V-8 ($26). M20 four-speed wide-ratio manual transmission ($200). M21 four-speed close-ratio manual transmission ($200). M22 heavy-duty four-speed close-ratio manual transmission. M35 Powerglide automatic transmission with six-cylinder engine ($174). M35 Powerglide automatic transmission with V-8 engine ($185). M40 Turbo-Hydra-Matic automatic transmission with Z/28 ($297). M40 Turbo-Hydra-Matic automatic transmission with Camaros SS with optional LS3 V-8 ($231). M40 Turbo-Hydra-Matic automatic transmission with other Camaros ($210). NK4 sport steering wheel ($15). N33 Comfortilt steering wheel ($44). N40 power steering ($130). PL3 E-78-14 white sidewall tires ($28). PL4 F70-14 white-letter tires ($82.85). PY4 F70-14 white sidewall tires ($69.85). PO1 bright metal wheel trim covers ($26). P02 custom wheel trim covers ($82). U35 electric clock ($16). U63 AM radio ($65). U69 AM/FM radio ($135). U80 rear seat speaker ($15). VF3 deluxe front and rear bumpers ($36). V01 heavy-duty radiator ($14). YD1 trailering axle ratio ($12). YF5 California emissions test ($15). ZJ7 Rally wheels with trim rings ($44). ZJ9 auxiliary lighting ($17.50). ZJ9 auxiliary lighting with Z54 Quiet Sound group or Type LT ($15). Z21 style trim ($56). Z22 Rally Sport package ($118). Z27 Camaro Super Sport package ($306.35). Z/28 special performance package ($769.15). Z87 custom interior ($113).

1973

AK1 color-keyed seat and shoulder belts ($14.50). AN6 adjustable seat back ($18). A01 Soft-Ray tinted glass ($39). A31 power windows ($75). B37 color-keyed floor mats ($12). B84 body-side moldings ($33). B93 door edge guard moldings ($6). C08 vinyl roof cover ($87). C24 Hide-A-Way windshield wipers ($21). C50 rear window defogger ($31). C60 Four-Season air conditioning ($397). D34 visor-vanity mirror ($3). D35 sport mirrors ($26). D55 center console ($57). D80 front and rear spoilers ($77). D88 black striping ($77). F41 sport suspension ($30). G80 positraction rear axle ($45). J50 power brakes ($46). L48 350-cid 175-hp four-barrel V-8 in base Sport Coupe ($102). L48 350-cid 175-hp four-barrel V-8 in Type LT coupe ($76). L65 350-cid 145-hp V-8 ($26). M20 four-speed wide-ratio manual transmission ($200). M21 four-speed close-ratio manual transmission ($200). M40 Turbo-Hydra-Matic automatic transmission with Z/28 ($297). M40 Turbo-Hydra-Matic automatic transmission with Camaros except Z/28 ($210). N33 Comfortilt steering wheel ($44). N40 power steering ($113). N65 Space-Saver spare tire ($14.16). N95 wire wheel covers ($82). PE1 Turbine I wheels and trim with Sport Coupe ($110.50). PE1 Turbine I wheels with wheel trim on Type LT ($75). PO1 full wheel covers ($26). QEH E78-14 white sidewall tires on Sport Coupe with Stowaway spare ($22.40). QEH E78-14 white sidewall tires on Sport Coupe without Stowaway spare ($28). QFC F70-14 white sidewall tires on Type LT with Space-Saver spare ($51). QFC F70-14 white sidewall tires on Type LT coupe with Space-Saver spare ($65). QFC F70-14 white sidewall tires on Sport Coupe with Space-Saver spare ($56). QFC F70-14 white sidewall tires on Sport Coupe with Space-Saver spare ($70). QFD F70-14 white-letter tires on Type LT coupe with Space-Saver spare ($61.40). QFD F70-14 white-letter tires on Type LT coupe without Space-Saver spare ($78). QFD F70-14 white-letter tires on Sport Coupe with Space-Saver spare ($66.40). QFD F70-14 white-letter tires on Sport Coupe without Space-Saver spare ($83). UA1 heavy-duty battery ($15). U14 Special Instrumentation ($82). U35 electric clock ($16). U63 AM radio ($65). U69 AM/FM radio ($135). U80 rear seat speaker ($15). V01 heavy-duty radiator without Z/28 ($14). V01 heavy-duty radiator with Z/28 ($7.50). YA7 California emissions equipment ($15). YD1 trailering axle ratio ($12). ZJ4 trailer towing package ($41). ZJ7 Rally wheels with trim rings ($44). ZJ9 auxiliary lighting ($17.50). ZJ9 auxiliary lighting with Z54 Quiet Sound group or Type LT ($15). Z21 style trim ($56). Z22 Rally Sport package on base Sport Coupe ($118). Z22 Rally Sport package on Type LT ($97). Z/28 special performance package with base Sport Coupe ($598.05). Z/28 special performance package with Type LT ($502.05). Z54 Quiet Sound interior décor group ($35).

1974

AK1 color-keyed seat and shoulder belts ($14.50). AN6 adjustable seatback ($18). A01 Soft-Ray tinted glass ($39). A31 power windows ($75). B37 color-keyed floor mats ($12). B84 body side moldings ($33). B93 door edge guard moldings ($6). C08 vinyl roof cover ($87). C24 Hide-A-Way windshield wipers ($21). C50 rear window defogger ($31). C60 Four-Season air conditioning ($397). D34 visor-vanity mirror ($3). D35 sport mirrors ($26). D55 center console ($57). D80 front and rear spoilers ($77). D88 black striping ($77). F41 sport suspension ($30). G80 positraction rear axle ($45). G92 high-altitude rear axle ($12). J50 power brakes ($46). LM1 350-cid 160-hp four-barrel V-8 ($46). L48 350-cid 185-hp four-barrel V-8 ($76). M20 four-speed wide-ratio manual transmission ($200). M21 four-speed close-ratio manual transmission ($200). M40 Turbo-Hydra-Matic automatic transmission with Z/28 ($297). M40 Turbo-Hydra-Matic automatic transmission with Camaros except Z/28 ($210). N33 Comfortilt steering wheel ($44). N41 power steering ($113). N65 Space-Saver spare tire ($14.16). PE1 Turbine I wheels and trim with Sport Coupe ($110.50). PE1 Turbine I wheels with wheel trim on Type LT ($75). PO1 full wheel covers ($26). QBT FR78-14 white-letter tires without Space-Saver spare ($147.15). QBT FR78-14 white-letter tires on Sport Coupe with Space-Saver spare ($117.72). QBT FR78-14 white-letter tires on Type LT with Space-Saver spare ($116.72). QDV FR78-14 black sidewall tires without Space-Saver spare ($104.15). QDV FR78-14 black sidewall tires on Sport Coupe with Space-Saver spare ($83.32). QDV FR78-14 black sidewall tires on Type LT with Space-Saver spare ($82.32). QDW FR78-14 white sidewall tires without Space-Saver spare ($134.15). QDW FR78-14 white sidewall tires on Sport Coupe with Space-Saver spare ($107.32). QDW FR78-14 white sidewall tires on Type LT with Space-Saver spare ($106.32). QEH E78-14 white sidewall tires on Sport Coupe with Stowaway spare ($22.40). QEH E78-14 white sidewall tires on Sport Coupe without Stowaway spare ($28). QFC F70-14 white sidewall tires on Sport Coupe with Space-Saver spare ($56). QFC F70-14 white sidewall tires on Sport Coupe with Space-Saver spare ($70). QFD F70-14 white-letter tires on Sport Coupe with Space-Saver spare ($66.40). QFD F70-14 white-letter tires on Sport Coupe without Space-Saver spare ($83). UA1 heavy-duty battery ($15). U05 dual horns ($4). U14 Special Instrumentation ($82). U35 electric clock ($16). U58 AM/FM stereo radio ($233). U63 AM stereo radio ($65). U69 AM/FM radio ($135). U80 rear seat speaker ($15). V01 heavy-duty radiator without Z/28 ($14). V01 heavy-duty radiator with Z/28 ($7.50). V30 front and rear bumper guards ($31). YF5 California emissions equipment ($15). ZJ4 trailer towing package ($41). ZJ7 Rally wheels with trim rings ($44). ZJ9 auxiliary lighting ($17.50). ZJ9 auxiliary lighting with Z54 Quiet Sound group or Type LT ($15). Z21 style trim ($52). Z/28 special performance package with base Sport Coupe ($572.05). Z/28 special performance package with Type LT ($502.05). Z54 Quiet Sound interior décor group ($35).

1975

AK1 color-keyed seat and shoulder belts ($16). AN6 adjustable seatback ($18). AU3 power door lock system ($56). A01 Soft-Ray tinted glass ($45). A31 power windows ($91). B37 color-keyed floor mats ($14). B84 body side moldings ($38). B93 door edge guard moldings ($7). C09 vinyl roof cover ($87). C24 Hide-A-Way windshield wipers ($21). C50 rear window defogger ($41). C60 Four-Season air conditioning ($435). D34 visor-vanity mirror ($3). D35 sport mirrors ($27). D55 center console ($68). D80 front and rear spoilers ($77). D88 black striping ($77). FE8 Radial Tuned Suspension ($35). G80 positraction rear axle ($49). G92 high-altitude rear axle ($12). G96 highway axle ($12). J50 power brakes ($55). LM1 350-cid four-barrel V-8 ($54). M20 four-speed wide-ratio manual transmission ($219). M40 Turbo-Hydra-Matic automatic transmission ($235). N33 Comfortilt steering wheel ($49). N65 Stowaway spare tire ($14.10). PE1 turbine wheels and trim with Sport Coupe ($110.50). PE1 turbine styled wheels with wheel trim on Type LT ($75). PO1 full wheel covers ($30). QBT FR78-14 white-letter tires ($46). QDW FR78-14 white sidewall tires with ($33). QEG E78-14 black sidewall tires on Sport Coupe with Stowaway spare ($105.42 credit). QEG E78-14 black sidewall tires on Sport Coupe without Stowaway spare ($105.90 credit). QEH E78-14 white sidewall tires on Sport Coupe with Stowaway spare ($74.42 credit). QEH E78-14 white sidewall tires on Sport Coupe without Stowaway spare ($74.90 credit). UA1 heavy-duty battery ($15). UM1 AM stereo radio with 8-track tape ($199). UM2 AM/FM stereo sound system with tape player ($363). U05 dual horns ($4). U14 Special Instrumentation ($88). U35 electric clock ($17). U58 AM/FM stereo radio ($233). U63 AM stereo radio ($69). U69 AM/FM radio ($135). U80 rear seat speaker ($19). V01 heavy-duty radiator ($15). V30 front and rear bumper guards ($34). YF5 California emissions equipment ($45). ZJ7 Rally wheels with trim rings ($46). ZJ9 auxiliary lighting ($22.50). ZJ9 auxiliary lighting with Z54 Quiet Sound group or Type LT ($20). Z21 Z08 Sport décor package for Sport Coupe with Z21 ($40). Z08 Sport décor package for Sport Coupe without Z21 ($42). Z08 Sport décor package for Type LT with Z21 ($13). Z08 Sport décor package for Type LT without Z21 ($15). Z21 style trim ($55). Z54 Quiet Sound interior décor group ($35). Z85 Rally Sport package on Sport Coupe ($238). Z85 Rally Sport package on Type LT ($165). Z86 Gymkhana suspension without Rally Sport package ($112). Z86 Gymkhana suspension with Rally Sport package ($66). Z86 Gymkhana suspension with Type LT ($66).

1976

AK1 color-keyed seat and shoulder belts ($17). AN6 adjustable seatback ($19). AU3 power door lock system ($62). A01 Soft-Ray tinted glass ($46). A31 power windows ($99). B37 color-keyed floor mats ($15). B80 roof drip moldings ($16). B84 body side moldings ($38). B93 door edge guard moldings ($7). C24 Hide-A-Way windshield wipers ($22). C50 rear window defogger ($43). C60 Four-Season air conditioning ($470 without V-8; $452 with V-8). D35 sport mirrors ($27). D55 center console ($71). D80 front and rear spoilers ($81). F41 sport suspension ($32). G80 Positraction rear axle ($51). G92 high-altitude rear axle ($13). J50 power brakes ($58). K30 cruise control ($73). LG3 305-cid V-8 (standard V-8). LM1 350-cid V-8 ($85). M20 four-speed wide-ratio manual transmission ($242). M40 Turbo-Hydra-Matic automatic transmission ($260). N33 Comfortilt steering wheel ($57). N65 Stowaway spare tire ($15.11 without radial tires or $1.13 credit on cars with radial tires). PE1 custom styled wheels without Rally Sport package ($116). PE1 custom styled wheels with Rally Sport package ($79). PE1 custom styled wheels with Type LT Camaro ($79). PO1 full wheel covers ($30). QBT FR78-14 white-letter tires with Stowaway spare ($39). QBT FR78-14 white-letter tires without Stowaway spare ($49). QDW FR78-14 white sidewall tires with Stowaway spare ($28). QDW FR78-14 white sidewall tires without Stowaway spare ($35). QEG E78-14 black sidewall tires with Stowaway spare ($84.40 credit). QEG E78-14 black sidewall tires without Stowaway spare ($105.75 credit). QEH E78-14 white sidewall tires with Stowaway spare ($72.75 credit). QEH E78-14 white sidewall tires without Stowaway spare ($58.40 credit). UA1 heavy-duty battery ($16). UM1 AM stereo radio with 8-track tape ($209). UM2 AM/FM stereo sound system with tape player ($324). U05 dual horns ($6). U14 Special Instrumentation ($92). U35 electric clock ($18). U58 AM/FM stereo radio ($226). U63 AM stereo radio ($75). U69 AM/FM radio ($137). U76 windshield antenna ($16). U80 rear seat speaker ($21). V01 heavy-duty radiator ($27). V30 front and rear bumper guards ($36). YF5 California emissions equipment ($50). ZJ7 Rally Sport wheels ($60). ZJ9 auxiliary lighting ($30). ZJ9 auxiliary lighting with Z54 Quiet Sound group or Type LT ($26). Z21 style trim ($58). Z54 Quiet Sound interior décor group ($53). Z85 Rally Sport package on Sport Coupe ($260). Z85 Rally Sport package on Type LT ($173).

1977

AK1 color-keyed seat and shoulder belts ($19). AN6 adjustable seat back ($20). AU3 power door lock system ($68). A01 Soft-Ray tinted glass ($50). A31 power windows ($108). B37 color-keyed floor mats ($16). B80 roof drip moldings ($17). B84 body side moldings ($40). B93 door edge guard moldings ($8). CD4 intermittent windshield wipers ($30). C50 rear window defogger ($48). C60 Four-Season air conditioning ($507 without V-8; $478 with V-8). D35 sport mirrors ($30). D55 center console ($75). D80 rear deck lid spoiler ($87). F41 sport suspension ($36). G80 Positraction rear axle ($54). G92 performance ratio rear axle ($14). J50 power brakes ($61). K30 cruise control ($80). LG3 305-cid 145-hp/135-hp California. V-8 ($120). LM1 350-cid 170-hp/160-hp in California. V-8 ($210). M20 four-speed wide-ratio manual transmission ($252). M21 four-speed close-ratio manual transmission with Z28 ((no cost). M40 Turbo-Hydra-Matic automatic transmission in Z28 ($30). M40 Turbo-Hydra-Matic automatic transmission in Camaros except Z28 ($282). NA6 high-altitude emissions ($22). N33 Comfortilt steering wheel ($57). N65 Stowaway spare tire (no cost). PE1 custom styled wheels without Rally Sport package ($125). PE1 custom styled wheels with Rally Sport package ($85). PE1 custom styled wheels with Type LT Camaro ($85). PO1 full wheel covers ($33). QBT FR78-14 white-letter tires with Stowaway spare ($44). QBT FR78-14 white-letter tires without Stowaway spare ($55). QDW FR78-14 white sidewall tires with Stowaway spare ($33). QDW FR78-14 white sidewall tires without Stowaway spare ($41). QEG E78-14 black sidewall tires with Stowaway spare ($86.94 credit). QEG E78-14 black sidewall tires without Stowaway spare ($107.10 credit credit). QEH E78-14 white sidewall tires with Stowaway spare ($55.94 credit). QEH E78-14 white sidewall tires without Stowaway spare ($68.10 credit). UA1 heavy-duty battery ($17). UM1 AM stereo radio with 8-track tape ($209). UM2 AM/FM stereo sound system with tape player ($324). U05 dual horns ($6). U14 special instrumentation ($99). U35 electric clock ($19). U58 AM/FM stereo radio ($226). U63 AM stereo radio ($72). U69 AM/FM radio ($137). U76 windshield antenna ($17). U80 rear seat speaker ($23). V01 heavy-duty radiator ($29). V30 front and rear bumper guards ($39). YF5 California emissions equipment ($70). ZJ7 Rally Sport wheels ($65). ZJ9 auxiliary lighting ($32). ZJ9 auxiliary lighting with Z54 Quiet Sound group or Type LT ($27). Z21 style trim ($61). Z54 Quiet Sound interior décor group ($57). Z85 Rally Sport package on Sport Coupe ($281). Z85 Rally Sport package on Type LT ($186).

1978

AK1 color-keyed seat and shoulder belts ($21). AN6 adjustable seat back ($21). AU3 power door lock system ($80). A01 Soft-Ray tinted glass ($56). A31 power windows ($124). B37 color-keyed floor mats ($20). B80 roof drip moldings ($23). B84 body side moldings ($42). B93 door edge guard moldings ($11). CC1 removable glass roof panels ($625). CD4 intermittent windshield wipers ($32). C50 rear window defogger ($51). C60 Four-Season air conditioning ($539 without V-8; $508 with V-8). D35 sport mirrors ($33). D55 center console ($80). D80 rear deck lid spoiler ($55). F41 Sport suspension ($38). G80 positraction rear axle ($59). G92 performance ratio rear axle ($15). J50 power brakes ($69). K30 cruise control ($90). LG3 305-cid 145-hp/135-hp California V-8 ($185). LM1 350-cid 170-hp/160-hp in California V-8 ($300). MM4 four-speed wide-ratio manual transmission ($125). MX1 automatic transmission in Z28 ($45). MX1 automatic transmission in Camaros except Z28 ($307). M21 close-ratio four-speed manual transmission in Z28 (no cost). NA6 high-altitude emissions ($33). N33 Comfortilt steering wheel ($69). N65 Stowaway spare tire (no cost). PE1 custom styled wheels with Camaro Sport Coupe ($133). PE1 custom styled wheels with Type LT or Rally Sport ($91). PO1 full wheel covers ($37). QBT FR78-14 white letter tires with Stowaway spare ($49). QBT FR78-14 white letter tires without Stowaway spare ($61). QDW FR78-14 white sidewall tires with Stowaway spare ($37). QDW FR78-14 white sidewall tires without Stowaway spare ($46). QEG E78-14 black sidewall tires with Stowaway spare ($89.56 credit). QEG E78-14 black sidewall tires without Stowaway spare ($112.95 credit). QEH E78-14 white sidewall tires with Stowaway spare ($54.56 credit). QEH E78-14 white sidewall tires without Stowaway spare ($68.95 credit). UA1 heavy-duty battery ($18). UM1 AM stereo radio with 8-track tape ($229). UM2 AM/FM stereo sound system with tape player ($328). U05 dual horns ($7). U14 Special Instrumentation ($106). U35 electric clock ($20). U58 AM/FM stereo radio ($229). U63 AM stereo radio ($79). U69 AM/FM radio ($149). U76 windshield antenna ($25). U80 rear seat speaker ($24). V01 heavy-duty radiator ($31). YF5 California emissions equipment ($75). YJ8 Color-keyed aluminum wheels with Sport Coupe ($265). YJ8 Color-keyed aluminum wheels with Z28 ($195). YJ8 Color-keyed aluminum wheels with Rally Sport or Type LT ($180). ZJ7 Rally wheels trim ($85). ZJ9 auxiliary lighting ($34). ZJ9 auxiliary lighting with Z54 Quiet Sound group or Type LT ($28). Z21 style trim ($70). Z54 Quiet Sound interior décor group ($61). J-2 cloth seats with Sport Coupe or Z28 ($21). F-2 Custom cloth seats with Type LT ($21). F-2 Custom cloth seats with Z28 ($315). S-2 custom cloth seats with Type LT ($21). S-2 custom sport seats with Z28 ($315). X-2 custom vinyl seats with Z28 ($294).

1979

AK1 color-keyed seat and shoulder belts ($23). AN6 adjustable seat back ($23). AU3 power door lock system ($86). A01 Soft-Ray tinted glass ($64). A31 power windows ($132). B37 color-keyed floor mats ($23). B80 roof drip moldings ($24). B84 body side moldings ($43). B93 door edge guard moldings ($13). CC1 removable glass roof panels ($655). CD4 intermittent windshield wipers ($38). C49 rear window defogger ($99). C60 Four-Season air conditioning ($562 without V-8; $529 with V-8). D35 sport mirrors ($43). D55 center console ($80). D80 rear deck lid spoiler ($58). F41 Sport suspension ($41). G80 Positraction rear axle ($64). G92 performance ratio rear axle ($18). J50 power brakes ($76). K30 cruise control ($103). LG3 305-cid 135-hp/130-hp Calif. V-8 ($235). LM1 350-cid 170-hp/165-hp in Calif. V-8 ($360). MM4 four-speed wide-ratio manual transmission ($135). MX1 automatic transmission in Z28 ($59). MX1 automatic transmission in Camaros except Z28 ($335). M21 close-ratio four-speed manual transmission in Z28 (no cost). N33 Comfortilt steering wheel ($75). N65 Stowaway spare tire (no cost). N90 aluminum wheels with Berlinetta ($172). N90 aluminum wheels with Sport Coupe ($315). N90 aluminum wheels with Z28 ($242). N90 aluminum wheels with Z28 ($222). PE1 custom styled wheels with Camaro Sport Coupe ($143). PE1 custom styled wheels with Rally Sport ($100). PO1 full wheel covers ($43). QBT FR78-14 white letter tires on Camaro Sport Coupe or Rally Sport with Stowaway spare ($52). QBT FR78-14 white letter tires on Camaro Sport Coupe or Rally Sport without Stowaway spare ($65). QBT FR78-14 white letter tires on Berlinetta with Stowaway spare ($13). QBT FR78-14 white-letter tires on Berlinetta without Stowaway spare ($16). QDW FR78-14 white sidewall tires with Stowaway spare ($40). QDW FR78-14 white sidewall tires without Stowaway spare ($49). QEG E78-14 black sidewall tires with Stowaway spare ($94.56 credit). QEG E78-14 black sidewall tires without Stowaway spare ($118.95 credit). QEH E78-14 white sidewall tires with Stowaway spare ($57.56). QEH E78-14 white sidewall tires without Stowaway spare ($71.95). TR9 auxiliary lighting ($39). TR9 auxiliary lighting with Berlinetta or Quiet Sound Group ($31). UA1 heavy-duty battery ($20). UM1 AM stereo radio with 8-track tape ($248). UM2 AM/FM stereo sound system with tape player ($335). UN3 AM/FM stereo radio with cassette player ($341). UP5 AM/FM radio with CB ($489). UP6 AM/FM stereo radio with CB ($570). UY8 AM/FM stereo radio with clock with Z28, Special Instrumentation or Berlinetta ($372). U05 dual horns ($9). U14 Special Instrumentation ($112). U35 electric clock ($23). U58 AM/FM stereo radio ($232). U63 AM stereo radio ($85). U69 AM/FM radio ($158). U75 power antenna ($47). U76 windshield antenna ($27). U80 rear seat speaker ($25). V01 heavy-duty radiator ($33). YF5 California emissions equipment ($83). ZJ7 Rally wheels with wheel trim rings ($93). Z21 style trim ($73). Z54 Quiet Sound interior décor group ($64). J-2 cloth seats with Sport Coupe, Rally Sport or Z28 ($23). S-2 custom cloth seats with Berlinetta ($23). S-2 custom cloth seats with Sport Coupe, Rally Sport or Z28 ($330). X-2 custom vinyl seats with Sport Coupe, Rally Sport or Z28 ($307).

1980

AN6 adjustable seat back ($25). AU3 power door lock system ($93). A01 Soft-Ray tinted glass ($68). A31 power windows ($143). B37 color-keyed floor mats ($25). B80 roof drip moldings ($26). B84 body side moldings ($46). B93 door edge guard moldings ($14). CC1 removable glass roof panels ($695). CD4 intermittent windshield wipers ($41). C49 rear window defogger ($107). C60 Four-Season air conditioning ($566). D35 sport mirrors ($46). D80 rear deck lid spoiler ($62). F41 sport suspension ($44). G80 Positraction rear axle ($68). G92 performance ratio rear axle ($19). J50 power brakes ($81). K35 cruise control ($112). LG4 305-cid 155-hp V-8 ($295). LG4 305-cid 165-hp V-8 with Z28 ($50 credit in Z28 in place of standard LM1 350-cid V-8). LM1 350-cid 175-hp V-8 with Z28 (no cost). L39 267-cid 115-hp V-8 ($180). MM4 four-speed wide-ratio manual transmission in Z28 (no cost); in other Camaros ($144). MX1 automatic transmission in Z28 ($63). MX1 automatic transmission, in Camaros except Z28 ($358). N33 Comfortilt steering wheel ($81). N65 Stowaway spare tire (no cost). N90 aluminum wheels on Camaro Berlinetta ($184). N90 aluminum wheels on base Camaro Sport Coupe ($337). N90 aluminum wheels on Camaro Rally Sport ($237). N90 aluminum wheels on Camaro Z28 ($257). PE1 custom styled wheels on base Camaro Sport Coupe ($153). PE1 custom styled wheels on Camaro Rally Sport ($107). PQ1 full wheel covers ($46). QGR P255/70R-15 white-letter tires on Z28 (no cost). QJY P20575R14 white sidewall tires on Berlinetta (no cost). QJY P20575R14 white sidewall tires on Camaros other than Berlinetta without Stowaway spare ($63). QJY P20575R14 white sidewall tires on Camaros other than Berlinetta with Stowaway spare ($65). QKL P205/75R14 tires with Berlinetta ($15). QKL P205/75R14 tires on Camaros other than Berlinetta with Stowaway spare ($65). QKL P205/75R14 tires on Camaros other than Berlinetta without Stowaway spare ($81). TR9 auxiliary lighting with Berlinetta or Quiet Sound Group ($40). TR9 auxiliary lighting without Berlinetta or Quiet Sound Group ($33). UA1 heavy-duty battery ($21). UM1 AM stereo radio with 8-track tape ($249). UM2 AM/FM stereo sound system with 8-track player ($272). UN3 AM/FM stereo radio with cassette player ($285). UP5 AM/FM radio with CB ($473). UP6 AM/FM stereo radio with CB ($525). UY8 AM/FM stereo radio with clock ($328-353). U05 dual horns ($10). U14 gauge package with tachometer ($120). U35 electric clock ($25). U58 AM/FM stereo radio ($192). U63 AM stereo radio (97). U69 AM/FM radio ($153). U75 power antenna ($51). U76 windshield antenna ($27). U80 rear seat speaker ($20). V08 heavy-duty cooling without air conditioning ($63). V08 heavy-duty cooling with air conditioning ($36). YF5 California emissions equipment ($250). ZJ7 Rally wheels with wheel trim rings ($100). Z21 style trim ($78). Z54 Quiet Sound interior décor group ($69). C-2 cloth seats with Sport Coupe, Rally Sport or Z28 ($25). F-2 custom cloth seats with Berlinetta ($25). F-2 custom cloth seats with Sport Coupe, Rally Sport or Z28 ($353). X-2 custom vinyl seats with Sport Coupe, Rally Sport or Z28 ($328).

1981

AN6 adjustable seatback ($24). AU3 power door lock system ($93). A01 Soft-Ray tinted glass ($75). A31 power windows ($140). B37 color-keyed floor mats ($25). B80 roof drip moldings ($25). B84 body side moldings ($44). B93 door edge guard moldings ($13) CC1 removable glass roof panels ($695). CD4 intermittent windshield wipers ($41). C49 rear window defogger ($107). C60 Four-Season air conditioning ($560). D35 sport mirrors ($47). D80 rear deck lid spoiler ($60). F41 Sport suspension ($43). G80 positraction rear axle ($67). G92 performance ratio rear axle ($19). K35 cruise control with resume feature ($132). LG4 305-cid 150-hp V-

8 ($50). LG4 305-cid 165-hp V-8 with Z28 (no cost replacement for standard LM1 V-8). LM1 350-cid 175-hp V-8 with Z28 (standard equipment). L39 267-cid 115-hp V-8 ($50). MM4 four-speed wide-ratio manual transmission in Z28 (no cost); in other Camaros ($141). MX1 automatic transmission in Z28 ($61). MX1 automatic transmission, in Camaros except Z28 ($349). N18 wheel cover locks ($34). N33 Comfortilt steering wheel ($81). N90 aluminum wheels on Berlinetta ($180). N90 aluminum wheels on base Sport Coupe ($331). N90 aluminum wheels on Z28 ($253). PE1 custom styled wheels ($151). PQ1 full wheel covers ($46). QGR P225/70R-15 white-letter tires on Z28 (no cost). QJY P20575R14 white sidewall tires on Berlinetta (no cost). QJY P20575R14 white sidewall tires on Camaros other than Berlinetta ($54). QKL P205/75R14 tires with Berlinetta ($15). QKL P205/75R14 tires on Camaros other than Berlinetta ($69). TR9 auxiliary lighting with Berlinetta or Quiet Sound Group ($33). TR9 auxiliary lighting without Berlinetta or Quiet Sound Group ($39). TT4 halogen headlights ($36). UA1 heavy-duty battery ($20). UM2 AM/FM stereo sound system with 8-track player ($252). UN3 AM/FM stereo radio with cassette player ($264). UP6 AM/FM stereo radio with CB ($487). U05 dual horns ($10). U14 gauge package with tachometer ($118). U35 electric clock ($23). U58 AM/FM stereo radio ($178). U63 AM stereo radio (90). U69 AM/FM radio ($142). U75 power antenna ($47). U76 windshield antenna ($25). U80 rear seat speaker ($19). V08 heavy-duty cooling without air conditioning ($61). V08 heavy-duty cooling with air conditioning ($34). YF5 California emissions equipment ($46). ZJ7 Rally wheels with wheel trim rings ($99). Z21 style trim ($76). Z54 Quiet Sound interior décor group ($67). C-2 cloth seats with Sport Coupe or Z28 ($26). F-2 custom cloth seats with Berlinetta ($26). F-2 custom cloth seats with Sport Coupe or Z28 ($330). X-2 custom vinyl seats with Sport Coupe or Z28 ($304).

1982

LC1 173-cid V-6 ($125). LG4 305-cid four-barrel base V-8 ($170 in Berlinetta; $295 in Sport Coupe). LU5 305-cid Cross-Fire fuel-injected V-8, Camaro Z28 only ($450). MXO four-speed overdrive automatic transmission in Berlinetta or Z28 ($295). MXO four-speed overdrive automatic transmission in base Camaro Sport Coupe ($525). MX3 three-speed automatic transmission in base Sport Coupe ($425). MX3 three-speed automatic transmission in Berlinetta ($195). MM5 five-speed manual transmission, in base Camaro Sport Coupe ($125). AG9 six-way power seat ($197). AU3 power door locks ($106). AO1 tinted glass ($88). A90 power hatch release ($32). BS1 Quiet Sound group ($72-$80). B34 color-keyed front floor mats ($16). B35 color-keyed rear floor mats ($11). B84 body side moldings ($47). CC1 removable glass roof panels ($790). CD4 intermittent windshield wipers ($47). C25 rear window wiper and washer ($117). C49 electric rear window defogger ($125). C60 air conditioning ($675). D67 twin electric remote-control sport style outside rearview mirrors ($88-$137). D80 rear deck lid spoiler ($69). F41 Sport suspension system ($49). G80 limited-slip differential ($76). J65 four-wheel power disc brakes ($179). N33 Comfortilt steering wheel ($95). UO5 dual horns ($12). UO5 gauge package ($149). ZJ7 Rally wheels ($112). PO1 full-wheel covers ($52).

1983

LC1 173-cid V-6 ($150). LG4 305-cid four-barrel base V-8 ($225 in Berlinetta; $350 in Sport Coupe). LB9 305-cid Cross-Fire Injected V-8, Camaro Z28 only ($450). L69 305-cid H.). four-barrel V-8 ($505). MXO four-speed overdrive automatic transmission in Berlinetta or Z28 ($295). MXO four-speed overdrive automatic transmission in base Camaro Sport Coupe ($525). MX3 three-speed automatic transmission in Base Sport Coupe ($425). MX3 three-speed automatic transmission in Berlinetta ($195). MM5 five-speed manual transmission, in base Camaro Sport Coupe ($125). AG9 six-way power seat ($210). AU3 power door locks ($120). AO1 tinted glass ($105). A90 power hatch release ($40). BS1 Quiet Sound Group ($72-$82). B34 color-keyed front floor mats ($20). B35 color-keyed rear floor mats ($15). CC1 removable glass roof panels ($825). CD4 intermittent windshield wipers ($49). C25 rear window wiper and washer ($120). C49 electric rear window defogger ($135). C60 air conditioning ($725). D67 twin electric remote-control sport style outside rearview mirrors ($89-$137). D80 rear deck lid spoiler ($69). F41 Sport suspension system ($49). G80 limited-slip differential ($95). J65 four-wheel power disc brakes ($179). N33 Comfortilt steering wheel ($105). UO5 dual horns ($12). UO5 gauge package ($149). ZJ7 Rally wheels ($112). PO1 full wheel covers ($52).

1984

173-cid two-barrel V-6 ($250). 305-cid four-barrel V-8 ($550). 305-cid four-barrel H.O. V-8 in Z28 ($530). Five-speed manual transmission in base Camaro ($125). Four-speed overdrive automatic transmission in base Camaro ($525). Limited-slip differential ($95). Performance axle ratio ($21). Power four-wheel disc brakes in Camaro V-8 ($179). F41 Sport suspension ($49). Heavy-duty cooling ($40-$70). Engine block heater ($20). Air conditioning ($730). Rear defogger, electric ($140). Cruise control ($175-$185). Tinted glass ($110). Comfortilt steering wheel ($110). Six-way power driver's seat ($215). Power windows ($185). Power door locks ($125). Power hatch release ($40). Electric clock ($35). Gauge package with tachometer ($149). Intermittent windshield wipers ($50). Rear wiper/washer ($120). Quiet Sound group ($72-$82). Halogen high-beam headlamps ($10). Auxiliary ($37-$72). Dual horns ($12). Twin sport mirrors left-hand remote controlled, on base Camaro ($53). Twin electric remote sport mirrors ($91-$139). AM radio ($112). AM/FM radio ($171). Electronic-tuning AM/FM stereo radio ($263); with clock ($267-$302); with cassette and clock ($367-$402); with cassette, clock and seek/scan ($570-$605). Dual rear speakers ($30). Fixed mast antenna, included with radios ($41). Power antenna ($60). Removable glass roof panels ($825). Rear spoiler ($69). Black body side moldings ($55). Door edge guards ($15). Roof drip molding ($29). Console ($50). Cloth bucket seats ($28). Custom cloth or vinyl bucket seats in base Camaro ($359); in Z28 ($287). Cloth LS contour bucket seats ($375). Custom cloth LS contour bucket seats Camaro ($650). Front mats with carpeted inserts ($20). Rear mat with carpeted inserts ($15). Cargo area cover ($69). Deluxe trunk trim in Camaro ($164); in Z28 ($84). Locking rear storage cover ($80). Rally wheels ($112). Full wheel covers ($52). Wire wheel covers: Monte ($159). Wheel cover locks: Monte ($39). P195/75R14 GBR WSW: Camaro ($62). P195/75R14 SBR WSW: Monte ($62). P205/70R14 steel-belted radial black sidewall tires on base Camaro ($58). P205/70R14 steel-belted radial white sidewall tires ($124). P205/70R14 white-letter steel-belted radial tires ($146). P215/65R15 steel-belted black sidewall tires on Z28 ($92 credit).

1985

IROC-Z sport equipment package for Camaro Z28 ($659). Air conditioning ($730). Rear defogger ($140). Cruise control with resume ($175-$185). Tinted glass ($110). Comfortilt steering wheel ($110). Six-way power driver's seat ($215). Power windows ($185). Power door locks ($125). Power hatch release ($40). Electric clock ($35). Gauge package including tachometer in Camaro Sport Coupe ($149). Intermittent wipers ($50). Rear wiper/washer on Camaro Sport Coupe ($120). Quiet sound group in Camaro ($72-$82). Halogen headlamps ($22). Auxiliary lighting: Camaro ($37-$72). Dual horns with Camaro Sport Coupe ($12). Twin sport mirrors (left remote control) with Camaro Sport Coupe ($53). Twin electric remote sport mirrors with Camaro Sport Coupe ($91-$139). AM/FM radio ($82). Electronic-tuning AM/FM stereo radio with Camaro Sport Coupe or Z28 ($173); with clock ($177-$212); with cassette, clock and seek-and-scan ($319-$354). AM stereo/FM with cassette, graphic equalizer and clock ($469-$504). Seek-and-scan AM/FM stereo with remote control in Berlinetta ($242). Dual rear speakers ($30). Power antenna ($60). Radio delete in Camaro Sport Coupe ($56 credit); in Berlinetta ($256 credit). Removable glass roof panels ($825). Rear spoiler on Camaro Sport Coupe ($69). Black body side moldings on Camaro Sport Coupe ($55). Door edge guards ($15). Roof console in Camaro Sport Coupe/Z28 ($50). Cloth bucket seats in Camaro Sport Coupe ($28). Custom cloth bucket seats in Camaro Sport Coupe or Z28 ($359). Custom cloth LS conteur bucket seats in Camaro Sport Coupe or Z28 ($650). Split folding back seat with Camaro Sport Coupe ($50). Mats with carpeted inserts for Camaro Sport Coupe front ($20); rear ($15). Cargo area cover with Camaro Sport Coupe ($69). Deluxe trunk trim with Camaro Sport Coupe ($164); with Z28 ($84). Locking rear storage cover for Camaro Sport Coupe ($80). Aluminum wheels, standard Z28, other models ($225). Rally wheels on Camaro Sport Coupe ($112). Full wheel covers on Camaro Sport Coupe ($52). P195/75R14 steel-belted-radial white sidewall on Camaro Sport Coupe ($62). P205/70R14 steel-belted-radial black sidewall on Camaro Sport Coupe ($58). P205/70R14 steel-belted-radial white sidewall on Camaro Sport Coupe ($124); on Berlinetta ($66). P205/70R14 steel-belted-radial white-letter on Camaro Sport Coupe ($146). P235/60VR15 steel-belted-radial black sidewall: Z28 ($85). LB8 173-cid V-6 in Camaro Sport Coupe ($435). LG4 305-cid V-8 in Camaro Sport Coupe ($635); in Berlinetta ($300). L69 305-cid H.O. V-8 in IROC-Z ($680). LB9 350-cid TPI V-8 in Z28 or IROC-Z ($680). Five-speed manual transmission in Camaro Sport Coupe (no cost). Four-speed overdrive automatic transmission ($395). Limited-slip differential ($95). Performance axle ratio ($21). Power four-wheel disc brakes ($179). F41 heavy-duty suspension: ($49). Heavy-duty cooling ($40-$70). Engine block heater ($20). Heavy-duty battery ($26). California emission system ($99).

1986

IROC-Z sport equipment package for Camaro Z28 ($659). Air conditioning ($750). Electric rear window defogger ($145). Cruise control with resume ($175-$185). Tinted glass ($115). Comfortilt steering wheel ($115). Six-way power driver's seat ($225). Power windows ($195). Power door locks ($130). Power hatch release ($40). Gauge package including tachometer in Camaro Sport Coupe ($149). Intermittent windshield wipers ($50). Rear wiper/washer ($125). Quiet sound group ($82). Halogen fog lamps ($60). Auxiliary lighting ($37-$72). Dual horns ($12). Twin electric remote sport mirrors ($91). Automatic day/night mirror ($80). AM radio with digital clock: base ($39). Electronic-tuning seek-and-scan AM/FM stereo radio in Camaro Sport Coupe ($193). Electronic-tuning seek-and-scan AM/FM stereo radio with clock ($197-$232); with cassette and clock ($319-$354); with AM/FM stereo and cassette ($469-$504). Seek-and-scan AM/FM stereo with remote control and cassette in Berlinetta ($242). Power antenna ($60). Radio delete ($56 credit) except Berlinetta ($256 credit); Z28 ($95 credit). Removable glass roof panels ($846). Rear spoiler ($69). Rear window louvers ($210). Black body side moldings ($55). Door edge guards ($15). Roof console in Camaro Sport Coupe or Z28 ($50). Cloth bucket seats ($28). Custom cloth bucket seats in Camaro Sport Coupe or Z28 ($359). Split folding back seat ($50). Mats with carpeted inserts: front ($20); rear ($15). Cargo area cover ($69). Deluxe trunk trim ($164); Z28 ($84). Locking rear storage cover in Z28 ($80). Aluminum wheels on Berlinetta ($225). Wheel locks on Berlinetta or Z28 ($16). P195/70R14 steel-belted-radial black sidewall Eagle GT tires on Berlinetta ($80). P205/70R14 steel-belted-radial white sidewall tires on Berlinetta ($66). P215/65R15 steel-belted-radial black sidewall tires on Z28 ($92 credit). P215/65R15 steel-belted-radial raised-white-letter tires on Camaro four ($92). P235/60VR15 steel-belted-radial black sidewall tires on Z28 ($85). LB8 173-cid V-6 in Camaro Sport Coupe ($350). LG4 305-cid V-8 in Camaro Sport Coupe ($750); in Berlinetta ($400). L69 305-cid H.O. V-8 in IROC-Z ($695). LB9 350-cid TPI V-8 in Z28 or IROC-Z ($680). Five-speed manual transmission in Camaro Sport Coupe (no cost). Four-speed overdrive automatic transmission ($695). Limited-slip differential. Performance axle ratio. Power four-wheel disc brakes ($179). F41 heavy-duty suspension: ($49). Heavy-duty cooling ($40-$70). Engine block heater ($20). Heavy-duty battery ($26). California emission system ($99).

1987

Air conditioning ($775). Heavy-duty battery ($26). Engine oil cooler ($110). Locking rear storage cover ($80). Rear defogger ($145). Power door locks ($145). California emissions pkg. ($99). Gauge package in Sport Coupe ($149). Tinted glass ($120). Rear window louvers ($210). Deluxe luggage compartment trim, Sport Coupe ($164). Z28 ($84). Body side moldings ($60). Power antenna ($70). T-top roof ($866). Split folding rear seat back ($50). Rear spoiler on Sport Coupe ($69). Cast aluminum wheels with locks ($215). AM/FM stereo cassette ($364). AM/FM stereo with electronic tuning and graphic equalizer ($242). AM/FM stereo electronic tuning with cassette and graphic equalizer ($514). Delco-GM/Bose music system ($1127). AM mono radio ($39). Sport Coupe option package 2 includes tinted glass, air conditioning, tilt steering column and AM/FM stereo ($1,212). AM/FM stereo cassette ($122). AM/FM stereo with cassette and graphic equalizer ($272). Delco-GM/Bose music system ($885). AM/FM stereo delete ($298 credit). Sport Coupe option package 3 includes package 2 plus four floor mats, body side moldings, intermittent wipers, rear spoiler, cruise control, AM/FM stereo w/cassette and extended range speakers ($1,628). Sport Coupe option package 4 includes package 3 plus power windows and door locks, power hatch release and cargo cover ($2,126). Halogen headlamps. Auxiliary lighting. Sound systems with Sport Coupe option packages 3 or 4. AM/FM stereo with cassette and graphic equalizer ($150). Delco-GM/Bose music system ($763). AM/FM stereo delete ($420 credit). LT option package 1, includes tinted glass, air conditioning, tilt steering column, AM-FM stereo, full wheel covers, body side stripes, custom interior and quiet sound group ($1,522). Sound systems with LT option package 1. AM/FM cassette ($122). AM/FM with cassette with graphic equalizer ($272). Delco-GM/Bose music system ($885). AM/FM delete ($298 credit). LT option package 2 includes package 1 plus floor mats, body side moldings, intermittent wipers, rear spoiler, cruise control, and electronic tuning AM/FM stereo cassette with extended-range speakers ($1,938). LP option package 3 includes package 2 plus power windows and door locks, power hatch release, cargo cover and halogen headlamps ($2,387). LT option package 4 includes package 3 plus power seat, interior roof console, automatic day/night mirror, power remote mirrors, and halogen fog lamps ($2,858). Sound systems with LT option package 2, 3 or 4: Electronic tuning AM/FM stereo with cassette and graphic equalizer ($150). Delco-GM/Bose music system ($763). AM/FM stereo ET cassette delete ($420 credit). Sound Systems in Z28: AM/FM ET cassette ($325); AM/FM stereo ET ($203); AM/FM with cassette and graphic equalizer ($475); Delco-GM/Bose music system ($1,088). Z28 option package 2 includes sport equipment, tinted glass, air conditioning, tilt steering wheel, floor mats, body side moldings, intermittent wipers, cruise control and AM/FM stereo electronic tuning cassette with extended range speakers ($1,999). Z28 option package 3 includes package 2 plus power windows and door locks, power hatch release, auxiliary lighting, halogen headlamps, cargo cover, power mirrors, power seat, automatic day/night mirror, interior roof console and halogen fog lamps ($2,470 without cargo area cover or $2,539 with cargo area cover). Sound system with Z28 option package 2 or 3 includes electronic tuning AM/FM stereo with cassette and graphic equalizer ($150). Delco-GM/Bose music system ($763). AM/FM electronic tuning with cassette deleted ($381 credit). IROC-Z option package 1 includes halogen fog lamps, uprated suspension and P245/50VR16 tires on aluminum wheels ($669). Sound systems with IROC-Z package 1 includes electronic tuning AM/FM stereo with cassette ($325). Electronic tuning AM/FM stereo ($203). Electronic tuning AM-FM stereo with cassette and graphic equalizer ($475). Delco-GM/Bose music system ($1,088). IROC-Z option package 2 includes package 1 plus sport equipment, tinted glass, air conditioning, tilt steering column, floor mats, intermittent wipers, AM/FM stereo electronic tuning cassette with extended range speakers, power windows and door locks and power hatch release ($2,409). Sound Systems with IROC-Z package 2 includes electronic tuning AM/FM stereo with cassette and graphic equalizer ($150). Delco-GM/Bose music system ($763). Electronic tuning AM/FM stereo with cassette and graphic equalizer ($150). Delco-GM/Bose music system

($763). Electronic tuning AM/FM stereo with cassette, deleted for credit ($381 credit). IROC-Z option package 3 includes package 2 plus power mirrors, cruise control, body side moldings, cargo cover, auxiliary lighting, automatic day/night mirror, power seat, interior roof console, electronic tuning AM/FM stereo with cassette and graphic equalizer and extended range speakers ($3,273 with cargo cover or $3,204 without cargo cover). Sound systems with IROC-Z package 3 includes Delco-GM/Bose music system ($613). Electronic tuning AM/FM stereo with cassette and graphic equalizer deleted for credit ($531 credit). 5.0-liter four-barrel V-8 ($400). 5.0-liter TPI V-8 in Camaro or Z28 ($745). 5.7-liter TPI V-8 in IROC-Z only ($1,045). Four-speed overdrive automatic transmission ($490). Performance axle ratio ($21). Power four-wheel disc brakes ($179).

1988

Air conditioning ($775). Heavy-duty battery ($26). Engine oil cooler ($110). Locking rear storage cover ($80). Rear defogger ($145). Power door locks ($145). California emissions package ($99). Gauge package in Sport Coupe ($149). Tinted glass ($120). Rear window louvers ($210). Deluxe luggage compartment trim for Sport Coupe ($164). Body side moldings ($60). Power antenna ($70). T-top roof ($866). Split folding rear seat back ($50). Rear spoiler in Sport Coupe ($69). Cast aluminum wheels with locks ($215). AM/FM stereo cassette ($364). Electronic-tuning AM/FM stereo ET with graphic equalizer ($242). Electronic-tuning AM/FM stereo with cassette and graphic equalizer ($514). Delco-GM/Bose music system ($1,127). AM mono radio ($39). Sport Coupe option package 2 includes tinted glass, air conditioning, tilt steering column and AM/FM stereo ($1,212). Sound systems with Sport Coupe package 2, AM/FM stereo cassette ($122). AM/FM stereo with cassette graphic equalizer ($272). Delco-GM/Bose music system ($885). AM/FM stereo delete ($298 credit). Sport Coupe option package 3 ($1,628) includes package 2 plus four floor mats, body side moldings, intermittent wipers, rear spoiler, cruise control, AM/FM stereo w/cassette and extended range speakers. Sport Coupe option package 4 ($2,126) includes package 3 plus power windows and door locks, power hatch release and cargo cover. Halogen headlamps. Auxiliary lighting. Sound systems with Sport Coupe option packages 3 or 4, AM/FM stereo with cassette and graphic equalizer ($150). Delco-GM/Bose music system ($763). AM/FM stereo delete ($420 credit). IROC-Z option package 1 ($669) includes halogen fog lamps, up-rated suspension and P245/50VR16 tires on aluminum wheels. Sound systems with IROC package 1, AM/FM stereo ET with cassette ($325). Electronic-tuning AM/FM stereo ($203). AM-FM stereo ET with cassette and graphic equalizer ($475). Delco-GM/Bose music system ($1,088). IROC option package 2 ($2,409), includes package 1 plus sport equipment, tinted glass, air conditioning, tilt steering column, floor mats, intermittent wipers, AM/FM stereo ET cassette with extended range speakers, power windows and door locks, and power hatch release. Sound Systems with IROC package 2, electronic-tuning AM/FM stereo with cassette and graphic equalizer ($150). Delco-GM/Bose music system ($763). Electronic-tuning AM/FM stereo with cassette and graphic equalizer ($150). Delco-GM/Bose music system ($763). AM/FM stereo ET with cassette deleted ($381 credit). IROC option package 3 ($3,273 or without cargo area cover $3,204) includes package 2 plus power mirrors, cruise control, body side moldings, cargo cover, auxiliary lighting, automatic day/night mirror, power seat, interior roof console, electronic-tuning AM/FM stereo with cassette and equalizer and extended range speakers. Sound systems with IROC package 3, Delco-GM/Bose music system ($613). Electronic-tuning AM/FM stereo with cassette and graphic equalizer delete ($531 credit).

1989

RS coupe preferred equipment group 1 including heavy-duty battery, tinted glass, auxiliary lighting and body side moldings ($255). RS coupe preferred equipment group 2: including air conditioning, power door locks, a heavy-duty battery, front and rear color-keyed carpet mats, tinted glass, auxiliary lighting, body side moldings, electronically tuned AM/FM stereo radio (with seek-and-scan, stereo cassette tape, digital clock and extended-range sound system), speed control with resume feature, a Comfortilt steering wheel and an intermittent windshield wiper system ($1,727). RS coupe preferred equipment group 3, including air conditioning, a heavy-duty battery, a cargo cover, a power door lock system, front and rear carpet mats, tinted glass, halogen headlamps, high and low-beam auxiliary lighting, a mirror with dual reading lamps, body side moldings, an electronically tuned AM/FM stereo radio (with seek-and-scan, stereo cassette tape, digital clock and extended-range sound system), electronic speed control with resume speed feature, a Comfortilt steering wheel and an intermittent windshield wiper system. IROC-Z preferred equipment group 1 including tinted glass, a heavy-duty battery, auxiliary lighting and body side moldings (without 5.7-liter engine $255; with 5.7-liter engine $229). IROC-Z preferred equipment group 2 including air conditioning, a power door lock system, front and rear carpet mats, tinted glass, a power hatch release, auxiliary lighting, body side moldings, electronically tuned AM/FM stereo radio (with seek-and-scan, stereo cassette tape, digital clock and extended-range sound system), speed control with resume feature, a heavy-duty battery, a Comfortilt steering wheel and an intermittent windshield wiper system, without 5.7-liter engine ($1,777). IROC-Z preferred equipment group 3, including air conditioning, power door lock system, a cargo cover, color-keyed front and rear carpet mats, tinted glass, halogen high- and low-beam headlamps, a power hatch release, auxiliary lighting, a mirror with dual reading lamps, twin remote-control sport-style outside rearview mirrors, body side moldings, an electronically tuned AM/FM stereo radio (with seek-and-scan, stereo cassette tape, search-and-repeat, graphic equalizer, digital clock and extended-range sound system), a power driver's seats, electronic speed control with resume speed, a heavy-duty battery, a Comfortilt steering wheel, power windows and an intermittent windshield wiper system (without 5.7-liter engine $2,605, with 5.7-liter engine $2,579). Camaro RS convertible preferred equipment group 1, including heavy-duty battery, tinted glass and body side moldings ($206). RS convertible preferred equipment group 2, includes air conditioning, heavy-duty battery, power door lock system, front and rear color-keyed carpet mats, tinted glass, body side moldings, electronically tuned AM/FM stereo radio, (with seek-and-scan, stereo cassette tape, digital clock, and extended-range sound system, electronic speed control, with resume feature, a Comfortilt steering wheel and an intermittent windshield wiper system ($1.678). RS convertible preferred equipment group 3, including air conditioning, a heavy-duty battery, a power door lock system, color-keyed front and rear carpet mats. Tinted glass, halogen high- and low-beam headlights, body side moldings, an electronically tuned AM/FM stereo radio (with seek-and-scan, cassette tape player, digital clock and an extended-range sound system). Electronic speed control with resume speed, a Comfortilt steering wheel, power windows and an intermittent windshield wiper system ($1,923). IROC-Z convertible preferred equipment group 1, including heavy-duty battery, tinted glass and body side moldings ($206). IROC-Z convertible preferred equipment group 2, including air conditioning, heavy-duty battery, power door lock system, front and rear carpet mats, tinted glass, body side moldings, electronically tuned AM/FM stereo radio (with seek-and-scan, cassette, digital clock and extended-range sound system), speed control with resume, Comfortilt steering wheel and intermittent windshield wiper system ($1,678). IROC-Z convertible preferred equipment group 3 including air conditioning, heavy-duty battery, power door lock system, front and rear carpet mats, tinted glass, halogen high- and low-beam headlamps, twin remote sport mirrors, body side moldings, electronically tuned AM/FM stereo radio (with seek-and-scan, stereo cassette tape, search-and-repeat, graphic equalizer, digital clock and extended-range sound system), power driver's seat, speed control with resume feature, Comfortilt steering wheel, power windows, and intermittent windshield wiper system ($2,414). Custom cloth bucket seats ($277). Custom leather bucket seats ($750). Air conditioning ($795). Limited-slip differential ($100). Performance axle ratio including dual exhausts ($177). Front license plate bracket (no cost). Power four-wheel disc brakes ($179). Engine oil cooler ($110). Locking rear storage cover ($80). Decal and stripe delete ($60 credit). Electric rear window defogger ($150). Power door lock system ($155). California emission system ($100). Power hatch release ($50). Engine block heater ($20). Rear window louvers ($210). Deluxe luggage compartment trim, RS coupe only, includes locking rear compartment storage cover ($164). IROC-Z coupe ($84). Sport twin remote mirrors ($91). Black door edge guards ($15). Electronically tuned AM/FM stereo radio (with seek-and-scan, stereo cassette tape, search-and-repeat, graphic equalizer and digital clock ($150/$272). Electronically tuned AM/FM stereo with seek-and-scan, stereo cassette tape and digital clock ($122). Electronically tuned GM Delco/Bose music system, including AM/FM stereo with seek-and-scan, stereo cassette tape, digital clock, special tone and balance control and four speakers ($613/$885). Electronically tuned AM/FM stereo radio (with seek-and-scan, compact disc player and digital clock ($124/$396). Power antenna ($70). Removable roof panels, including locks ($866). Split folding rear seatback ($50). Cast-aluminum 16-in. wheels with wheel locks and P245/50 VF16 SBR black sidewall tires ($520).

1990

RS coupe base equipment group included with model (no cost). RS coupe base equipment group with UM6 radio (add $140). RS coupe base equipment group with UU8 radio (add $1,015). RS coupe base equipment group with UL5 radio delete ($165 credit). RS coupe preferred equipment group number 1, including air conditioning, ETR AM/FM stereo (with seek-and-scan, cassette tape, digital clock and extended-range sound system), power door locks, speed control with resume, body side moldings and front and rear color-keyed carpeted floor mats for package price of $1,410 or $875 additional with UU8 radio. RS coupe preferred equipment group number 2, including air conditioning, ETR AM/FM stereo (with seek-and-scan, cassette tape, digital clock and extended-range sound system), power door locks, speed control with resume, power hatch release, cargo area cover, body side moldings, front and rear color-keyed carpeted floor mats and mirror with dual reading lamps for package price of $1,782 or $875 additional with UU8 radio. IROC-Z base equipment group included with model (no cost). IROC-Z base equipment group with UM6 radio (add $140). IROC-Z base equipment group with UU8 radio (add $1,015). IROC-Z base equipment group with UL5 radio delete ($165 credit). IROC-Z preferred equipment group number 1 includes air conditioning and body side moldings for package price of $865 (with UM6 radio add $140 or with UU8 radio add $1,015). IROC-Z coupe preferred equipment group number 2, including air conditioning, ETR AM/FM stereo (with seek-and-scan, cassette tape, digital clock and extended-range sound system), power door locks, speed control with resume, power hatch release, cargo area cover, body side moldings and front and rear color-keyed carpeted floor mats for package price of $1,759 or $875 additional with UU8 radio. IROC-Z coupe preferred equipment group number 3, including air conditioning, ETR AM/FM stereo (with seek-and-scan, cassette tape, digital clock and extended-range sound system), power windows, power driver's seat, power door locks, speed control with resume, power hatch release, dual power sport-type outside rearview mirrors, cargo area cover, body side moldings, front and rear color-keyed carpeted floor mats and mirror with dual reading lamps for package price of $2,143 or $875 additional with UU8 radio. RS convertible base equipment group (no cost) RS convertible base equipment group with UM6 radio (add $140). RS convertible base equipment group with UL5 radio delete ($165 credit). RS convertible preferred equipment group number 1, including air conditioning, ETR AM/FM stereo (with seek-and-scan, cassette tape, digital clock and extended-range sound system), body side moldings and front and rear color-keyed carpeted floor mats for package price of $1,040. RS convertible preferred equipment group number 2, including air conditioning, ETR AM/FM stereo (with seek-and-scan, cassette tape, digital clock and extended-range sound system), power windows, power door locks, speed control with resume, body side moldings and front and rear color-keyed carpeted floor mats for package price of $1,640. IROC-Z convertible base equipment group (no cost) IROC-Z convertible base equipment group with UM6 radio (add $140). IROC-Z convertible base equipment group with UL5 radio delete ($165 credit). IROC-Z convertible preferred equipment group number 1, including air conditioning and body side moldings for package price of $865 or add $140 for UM6 radio. IROC-Z convertible preferred equipment group number 2, including air conditioning, ETR AM/FM stereo (with seek-and-scan, cassette tape, digital clock and extended-range sound system), power windows, power door locks, speed control with resume, body side moldings and front and rear color-keyed carpeted floor mats for package price of $1,640. IROC-Z convertible preferred equipment group number 3, including air conditioning, ETR AM/FM stereo (with seek-and-scan, cassette tape, digital clock and extended-range sound system), power windows, power driver's seat, power door locks, speed control with resume, dual power sport-type outside rearview mirrors, body side moldings and front and rear color-keyed carpeted floor mats for package price of $2,001. C2 cloth bucket seats (no cost). F2 custom cloth bucket seats ($327). A2 custom leather bucket seats ($800). Solid color exterior paint (no cost). LH0 3.1-liter MFI V-6 in RS coupe only, as standard equipment (no cost). LB9 5.0-liter TPI V-8 in IROC-Z coupe and convertible only, as standard equipment (no cost). L03 5.0-liter EFI V-8, standard in RS convertible, in RS coupe ($350). B2L 5.7-liter V-8 in IROC-Z ($300). C60 air conditioning, including increased-capacity cooling system ($805). G92 performance ratio and dual exhausts ($466). VK3 front license plate bracket (no cost). DX3 decals and stripes delete ($60 credit). C49 electric rear window defogger ($160). AU3 electric power door lock system ($175). YF5 California emissions requirements, including all testing and certification necessary for registration in California ($100). NA5 standard emissions equipment (no cost). A90 power hatch release ($50). K05 engine block heater ($20). DE1 rear window louvers ($210). DG7 electric twin remote sport mirrors ($91). [Note: All stereo radios include extended-range sound system. UM6 ETR AM/FM stereo with seek-and-scan, cassette tape and digital clock (available in packages only)]. UU8 ETR Delco-Bose music system, including AM/FM ETR stereo with seek-and-scan, stereo cassette tape, digital clock, special tone balance and four speakers (available in packages only). UL5 radio delete (available in packages only). CC1 removable glass roof panels including, locks ($866). QYZ P215/65R15 steel-belted radial-ply black sidewall tires (no cost). QLC P245/50ZR16 steel-belted radial-ply black sidewall tires (no cost). MM5 five-speed manual transmission (no cost). MXO automatic overdrive transmission ($515). N96 16-in. cast-aluminum wheels with locks and P245/50ZR16 steel-belted radial-ply black sidewall tires ($520).

1991

RS coupe base equipment group included with model (no cost). RS coupe base equipment group with UN6 radio (add $160). RS coupe base equipment group with U1C radio (add $396). RS coupe base equipment group with UL5 radio delete ($165 credit). RS coupe preferred equipment group number 1, including air conditioning, ETR AM/FM stereo (with seek-and-scan, cassette tape, digital clock and extended-range sound system), body side moldings and front and rear color-keyed carpeted floor mats for package price of $1,060 or $236 additional with U1C radio. RS coupe preferred equipment group number 2 includes air conditioning, ETR AM/FM stereo (with seek-and-scan, cassette tape, digital clock and extended-range sound system), body side moldings and front and rear color-keyed carpeted floor mats, power door locks, speed control with resume, power hatch release, cargo area cover and mirror with dual reading lamps for package price of $1,847 or $236 additional with U1C radio. Z28 base equipment group included with model (no cost). Z28 base equipment group with UN6 radio (add $160). Z28 base equipment group with U1C radio (add $396). Z28 base equipment group with UL5 radio delete ($165 credit). Z28 preferred equipment group number 1 includes air conditioning, body side moldings and front and rear color-keyed carpet mats for package price of $900 (with UN6 radio add $160 or with U1C radio add $396). Z28 coupe preferred equipment group number 2, including air conditioning, body side moldings, front and rear color-keyed carpet mats, ETR AM/FM stereo (with seek-and-scan, cassette tape, digital clock and extended-range sound system), power door locks, speed control with resume, power hatch release, cargo area cover, body side moldings and front and rear color-keyed carpeted floor mats for package price of $1,847 or $236 additional with U1C radio. Z28 coupe preferred equipment group number 3, including air conditioning, ETR AM/FM stereo (with seek-and-scan, cassette tape, digital clock and extended-range sound system), power windows, power driver's seat, power door locks, speed control with resume, power hatch release, dual power sport-type outside rearview mirrors, cargo area cover, body side moldings, front and rear color-keyed carpeted floor mats and mirror with dual reading lamps for package price of $2,228 or $236 additional with U1C radio. RS convertible base equipment group (no cost). RS convertible base equipment group with UN6 radio (add $160). RS convertible base equipment group with U1C radio (add $236). RS convertible base equipment group with UL5 radio delete ($165 credit). RS convertible preferred equipment group number 1, including air conditioning, ETR AM/FM stereo (with seek-and-scan, cassette tape, digital clock and extended-range sound system), body side moldings and front and rear color-keyed carpeted floor mats for package price of $1,060 (or $236 additional with U1C radio). RS convertible preferred equipment group number 2, including air conditioning, ETR AM/FM stereo (with seek-and-scan, cassette tape, digital clock and extended-range sound system), power windows, power door locks, speed control with resume, body side moldings and front and rear color-keyed carpeted floor mats for package price of $1,705 (or $236 additional with U1C radio). Z28 convertible base equipment group (no cost) Z28 convertible base equipment group with UN6 radio (add $160). Z28 convertible base equipment group with UL5 radio delete ($165 credit). Z28 convertible preferred equipment group number 1, including air conditioning, body side moldings and front and rear color-keyed carpet mats for package price of $900 (add $160 for UN6 radio or $236 for U1C radio). Z28 convertible preferred equipment group number 2, including air conditioning, ETR AM/FM stereo (with seek-and-scan, cassette tape, digital clock and extended-range sound system), power windows, power door locks, speed control with resume, body side moldings and front and rear color-keyed carpeted floor mats for package price of $1,705. Z28 convertible preferred equipment group number 3 including air conditioning, ETR AM/FM stereo (with seek-and-scan, cassette tape, digital clock and extended-range sound system), power windows, power driver's seat, power door locks, speed control with resume, dual power sport-type outside rearview mirrors, body side moldings and front and rear color-keyed carpeted floor mats for package price of $2,086 (or $236 additional with U1C radio. C2 cloth bucket seats (no cost). F2 custom cloth bucket seats ($327). F2 custom cloth bucket seats $(327). A2 custom leather bucket seats ($800). Solid color exterior paint (no cost). LHO 3.1-liter MFI V-6 in RS coupe only, as standard equipment (no cost). LB9 5.0-liter TPI V-8 in Z28 coupe and convertible only, as standard equipment (no cost). L03 5.0-liter EFI V-8, standard in RS convertible, optional in RS coupe ($350). B2L 5.7-liter V-8 in Z28 ($300). C60 air conditioning, including increased-capacity cooling system ($805). G92 performance ratio, includes performance exhaust system, without C60 air conditioning ($675). G92 performance ratio, includes performance exhaust system, with C60 air conditioning ($267). VK3 front license plate bracket (no cost). C49 electric rear window defogger ($160). AU3 electric power door lock system ($190). YF5 California emissions requirements, including all testing and certification necessary for registration in California ($100). NA5 standard emissions equipment (no cost). A90 power hatch release ($50). K05 engine block heater ($20). DE1 rear window louvers ($210). DG7 electric twin remote Sport mirrors ($91). Note: All stereo radios include extended-range sound system. UN6 ETR AM/FM stereo with seek-and-scan, cassette tape and digital clock (available in packages only). U1C ETR stereo with seek-and-scan, stereo cassette tape, search-and-repeat and digital clock (available in packages only). UL5 radio delete (available in packages only). CC1 removable glass roof panels including locks ($866). QMT P235/55R16 steel-belted radial-ply black sidewall tires, standard on Z28, on RS ($170 extra). QLC P245/50ZR16 steel-belted radial-ply black sidewall tires ($400). MM5 five-speed manual transmission, standard on Z28 coupe and convertible ($515 credit). MXO automatic overdrive transmission, standard on RS coupe and convertible ($515). N96 16-in. cast-aluminum wheels with locks and P245/50ZR16 steel-belted radial-ply black sidewall tires (no cost).

1992

RS coupe base equipment group included with model (no cost). RS coupe base equipment group with UN6 radio (add $160). RS coupe base equipment group with U1C radio (add $396). RS coupe base equipment group with UL5 radio delete ($165 credit). RS coupe preferred equipment group number 1, including air conditioning, ETR AM/FM stereo (with seek-and-scan, cassette tape, digital clock and extended-range sound system), body side moldings and front and rear color-keyed carpeted floor mats for package price of $1,085 or $855 additional with UU8 radio or $236 additional with U1C radio. RS coupe preferred equipment group number 2 air conditioning, ETR AM/FM stereo (with seek-and-scan, cassette tape, digital clock and extended-range sound system), body side moldings and front and rear color-keyed carpeted floor mats, power door locks, speed control with resume, power hatch release, cargo area cover and mirror with dual reading lamps for package price of $1,937 or $855 additional with UU8 radio or $236 additional with U1C radio. Z28 base equipment group included with model (no cost). Z28 base equipment group with UN6 radio (add $160). Z28 base equipment group with U1C radio (add $396). Z28 base equipment group with UL5 radio delete ($165 credit). Z28 preferred equipment group number 1 includes air conditioning, body side moldings and front and rear color-keyed carpet mats for package price of $925 (with UN6 radio add $160, with UU8 radio add $1,015 and with U1C radio add $396). Z28 coupe preferred equipment group number 2 includes air conditioning, ETR AM/FM stereo (with seek-and-scan, cassette tape, digital clock and extended-range sound system), body side moldings and front and rear color-keyed carpeted floor mats, power door locks, speed control with resume, power hatch release, cargo area cover and mirror with dual reading lamps for package price of $1,937 or $855 additional with UU8 radio or $236 additional with U1C radio. Z28 coupe preferred equipment group number 3, including air conditioning, ETR AM/FM stereo (with seek-and-scan, cassette tape, digital clock and extended-range sound system), power windows, power driver's seat, power door locks, speed control with resume, power hatch release, dual power sport-type outside rearview mirrors, cargo area cover, body side moldings, front and rear color-keyed carpeted floor mats and mirror with dual reading lamps for package price of $2,332 or $855 additional with UU8 radio or $236 additional with U1C radio. RS convertible base equipment group (no cost). RS convertible base equipment group with UN6 radio (add $160). RS convertible base equipment group with U1C radio (add $236). RS convertible base equipment group with UL5 radio delete ($165 credit). RS convertible preferred equipment group number 1, including air conditioning, ETR AM/FM stereo (with seek-and-scan, cassette tape, search-and-repeat, digital clock and extended-range sound system), body side moldings and front and rear color-keyed carpeted floor mats for package price of $1,085 (or $236 additional with U1C radio). RS convertible preferred equipment group number 2, including air conditioning, ETR AM/FM stereo (with seek-and-scan, cassette tape, digital clock and extended-range sound system), body side moldings and front and rear color-keyed carpeted floor mats, power door locks, speed control with resume for package price of $1,785 or $236 additional with U1C radio. Z28 convertible base equipment group (no cost). Z28 convertible base equipment group with UN6 radio (add $160). Z28 convertible base equipment group with U1C radio (add $396). Z28 convertible base equipment group with UL5 radio delete ($165 credit). Z28 convertible preferred equipment group number 1, including air conditioning, body side moldings and front and rear color-keyed carpet mats for package price of $925 (add $160 for UN6 radio or $236 for U1C radio). Z28 convertible preferred equipment group number 2, including air conditioning, ETR AM/FM stereo (with seek-and-scan, cassette tape, digital clock and extended-range sound system), body side moldings and front and rear color-keyed carpeted floor mats, power door locks, speed control with resume for package price of $1,785 or $236 additional with U1C radio. Z28 convertible preferred equipment group number 3, including air conditioning, ETR AM/FM stereo (with seek-and-scan, cassette tape, digital clock and extended-range sound system), power windows, power driver's seat, power door locks, speed control with resume, dual power sport-type outside rearview mirrors, body side moldings and front and rear color-keyed carpeted floor mats for package price of $2,181 (or $236 additional with U1C radio). C2 cloth bucket seats (no cost). F2 custom cloth bucket seats ($327). A2 custom leather bucket seats ($850). Solid color exterior paint (no cost). LH0 3.1-liter MFI V-6 in RS coupe only, as standard equipment (no cost). LB9 5.0-liter TPI V-8 in Z28 coupe and convertible only, as standard equipment (no cost). L03 5.0-liter EFI V-8, standard in RS convertible, in RS coupe ($369). B2L 5.7-liter V-8 in Z28 ($300). C60 air conditioning including increased-capacity cooling system ($830). G92 performance ratio, includes performance exhaust system, without C60 air conditioning ($675). G92 performance ratio, includes performance exhaust system, with C60 air conditioning ($466). VK3 front license plate bracket (no cost). D42 rear compartment cover ($69). C49 electric rear window defogger ($170). R9W rear window defogger not desired (no cost). AU3 electric power door lock system ($190). YF5 California emissions requirements, including all testing and certification necessary for registration in California ($100). NA5 standard emissions equipment (no cost). B34 front color-keyed carpeted floor mats ($20). Rear color-keyed carpeted floor mats ($15). A90 power hatch release ($50). K05 engine block heater ($20). Z03 Heritage Edition appearance package, including striping and exterior badging, body-color grille and black headlamp pockets ($175). DE1 rear window louvers ($210). DC4 mirror with dual reading lamps ($23). DG7 electric twin remote Sport mirrors ($91). B84 body side moldings ($60). (Note: All stereo radios include extended-range sound system.) UN6 ETR AM/FM stereo with seek-and-scan, cassette tape and digital clock (available in packages only). UU8 GM Delco/Bose music system with ETR AM/FM stereo with seek-and-scan, stereo cassette tape with auto reverse and digital clock (available in packages only). U1C ETR stereo with seek-and-scan, stereo cassette tape, search-and-repeat and digital clock (available in packages only). UL5 radio delete (available in packages only). CC1 removable glass roof panels including locks ($895). AC3 power driver's seat ($305). K34 electric speed control ($225). QPH P215/65R15 steel-belted radial-ply black sidewall tires, standard on RS coupe and convertible (no cost). QMT P235/55R16 steel-belted radial black sidewall tires, standard on Z28 coupe and convertible ($219). QLC P245/50ZR16 steel-belted radial-ply black sidewall tires ($400). MM5 five-speed manual transmission, standard (no cost). MXO automatic overdrive transmission ($530). N96 16-in. cast-aluminum wheels with locks, standard Z28 coupe and convertible (no cost). A31 power windows ($265).

1993

Preferred equipment group No. 1 included air conditioning, electronic speed control with resume speed feature, fog lamps and remote hatch release (net price $1,240). Preferred equipment group No. 2 included air conditioning, electronic speed control with resume speed feature, fog lamps, remote hatch release, power door lock system, power windows with driver's side "express down" feature, twin remote electric sport mirrors, leather-wrapped steering wheel, leather-wrapped gear shifter handle and leather-wrapped parking brake handle (net price $1,901). B84 body side moldings ($60). CC1 transparent removable roof panels ($895). C60 air conditioning ($895). AU3 power door lock system ($220). AC3 6-way power driver's seat ($270). C49 rear window defogger ($170). UU8 Delco/Bose electronically tuned AM/FM radio with cassette player ($275). U1T Delco/Bose electronically tuned AM/FM radio with compact disc player ($531). K05 engine block heater ($20). G92 performance axle ratio ($110). MXO four-speed automatic transmission ($595). P245/50ZR16 performance tires ($144). The 1993 base Camaro could be ordered with the 1LE Special Performance Suspension package that included a 32-mm front stabilizer bar, a 21-mm rear stabilizer bar, higher-rate stabilizer bar bushings, higher-rate upper and lower control arm bushings, stiffer front and rear shock absorber valving and increased-capacity cooling system. There was also a special equipment option package SEO B4C for cars used in police work. It included the LT1 engine, a choice of the automatic or six-speed manual transmissions, the performance suspension, 16-in. aluminum wheels, P245/50ZR16 black sidewall tires, four-wheel disc brakes, a limited-slip axle (3.23:1 ratio with automatic transmission and 3.42:1 ratio with manual gearbox), an engine oil cooler, an automatic transmission cooler for cars so-equipped, a 140-amp alternator, air conditioning and a 150-mph speedometer.

1994

Coupe preferred equipment group No. 1 included air conditioning, electronic speed control with resume speed feature, fog lamps and remote hatch release (net price $1,240 with automatic transmission $1,350 with six-speed manual transmission). Coupe preferred equipment group No. 2 included air conditioning, electronic speed control with resume speed feature, fog lamps, remote hatch release, power door lock system, power windows with driver's side "express down" feature, twin remote electric sport mirrors, remote keyless entry, leather-wrapped steering wheel, leather-wrapped gear shifter handle and leather-wrapped parking brake handle (net price $2,036 with automatic transmission $2,146 with six-speed manual transmission). Convertible preferred equipment group No. 1 included air conditioning, electronic speed control with resume speed feature, fog lamps and remote hatch release (net price $1,240 with automatic transmission $1,350 with six-speed manual transmission). Convertible preferred equipment group No. 2 included air conditioning, electronic speed control with resume speed feature, fog lamps, remote hatch release, power door lock system, power windows with driver's side "express down" feature, twin remote electric sport mirrors, remote keyless entry, leather-wrapped steering wheel, leather-wrapped gear shifter handle and leather-wrapped parking brake handle (net price $2,036 with automatic transmission $2,146 with six-speed manual transmission). C2 cloth bucket seats (no cost). A2 leather bucket seats ($499). C60 air conditioning ($895). GU5 performance axle includes engine oil cooler, Z28 only ($65 with 1LE performance package or $175 without 1LE performance package). VK3 front license plate bracket (no cost). C49 rear window defogger ($170). R9W rear window defogger not desired (no cost). AU3 power door lock system ($220). YF5 California emissions ($100). FE9 federal emissions (no cost). NB8 California/New York override (no cost). NC7 federal emissions override (no cost). B35 rear floor covering ($15). B84 body side moldings ($60). 1LE Performance package including engine oil cooler and Special Handling suspension, Z28 coupe only ($310). [Note: All audio options include extended-range sound system UU8 Delco/Bose electronically tuned AM/FM radio with cassette player ($275 extra as part of all PEGs)]. U1T Delco/Bose electronically tuned AM/FM radio with compact disc player ($531 as part of all PEGs). U1C ETR AM/FM stereo with seek-and-scan, digital clock, CD player, extended-range speakers and Delco Loc II, in convertibles only ($226 as part of all convertible PEGs). CC1 transparent removable coupe roof panels with storage provisions

($970). AC3 six-way power driver's seat ($270). DE4 removable coupe roof sunshade panels ($25). QPE P215/60R16 steel-belted radial black sidewall tires on base coupe and convertible (no cost). QMT P235/55R16 steel-belted radial black sidewall tires on Z28 coupe and convertible (no cost). QLC P245/50ZR16 steel-belted radial black sidewall tires and 150-mph speedometer for Z28 coupe ($225). MXO four-speed automatic transmission ($750). MM5 five-speed manual transmission in base Camaro coupe or convertible (no cost) MN6 six-speed manual transmission in Z28 coupe or convertible (no cost). N96 cast-aluminum wheels with locks on Z28 coupe or convertible only ($275). QB3 16-in. cast steel wheels with bolt-on wheel covers for base coupe or convertible (no cost). L32 3.4-liter sequentially fuel-injected V-6 in base coupe or convertible (no cost). LT1 5.7-liter sequentially fuel-injected V-8 in Z28 coupe or convertible (no cost).

1995

1SA Coupe base equipment group (PEG) included with model, no radio upgrade allowed (no cost). Coupe preferred equipment group No. 1 included air conditioning, electronic speed control with resume speed feature, fog lamps and remote hatch release (net price $1,240 with automatic transmission). PEG 1 with UU8 radio upgrade ($350 additional). PEG 1 with U1T radio upgrade ($606 additional). PEG No. 2 included air conditioning, electronic speed control with resume speed feature, fog lamps, remote hatch release, power door lock system, power windows with driver's side "express down" feature, twin remote electric sport mirrors, remote keyless entry, leather-wrapped steering wheel, leather-wrapped gear shifter handle and leather-wrapped parking brake handle (net price $2,036 with automatic transmission $2,146 with six-speed manual transmission). PEG 1 with UU8 radio upgrade ($350 additional). PEG 1 with U1T radio upgrade ($606 additional). Convertible PEG No. 1 included air conditioning, electronic speed control with resume speed feature, fog lamps and remote hatch release (net price $1,240 with automatic transmission $1,350 with six-speed manual transmission). Convertible PEG No. 2 included air conditioning, electronic speed control with resume speed feature, fog lamps, remote hatch release, power door lock system, power windows with driver's side "express down" feature, twin remote electric sport mirrors, remote keyless entry, leather-wrapped steering wheel, leather-wrapped gear shifter handle and leather-wrapped parking brake handle (net price $2,036 with automatic transmission $2,146 with six-speed manual transmission). C2 cloth bucket seats (no cost). A2 leather bucket seats ($499). C60 air conditioning ($895). GU5 performance axle includes engine oil cooler, Z28 only ($65 with 1LE performance package or $175 without). 1LE performance package. VK3 front license plate bracket (no cost). C49 rear window defogger ($170). R9W rear window defogger not desired (no cost). AU3 power door lock system ($220). YF5 California emissions ($100). FE9 federal emissions (no cost). NB8 California/New York override (no cost). NC7 federal emissions override (no cost). B35 rear floor covering ($15). B84 body side moldings ($60). 1LE Performance package including engine oil cooler and Special Handling suspension, Z28 coupe only ($310). [Note: All audio options include extended-range sound system UU8 Delco/Bose electronically tuned AM/FM radio with cassette player ($275 extra as part of all PEGs).] U1T Delco/Bose electronically tuned AM/FM radio with compact disc player ($531 as part of all PEGs). U1C ETR AM/FM stereo with seek-and-scan, digital clock, CD player, extended-range speakers and Delco Loc II, in convertibles only ($226 as part of all convertible PEGs). CC1 transparent removable coupe roof panels with storage provisions ($970). AC3 six-way power driver's seat ($270). DE4 removable coupe roof sunshade panels ($25). QPE P215/60R16 steel-belted radial black sidewall tires on base coupe and convertible (no cost). QMT P235/55R16 steel-belted radial black sidewall tires on Z28 coupe and convertible (no cost). QLC P245/50ZR16 steel-belted radial black sidewall tires and 150-mph speedometer for Z28 coupe ($225). MXO four-speed automatic transmission ($750). MM5 five-speed manual transmission in base Camaro coupe or convertible (no cost) MN6 six-speed manual transmission in Z28 coupe or convertible (no cost). N96 cast-aluminum wheels with locks on Z28 coupe or convertible only ($275). QB3 16-in. cast steel wheels with bolt-on wheel covers for base coupe or convertible (no cost). L32 3.4-liter sequentially fuel-injected V-6 in base coupe or convertible (no cost). LT1 5.7-liter sequentially fuel-injected V-8 in Z28 coupe or convertible (no cost). L36 3.8-liter sequentially fuel-injected V-6 in base coupe or convertible

1996

1SA Camaro coupe base equipment group, included with model, no radio upgrades allowed (no cost). 1SB Camaro coupe preferred equipment group 1 includes air conditioning, fog lights, remote control hatch release and electric speed control with resume feature ($1,240). 1SB Camaro coupe preferred equipment group 1 includes air conditioning, fog lights, remote control hatch release and electric speed control with resume feature and UU8 radio upgrade ($1,590). 1SB Camaro coupe preferred equipment group 1 includes air conditioning, fog lights, remote control hatch release and electric speed control with resume feature and U1T radio upgrade ($1,846). 1SC Camaro coupe preferred equipment group 2 includes air conditioning, fog lights, remote control hatch release, electric speed control with resume feature, power lock system, leather-wrapped steering wheel, leather-wrapped brake handle, leather-wrapped shifter, electric sport mirrors, remote keyless entry with illuminated interior feature, theft deterrent alarm system and power windows with driver's side express down ($2,126). 1SC Camaro coupe preferred equipment group 2 includes air conditioning, fog lights, remote control hatch release, electric speed control with resume feature, power lock system, leather-wrapped steering wheel, leather-wrapped brake handle, leather-wrapped shifter, electric sport mirrors, remote keyless entry with illuminated interior feature, theft deterrent alarm system, power windows with driver's side express down and UU8 radio upgrade ($2,476). 1SC Camaro coupe preferred equipment group 2 includes air conditioning, fog lights, remote control hatch release, electric speed control with resume feature, power lock system, leather-wrapped steering wheel, leather-wrapped brake handle, leather-wrapped shifter, electric sport mirrors, remote keyless entry with illuminated interior feature, theft deterrent alarm system, power windows with driver's side express down and U1T radio upgrade ($2,732). 1SD Camaro convertible base equipment group, included with model (no cost). 1SD Camaro convertible base equipment group, included with model and U1C radio upgrade ($226). 1SE Camaro convertible preferred equipment group 1 includes power door lock system, fog lights, remote control trunk release and electric speed control with resume feature ($565). 1SE Camaro convertible preferred equipment group 1 includes power door lock system, fog lights, remote control trunk release, electric speed control with resume feature and U1C radio upgrade ($791). 1SF Camaro convertible preferred equipment group 2 includes power door lock system, fog lights, remote control trunk release, electric speed control with resume feature, leather-wrapped steering wheel, leather-wrapped brake handle, leather-wrapped shifter, electric sport mirrors, remote keyless entry with illuminated interior feature, theft-deterrent alarm system and power windows with driver's side express down ($1,231). 1SF Camaro convertible preferred equipment group 2 includes power door lock system, fog lights, remote control trunk release, electric speed control with resume feature, leather-wrapped steering wheel, leather-wrapped brake handle, leather-wrapped shifter, electric sport mirrors, remote keyless entry with illuminated interior feature, theft deterrent alarm system, power windows with driver's side express down and U1C radio upgrade ($1,457). 1SN Camaro RS coupe base equipment group, included with model, no radio upgrades allowed (no cost). 1SP Camaro RS coupe preferred equipment group 1 includes electric speed control with resume feature, power lock system, remote hatch release and fog lights ($565). 1SP Camaro RS coupe preferred equipment group 1 includes electric speed control with resume feature, power lock system, remote hatch release, fog lights and UU8 radio upgrade ($915). 1SP Camaro RS coupe preferred equipment group 1 includes electric speed control with resume feature, power lock system, remote hatch release, fog lights and U1T radio upgrade ($1,170). 1SQ Camaro RS coupe preferred equipment group 2 includes power door lock system, remote control hatch release, electric speed control with resume feature, fog lights, leather-wrapped steering wheel, leather-wrapped brake handle, leather-wrapped shifter, electric sport mirrors, remote keyless entry with illuminated interior feature, theft deterrent alarm system and power windows with driver's side express down ($1,231). 1SQ Camaro RS coupe preferred equipment group 2 includes power door lock system, remote control hatch release, electric speed control with resume feature, fog lights, leather-wrapped steering wheel, leather-wrapped brake handle, leather-wrapped shifter, electric sport mirrors, remote keyless entry with illuminated interior feature, theft deterrent alarm system, power windows with driver's side express down and UU8 radio upgrade ($1,581). 1SQ Camaro RS coupe preferred equipment group 2 includes power door lock system, remote control hatch release, electric speed control with resume feature, fog lights, leather-wrapped steering wheel, leather-wrapped brake handle, leather-wrapped shifter, electric sport mirrors, remote keyless entry with illuminated interior feature, theft deterrent alarm system, power windows with driver's side express down and U1T radio upgrade ($1,837). 1SR Camaro RS convertible base equipment group, included with model (no cost). 1SR Camaro RS convertible base equipment group, included with model and U1C radio upgrade ($226). 1SS Camaro RS convertible preferred equipment group 1 includes power door lock system, fog lights, remote control trunk release and electric speed control with resume feature ($565). 1SS Camaro RS convertible preferred equipment group 1 includes power door lock system, fog lights, remote control trunk release, electric speed control with resume feature and U1C radio upgrade ($791). 1SF Camaro RS convertible preferred equipment group 2 includes power door lock system, fog lights, remote control trunk release, electric speed control with resume feature, leather-wrapped steering wheel, leather-wrapped brake handle, leather-wrapped shifter, electric Sport mirrors, remote keyless entry with illuminated interior feature, theft-deterrent alarm system and power windows with driver's side express down ($1,231). 1SF Camaro RS convertible preferred equipment group 2 includes power door lock system, fog lights, remote control trunk release, electric speed control with resume feature, leather-wrapped steering wheel, leather-wrapped brake handle, leather-wrapped shifter, electric sport mirrors, remote keyless entry with illuminated interior feature, theft-deterrent alarm system, power windows with driver's side express down and U1C radio upgrade ($1,457). 1SG Camaro Z28 coupe base equipment group, included with model, no radio upgrades allowed (no cost). 1SH Camaro Z28 coupe preferred equipment group 1 includes electric speed control with resume feature, power lock system, remote hatch release, fog lights and four-way manual driver's seat adjustment ($600). 1SH Camaro Z28 coupe preferred equipment group 1 includes electric speed control with resume feature, power lock system, remote hatch release, fog lights, four-way manual driver's seat adjustment and UU8 radio upgrade ($950). 1SH Camaro Z28 coupe preferred equipment group 1 includes electric speed control with resume feature, power lock system, remote hatch release, fog lights, four-way manual driver's seat adjustment and U1T radio upgrade ($1,206). 1SJ Camaro Z28 coupe preferred equipment group 2 includes power door lock system, remote control hatch release, electric speed control with resume feature, fog lights, leather-wrapped steering wheel, leather-wrapped brake handle, leather-wrapped shifter, electric Sport mirrors, remote keyless entry with illuminated interior feature, theft deterrent alarm system, four-way manual driver's seat adjustment and power windows with driver's side express down ($1,266). 1SJ Camaro Z28 coupe preferred equipment group 2 includes power door lock system, remote control hatch release, electric speed control with resume feature, fog lights, leather-wrapped steering wheel, leather-wrapped brake handle, leather-wrapped shifter, electric Sport mirrors, remote keyless entry with illuminated interior feature, theft deterrent alarm system, power windows with driver's side express down, four-way manual driver's seat adjustment and UU8 radio upgrade ($1,616). 1SJ Camaro Z28 coupe preferred equipment group 2 includes power door lock system, remote control hatch release, electric speed control with resume feature, fog lights, leather-wrapped steering wheel, leather-wrapped brake handle, leather-wrapped shifter, electric sport mirrors, remote keyless entry with illuminated interior feature, theft deterrent alarm system, power windows with driver's side express down, four-way manual driver's seat adjustment and U1T radio upgrade ($1,872). 1SK Camaro Z28 convertible base equipment group, included with model (no cost). 1SK Camaro Z28 convertible base equipment group, included with model and U1C radio upgrade ($226). 1SL Camaro Z28 convertible preferred equipment group 1 includes power door lock system, fog lights, remote control trunk release and electric speed control with resume feature ($565). 1SL Camaro Z28 convertible preferred equipment group 1 includes power door lock system, fog lights, remote control trunk release, electric speed control with resume feature and U1C radio upgrade ($791). 1SM Camaro Z28 convertible preferred equipment group 2 includes power door lock system, fog lights, remote control trunk release, electric speed control with resume feature, leather-wrapped steering wheel, leather-wrapped brake handle, leather-wrapped shifter, electric sport mirrors, remote keyless entry with illuminated interior feature, theft-deterrent alarm system and power windows with driver's side express down ($1,231). 1SM Camaro Z28 convertible preferred equipment group 2 includes power door lock system, fog lights, remote control trunk release, electric speed control with resume feature, leather-wrapped steering wheel, leather-wrapped brake handle, leather-wrapped shifter, electric sport mirrors, remote keyless entry with illuminated interior feature, theft-deterrent alarm system, power windows with driver's side express down and U1C radio upgrade ($1,457). C60 air conditioning ($895). GU5 optional performance axle ($250). VK3 front license plate bracket (no cost). C49 rear window defogger ($170). R9W rear window defogger not desired in coupes (no cost). AU3 power door lock system ($220). FE9 federal emissions (no cost). NG1 New York and Massachusetts emissions (no cost). YF5 California emissions (no cost). NB8 California and Massachusetts emissions override (no cost). NC7 federal emissions override (no cost). B35 rear carpeted floor mats ($15). B84 color-keyed body side moldings ($60). 1LE performance package includes Special Handling suspension, larger stabilizer bars, stiffer springs, dual adjustable shocks and bushings, Z28 coupe only ($310). Y87 performance handling package includes limited-slip axle, four-wheel disc brakes, dual outlet exhaust and sport steering ration on base and RS models only ($400). UU8 Delco Bose music system (packages only). U1C ETR AM/FM stereo (with packages only). U1C ETR AM/FM stereo (with packages only). D82 monochromatic roof treatment including body-color roof and mirrors on base or RS coupe, requires CC1 roof panels or on Z28 replaces standard black roof (no cost). CC1 removable roof panels ($970). AGF1 six-way power driver's seat ($270). AR9 leather bucket seat ($499). DE4 sunshades for removable roof panels ($25). QCB P235/55R16 tires ($132). QLC P245/50ZR16 tires ($225). QFZ P245/50ZR16 performance tires for Z28s and convertibles ($225). MXO four-speed automatic transmission with brake/shift interlock ($790). N96 16-in. silver aluminum wheels ($275). N98 16-in. chrome wheels with Z28 ($500).

CAMARO SS OPTIONS: Performance exhaust system. Level II Bilstein Sport suspension .Torsen limited-slip differential includes performance lubricant package. Hurst six-speed short-throw shifter. Engine oil cooler. B.F. Goodrich Comp T/A 17-in. tires, available only as a second set shipped to Chevrolet dealer on 17-in. wheels and recommended for track usage by an experienced driver. Performance lubricants package with premium synthetic media engine oil filter, rear axle lube and semi-synthetic power steering fluid.

1997

1SA Camaro coupe base equipment group, included with model (no cost). 1SA Camaro coupe base equipment group with UL0 radio upgrade ($215). 1SA Camaro coupe base equipment group with UN0 radio upgrade ($315). 1SB Camaro coupe preferred equipment group 1 includes fog lights, remote control hatch release and electric speed control with resume feature ($345). 1SB Camaro coupe preferred equipment group 1 includes fog lights, remote control hatch release and electric speed control with resume feature and UL0 radio upgrade ($560). 1SB Camaro coupe preferred equipment group 1 includes fog lights, remote control hatch release and electric speed control with resume feature and UN0 radio upgrade ($660). 1SC Camaro coupe preferred equipment group 2 includes fog lights, remote control hatch release, electric speed control with resume feature, power lock system, leather-wrapped steering wheel, leather-wrapped brake handle, leather-wrapped shifter, electric Sport mirrors, remote keyless entry with illuminated interior feature, theft deterrent alarm system and power windows with driver's side express down ($1,231). 1SC Camaro coupe preferred equipment group 2 includes fog lights, remote control hatch release, electric speed control with resume feature, power lock system, leather-wrapped steering wheel, leather-wrapped brake handle, leather-wrapped shifter, electric Sport mirrors, remote keyless entry with illuminated interior feature, theft deterrent alarm system, power windows with driver's side express down and UL0 radio upgrade ($1,446). 1SC Camaro coupe preferred equipment group 2 includes fog lights, remote control hatch release, electric speed control with resume feature, power lock system, leather-wrapped steering wheel, leather-wrapped brake handle, leather-wrapped shifter, electric Sport mirrors, remote keyless entry with illuminated interior feature, theft deterrent alarm system, power windows with driver's side express down and UN0 radio upgrade ($1,546). 1SD Camaro convertible base equipment group, included with model (no cost). 1SD Camaro convertible base equipment group, included with model and UL0 radio upgrade ($215). 1SD Camaro convertible base equipment group, included with model and UN0 radio upgrade ($315). 1SE Camaro convertible preferred equipment group 1 includes power door lock system, fog lights, remote control trunk release and electric speed control with resume feature ($565). 1SE Camaro convertible preferred equipment group 1 includes power door lock system, fog lights, remote control trunk release, electric speed control with resume feature and UL0 radio upgrade ($780). 1SE Camaro convertible preferred equipment group 1 includes power door lock system, fog lights, remote control trunk release, electric speed control with resume feature and UL0 radio upgrade ($1,446). 1SE Camaro convertible preferred equipment group 1 includes power door lock system, fog lights, remote control trunk release, electric speed control with resume feature and UL0 radio upgrade ($1,446). 1SF Camaro convertible preferred equipment group 2 includes power door lock system, fog lights, remote control trunk release, electric speed control with resume feature, leather-wrapped steering wheel, leather-wrapped brake handle, leather-wrapped shifter, electric Sport mirrors, remote keyless entry with illuminated interior feature, theft deterrent alarm system and power windows with driver's side express down ($1,231). 1SF Camaro convertible preferred equipment group 2 includes power door lock system, fog lights, remote control trunk release, electric speed control with resume feature, leather-wrapped steering wheel, leather-wrapped brake handle, leather-wrapped shifter, electric Sport mirrors, remote keyless entry with illuminated interior feature, theft deterrent alarm system, power windows with driver's side express down and UL0 radio upgrade ($1,456). 1SF Camaro convertible preferred equipment group 2 includes power door lock system, fog lights, remote control trunk release, electric speed control with resume feature, leather-wrapped steering wheel, leather-wrapped brake handle, leather-wrapped shifter, electric Sport mirrors, remote keyless entry with illuminated interior feature, theft deterrent alarm system, power windows with driver's side express down and UL0 radio upgrade ($1,556). 1SN Camaro RS coupe base equipment group, included with model, no radio upgrades allowed (no cost). 1SN Camaro RS coupe base equipment group, included with UL0 radio upgrade ($215). 1SN Camaro RS coupe base equipment group, included with UN0 radio upgrade ($315). 1SP Camaro RS coupe preferred equipment group 1 includes electric speed control with resume feature, power lock system, remote hatch release and fog lights ($565). 1SP Camaro RS coupe preferred equipment group 1 includes electric speed control with resume feature, power lock system, remote hatch release, fog lights and UL0 radio upgrade ($780). 1SP Camaro RS coupe preferred equipment group 1 includes electric speed control with resume feature, power lock system, remote hatch release, fog lights and UN0 radio upgrade ($880). 1SQ Camaro RS coupe preferred equipment group 2 includes power door lock system, remote control hatch release, electric speed control with resume feature, fog lights, leather-wrapped steering wheel, leather-wrapped brake handle, leather-wrapped shifter, electric Sport mirrors, remote keyless entry with illuminated interior feature, theft deterrent alarm system and power windows with driver's side express down ($1,231). 1SQ Camaro RS coupe preferred equipment group 2 includes power door lock system, remote control hatch release, electric speed control with resume feature, fog lights, leather-wrapped steering wheel, leather-wrapped brake handle, leather-wrapped shifter, electric Sport mirrors, remote keyless entry with illuminated interior feature, theft deterrent alarm system, power windows with driver's side express down and UU8 radio upgrade ($1,446). 1SQ Camaro RS coupe preferred equipment group 2 includes power door lock system, remote control hatch release, electric speed control with resume feature, fog lights, leather-wrapped steering wheel, leather-wrapped brake handle, leather-wrapped shifter, electric Sport mirrors, remote keyless entry with illuminated interior feature, theft deterrent alarm system, power windows with driver's side express down and U1T radio upgrade ($1,546). 1SR Camaro RS convertible base equipment group, included with model (no cost). 1SR Camaro RS convertible base equipment group, included with model and UL0 radio upgrade ($215). 1SR Camaro RS convertible base equipment group, included with model and UN0 radio upgrade ($315). 1SS Camaro RS convertible preferred equipment group 1 includes power door lock system, fog lights, remote control trunk release and electric speed control with resume feature ($565). 1SS Camaro RS convertible preferred equipment group 1 includes power door lock system, fog lights, remote control trunk release, electric speed control with resume feature and UL0 radio upgrade ($780). 1SS Camaro RS convertible preferred equipment group 1 includes power door lock system, fog lights, remote control trunk release, electric speed control with resume feature and UN0 radio upgrade ($780). 1ST Camaro RS convertible preferred equipment group 2 includes power door lock system, fog lights, remote control trunk release, electric speed control with resume feature, leather-wrapped steering wheel, leather-wrapped brake handle, leather-wrapped shifter, electric Sport mirrors, remote keyless entry with illuminated interior feature, theft deterrent alarm system and power windows with driver's side express down ($1,231). 1ST Camaro RS convertible preferred equipment group 2 includes power door lock system, fog lights, remote control trunk release, electric speed control with resume feature, leather-wrapped steering wheel, leather-wrapped brake handle, leather-wrapped shifter, electric Sport mirrors, remote keyless entry with illuminated interior feature, theft deterrent alarm system, power windows with driver's side express down and UL0 radio upgrade ($1,446). 1ST Camaro RS convertible preferred equipment group 2 includes power door lock system, fog lights, remote control trunk release, electric speed control with resume feature, leather-wrapped steering wheel, leather-wrapped brake handle, leather-wrapped shifter, electric Sport mirrors, remote keyless entry with illuminated interior feature, theft deterrent alarm system, power windows with driver's side express down and UN0 radio upgrade ($1,446). 1SG Camaro Z28 coupe base equipment group, included with model (no cost). 1SG Camaro Z28 coupe base equipment group, plus UL0 radio upgrade ($215). 1SG Camaro Z28 coupe base equipment group, plus UN0 radio upgrade ($315). 1SH Camaro Z28 coupe preferred equipment group 1 includes electric speed control with resume feature, power lock system, remote hatch release, fog lights and four-way manual driver's seat adjustment ($600). 1SH Camaro Z28 coupe preferred equipment group 1 includes electric speed control with resume feature, power lock system, remote hatch release, fog lights, four-way manual driver's seat adjustment and UL0 radio upgrade ($815). 1SH Camaro Z28 coupe preferred equipment group 1 includes electric speed control with resume feature, power lock system, remote hatch release, fog lights, four-way manual driver's seat adjustment and UN0 radio upgrade ($915). 1SJ Camaro Z28 coupe preferred equipment group 2 includes power door lock system, remote control hatch release, electric speed control with resume feature, fog lights, leather-wrapped steering wheel, leather-wrapped brake handle, leather-wrapped shifter, electric Sport mirrors, remote keyless entry with illuminated interior feature, theft deterrent alarm system, four-way manual driver's seat adjustment and power windows with driver's side express down ($1,266). 1SJ Camaro Z28 coupe preferred equipment group 2 includes power door lock system, remote control hatch release, electric speed control with resume feature, fog lights, leather-wrapped steering wheel, leather-wrapped brake handle, leather-wrapped shifter, electric Sport mirrors, remote keyless entry with illuminated interior feature, theft deterrent alarm system, power windows with driver's side express down, four-way manual driver's seat adjustment and UU8 radio upgrade ($1,481). 1SJ Camaro Z28 coupe preferred equipment group 2 includes power door lock system, remote control hatch release, electric speed control with resume feature, fog lights, leather-wrapped steering wheel, leather-wrapped brake handle, leather-wrapped shifter, electric Sport mirrors, remote keyless entry with illuminated interior feature, theft deterrent alarm system, power windows with driver's side express down, four-way manual driver's seat adjustment and U1T radio upgrade ($1,581). 1SK Camaro Z28 convertible base equipment group, included with model (no cost). 1SK Camaro Z28 convertible base equipment group, included with model and UL0 radio upgrade ($215). 1SK Camaro Z28 convertible base equipment group, included with model and UN0 radio upgrade ($315). 1SL Camaro Z28 convertible preferred equipment group 1 includes power door lock system, fog lights, remote control trunk release and electric speed control with resume feature ($565). 1SL Camaro Z28 convertible preferred equipment group 1 includes power door lock system, fog lights, remote control trunk release, electric speed control with resume feature and UL0 radio upgrade ($780). 1SL Camaro Z28 convertible preferred equipment group 1 includes power door lock system, fog lights, remote control trunk release, electric speed control with resume feature and UL0 radio upgrade ($780). 1SM Camaro Z28 convertible preferred equipment group 2 includes fog lights, leather-wrapped steering wheel, leather-wrapped brake handle, leather-wrapped shifter, electric Sport mirrors, remote keyless entry with illuminated interior feature, theft deterrent alarm system, power windows with driver's side express down and U1C radio upgrade ($1,231). 1SM Camaro Z28 convertible preferred equipment group 2 includes fog lights, leather-wrapped steering wheel, leather-wrapped brake handle, leather-wrapped shifter, electric Sport mirrors, remote keyless entry with illuminated interior feature, theft deterrent alarm system, power windows with driver's side express down and UL0 radio upgrade ($1,456). 1SM Camaro Z28 convertible preferred equipment group 2 includes fog lights, leather-wrapped steering wheel, leather-wrapped brake handle, leather-wrapped shifter, electric Sport mirrors, remote keyless entry with illuminated interior feature, theft deterrent alarm system, power windows with driver's side express down and UL0 radio upgrade ($1,556). GU5 optional performance axle ($300). VK3 front license plate bracket (no cost). C49 rear window defogger ($170). R9W rear window defogger not desired in coupes (no cost). AU3 power door lock system ($220). FE9 federal emissions (no cost). NG1 New York and Massachusetts emissions (no cost). YF5 California emissions (no cost). NB8 California and Massachusetts emissions override (no cost). NC7 federal emissions override (no cost). LT36 3.8-liter SFI V-6 (no cost in base coupe and RS; not available in Z28). LT1 5.7-liter SFI V-8 (in Z28 no charge). B35 rear carpeted floor mats ($15). K05 engine block heater ($20). AU0 remote keyless entry, as a separate option ($225). B84 color-keyed body side moldings ($60). 1LE performance package includes special handling suspension, Z28 coupe only ($1,175). Y87 performance handling package includes limited-slip axle, four-wheel disc brakes, dual outlet exhaust and sport steering ration on base and RS models only ($400). UL0 ETR AM/FM stereo ($350). UN0 ETR AM/FM stereo and CG player ($450). U1S 12-disc CD player ($595). D82 monochromatic roof treatment includes body-color roof and mirrors on base or RS coupe requires CC1 roof panels or on Z28 replaces standard black roof (no cost). CC1 removable roof panels ($995). AGF1 six-way power driver's seat ($270). AR9 leather bucket seat ($499). Z4C 30th Anniversary Edition package includes white monochromatic exterior with orange stripes, white 5-spoke aluminum wheels, 30th Anniversary embroidered emblems on front floor mats and 30th Anniversary embroidered emblems on headrests ($575). QEA P215/60R16 black sidewall tires for standard coupe or convertible (no cost). QCB P235/55R16 tires ($132). QLC P245/50ZR16 tires ($225). QFZ P245/50ZR16 performance tires for Z28s and convertibles ($225). MN6 six-speed manual transmission (no cost). MM5 five-speed manual transmission (no cost). MXO four-speed automatic transmission with brake/shift interlock ($790). N96 16-in. silver aluminum wheels ($275). N98 16-in. chrome wheels with Z28 ($500). N98 16-in. chrome wheels with Z28 ($775).

CAMARO SS OPTIONS: Performance exhaust system. Level II Bilstein sport suspension. Torsen limited-slip differential includes performance lubricant package. Hurst six-speed short-throw shifter. Engine oil cooler. B.F. Goodrich Comp T/A 17-in. tires for Camaro SS Coupe, available only as a second set shipped to Chevrolet dealer on 17-in. wheels and recommended for track usage by an experienced driver. Performance lubricants package with premium synthetic media engine oil filter, rear axle lube and semi-synthetic power steering fluid. Fitted car cover with locking cable, tote bag and silk-screened Camaro SS logo on cover and bag (standard with 30th Anniversary package). Premium front floor mats with embroidered Camaro SS logo. Sebring Silver Metallic exterior color.

1998

U15 12-disc CD changer, requires ULO, not available with UNO ($595). GU5 3.23 performance axle ratio for Z28, requires QFZ or QLC, not available with MN6 ($300). MXO four-speed automatic transmission in base Camaro, includes second-gear start and 3.23 axle, not available with Y87 teamed with MM5 ($815). MN6 six-speed manual transmission in Z28, includes 3.42 axle, not available with GU5 (no cost). AG1 six-way power driver's seat in base Camaro ($270). NW9 acceleration slip regulation in Z28, QFC tires recommended, not available with 1SF ($450). YF5 California emissions ($170). B84 color-keyed body side moldings on base coupe ($60). C49 electric rear window defogger on coupes, not available with R9W ($170). Leather seating surface, not available with 1SF ($499). New York, Massachusetts, Connecticut emissions ($170). Y87 performance handling package with MM5, includes sport steering ratio, dual outlet exhaust and limited-slip differential, requires QCB and N96 or N98, not available with 1SA or 1SD ($225). 1LE Z28 coupe performance package, includes special handling suspension system, larger stabilizer bars, stiffer springs, dual adjustable shock absorbers and bushings and power steering cooler ($1,175). 1SA base coupe preferred equipment group includes vehicle with standard equipment (no cost). 1SB base coupe preferred equipment package includes electronic speed control, remote hatch release, power door lock system and fog lamps ($565). 1SC base coupe preferred equipment package includes electronic speed control with resume feature, remote hatch lid release, power door lock system, fog lamps, power windows with river's side express down, dual electric remote-control sport mirrors, a leather-wrapped steering wheel, a leather gearshift knob, remote keyless entry, illuminated entry, remote hatch release and theft-deterrent alarm system ($1,231). 1SD base convertible preferred equipment group includes vehicle with standard equipment (no cost). 1SE base convertible preferred equipment group includes power door lock system, electronic speed control with resume, remote hatch release, fog lamps, power windows with driver's side express down, electric dual remote control sport mirrors, leather-wrapped steering wheel, leather gearshift knob, remote keyless entry, illuminated entry, panic alarm, remote hatch release, theft-deterrent alarm system, color-keyed lower body side moldings and rear carpet floor mats ($1,306). 1SF Z28 coupe preferred equipment group, includes vehicle with standard equipment (no cost). 1SG Z28 coupe preferred equipment group includes power door lock system, electronic speed control with resume, remote hatch release, fog lamps, power windows with driver's side express down, electric dual remote control sport mirrors, leather-wrapped steering wheel, leather gearshift knob, remote keyless entry, illuminated entry, panic alarm, remote hatch release, theft-deterrent alarm system, six-way power driver's seat, color-keyed lower body side moldings and rear carpet floor mats ($1,576). 1SH Z28 convertible preferred equipment group includes power door lock system, electronic speed control with resume, remote hatch release, fog lamps, power windows with driver's side express down, electric dual remote control sport mirrors, leather-wrapped steering wheel, leather gearshift knob, remote keyless entry, illuminated entry, panic alarm, remote hatch release, theft-deterrent alarm system, six-way power driver's seat, color-keyed lower body side moldings and rear carpet floor mats (no cost). ULO AM/FM stereo with automatic tone control and cassette in coupes, includes digital clock, theft lock, speed-compensated volume, 200-watt amplifier and eight speakers ($350). ULO AM/FM stereo with automatic tone control and cassette in convertibles, includes digital clock, theft lock, speed-compensated volume, 200-watt amplifier and eight speakers ($215). UNO AM/FM stereo with Automatic Tone Control and CD in convertibles, includes digital clock, theft lock, speed-compensated volume, 200-watt amplifier and eight speakers ($315). UNO AM/FM stereo with Automatic Tone Control and CD in coupes, includes digital clock, theft lock, speed-compensated volume, 200-watt amplifier and eight speakers ($450). B35 rear carpet floor mats in base coupe ($15). R9W rear window defogger not desired in coupes (no cost). AUO remote keyless entry in base coupe, includes illuminated entry, theft-deterrent alarm system, panic alarm and remote hatch release ($225). Y3F Sport Appearance package for base Camaro, includes rocker and rear fascia moldings, 16-in. aluminum wheels and P235/55R15 all-season black sidewall tires ($1,755). Y3F Sport Appearance package for Z28 includes rocker moldings, front fascia moldings, rear fascia moldings, spoiler extension, 16-in. aluminum wheels and P235/55R16 all-season black sidewall tires ($1,348). WU8 SS performance and appearance package for Z28, includes 320-hp engine, forced air induction hood, a unique spoiler, 17-in. aluminum wheels, P275/40ZR17 Goodyear Eagle F1 tires, high performance ride & handling package and SS badging ($3,500). QCB P235/55R16 black sidewall tires on base Camaros ($132). QFZ P245/50ZR16 black sidewall all-season performance tires on Z28s ($225). QLC P245/50ZR16 black sidewall performance tires on Z28s ($225). CC1 transparent removable roof panels, includes locks, lockable stowage and sun shade ($995). N96 16-in. aluminum wheels on base Camaro ($275). N98 16-in chrome aluminum wheels on base Camaros ($775). N98 16-in. chrome aluminum wheels on Camaro Z28s ($500).

1999

U15 12-disc CD changer, requires ULO, not available with UNO ($595). GU5 3.23 performance axle ratio for Z28, requires QFZ or QLC, not available with MN6 ($300). MXO four-speed automatic transmission in base Camaro, includes second-gear start and 3.23 axle, not available with Y87 teamed with MM5 ($815). MN6 six-speed manual transmission in Z28, includes 3.42 axle, not available with GU5 (no cost). AG1 six-way power driver's seat in base Camaro ($270). NW9 acceleration slip regulation in Z28, QFC tires recommended, not available with 1SF ($450). YF5 California emissions ($170). B84 color-keyed body side moldings on base coupe ($60). C49 electric rear window defogger on coupes, not available with R9W ($170). Leather seating surface, not available with 1SF ($499). New York, Massachusetts, Connecticut emissions ($170). Y87 performance handling package with MM5, includes sport steering ratio, dual outlet exhaust and limited-slip differential, requires QCB and N96 or N98, not available with 1SA or 1SD ($225). 1LE Z28 coupe performance package, including special handling suspension system, larger stabilizer bars, stiffer springs, dual adjustable shock absorbers and bushings and power steering cooler ($1,175). 1SA base coupe preferred equipment group includes vehicle with standard equipment (no cost). 1SB base coupe preferred equipment package includes electronic speed control, remote hatch release, power door lock system and fog lamps ($565). 1SC base coupe preferred equipment package includes electronic speed control with resume feature, remote hatch lid release, power door lock system, fog lamps, power windows with river's side express down, dual electric remote-control sport mirrors, a leather-wrapped steering wheel, a leather gearshift knob, remote keyless entry, illuminated entry, remote hatch release and theft-deterrent alarm system ($1,231). 1SD base convertible preferred equipment group includes vehicle with standard equipment (no cost). 1SE base convertible preferred equipment group includes power door lock system, electronic speed control with resume, remote hatch release, fog lamps, power windows with driver's side express down, electric dual remote control sport mirrors, leather-wrapped steering wheel, leather gearshift knob, remote keyless entry, illuminated entry, panic alarm, remote hatch release, theft-deterrent alarm system, color-keyed lower body side moldings and rear carpet floor mats ($1,306). 1SF Z28 coupe preferred equipment group, includes vehicle with standard equipment (no cost). 1SG Z28 coupe preferred equipment group includes power door lock system, electronic speed control with resume, remote hatch release, fog lamps, power windows with driver's side express down, electric dual remote control sport mirrors, leather-wrapped steering wheel, leather gearshift knob, remote keyless entry, illuminated entry, panic alarm, remote hatch release, theft-deterrent alarm system, six-way power driver's seat, color-keyed lower body side moldings and rear carpet floor mats ($1,576). 1SH Z28 convertible preferred equipment group includes power door lock system, electronic speed control with resume, remote hatch release, fog lamps, power windows with driver's side express down, electric dual remote control sport mirrors, leather-wrapped steering wheel, leather gearshift knob, remote keyless entry, illuminated entry, panic alarm, remote hatch release, theft-deterrent alarm system, six-way power driver's seat, color-keyed lower body side moldings and rear carpet floor mats (no cost). ULO AM/FM stereo with automatic tone control and cassette in coupes, includes digital clock, theft lock, speed-compensated volume, 200-watt amplifier and eight speakers ($350). ULO AM/FM stereo with automatic tone control and cassette in convertibles, includes digital clock, theft lock, speed-compensated volume, 200-watt amplifier and eight speakers ($215). UNO AM/FM stereo with Automatic Tone Control and CD in convertibles, includes digital clock, theft lock, speed-compensated volume, 200-watt amplifier and eight speakers ($315). UNO AM/FM stereo with Automatic Tone Control and CD in coupes, includes digital clock, theft lock, speed-compensated volume, 200-watt amplifier and eight speakers ($450). B35 rear carpet floor mats in base coupe ($15). R9W rear window defogger not desired in coupes (no cost). AUO remote keyless entry in base coupe, includes illuminated entry, theft-deterrent alarm system, panic alarm and remote hatch release ($225). Y3F Sport Appearance package for base Camaro, includes rocker and rear fascia moldings, 16-in. aluminum wheels and P235/55R15 all-season black sidewall tires ($1,755). Y3F Sport Appearance package for Z28 includes rocker moldings, front fascia moldings, rear fascia moldings, spoiler extension, 16-in. aluminum wheels and P235/55R16 all-season black sidewall tires ($1,348). WU8 SS performance and appearance package for Z28, includes 320-hp engine, forced air induction hood, a unique spoiler, 17-in. aluminum wheels, P275/40ZR17 Goodyear Eagle F1 tires, high-performance ride & handling package and SS badging ($3,500). QCB P235/55R16 black sidewall tires on base Camaros ($132). QFZ P245/50ZR16 black sidewall all-season performance tires on Z28s ($225). QLC P245/50ZR16 black sidewall performance tires on Z28s ($225). CC1 transparent removable roof panels, includes locks, lockable stowage and sunshade ($995). N96 16-in. aluminum wheels on base Camaro ($275). N98 16-in chrome aluminum wheels on base Camaros ($775). N98 16-in. chrome aluminum wheels on Camaro Z28s ($500).

2000

U15 12-disc CD changer, requires ULO, not available with UNO ($595). GU5 3.23 performance axle ratio for Z28, requires QFZ or QLC, not available with MN6 ($300). MXO four-speed automatic transmission in base Camaro, includes second-gear start and 3.23 axle, not available with Y87 teamed with MM5 ($815). MN6 six-speed manual transmission in Z28, includes 3.42 axle, not available with GU5 (no cost). AG1 six-way power driver's seat in base Camaro ($270). NW9 acceleration slip regulation in Z28, QFC tires recommended, not available with 1SF ($450). YF5 California emissions ($170). B84 color-keyed body side moldings on base coupe ($60). C49 electric rear window defogger on coupes, not available with R9W ($170). Leather seating surface, not available with 1SF ($499). New York, Massachusetts, Connecticut emissions ($170). Y87 performance handling package with MM5, includes sport steering ratio, dual outlet exhaust and limited-slip differential, requires QCB and N96 or N98, not available with 1SA or 1SD ($225). 1LE Z28 coupe performance package, includes special handling suspension system, larger stabilizer bars, stiffer springs, dual adjustable shock absorbers and bushings and power steering cooler ($1,175). 1SA base coupe preferred equipment group includes vehicle with standard equipment (no cost). 1SB base coupe preferred equipment package includes electronic speed control, remote hatch release, power door lock system and fog lamps ($565). 1SC base coupe preferred equipment package includes electronic speed control with resume feature, remote hatch lid release, power door lock system, fog lamps, power windows with river's side express down, dual electric remote-control sport mirrors, a leather-wrapped steering wheel, a leather gearshift knob, remote keyless entry, illuminated entry, remote hatch release and theft-deterrent alarm system ($1,231). 1SD base convertible preferred equipment group includes vehicle with standard equipment (no cost). 1SE base convertible preferred equipment group includes power door lock system, electronic speed control with resume, remote hatch release, fog lamps, power windows with driver's side express down, electric dual remote control sport mirrors, leather-wrapped steering wheel, leather gearshift knob, remote keyless entry, illuminated entry, panic alarm, remote hatch release, theft-deterrent alarm system, color-keyed lower body side moldings and rear carpet floor mats ($1,306). 1SF Z28 coupe preferred equipment group, includes vehicle with standard equipment (no cost). 1SG Z28 coupe preferred equipment group includes power door lock system, electronic speed control with resume, remote hatch release, fog lamps, power windows with driver's side express down, electric dual remote control sport mirrors, leather-wrapped steering wheel, leather gearshift knob, remote keyless entry, illuminated entry, panic alarm, remote hatch release, theft-deterrent alarm system, six-way power driver's seat, color-keyed lower body side moldings and rear carpet floor mats ($1,576). 1SH Z28 convertible preferred equipment group includes power door lock system, electronic speed control with resume, remote hatch release, fog lamps, power windows with driver's side express down, electric dual remote control sport mirrors, leather-wrapped steering wheel, leather gearshift knob, remote keyless entry, illuminated entry, panic alarm, remote hatch release, theft-deterrent alarm system, six-way power driver's seat, color-keyed lower body side moldings and rear carpet floor mats (no cost). ULO AM/FM stereo with Automatic Tone Control and cassette in coupes, includes digital clock, TheftLock, speed-compensated volume, 200-watt amplifier and eight speakers ($350). ULO AM/FM stereo with Automatic Tone Control and cassette in convertibles, includes digital clock, TheftLock, speed-compensated volume, 200-watt amplifier and eight speakers ($215). UNO AM/FM stereo with Automatic Tone Control and CD in convertibles, includes digital clock, TheftLock, speed-compensated volume, 200-watt amplifier and eight speakers ($315). UNO AM/FM stereo with Automatic Tone Control and CD in coupes, includes digital clock, TheftLock, speed-compensated volume, 200-watt amplifier and eight speakers ($450). B35 rear carpet floor mats in base coupe ($15). R9W rear window defogger not desired in coupes (no cost). AUO remote keyless entry in base coupe, includes illuminated entry, theft-deterrent alarm system, panic alarm and remote hatch release ($225). Y3F Sport Appearance package for base Camaro, includes rocker and rear fascia moldings, 16-in. aluminum wheels and P235/55R15 all-season black sidewall tires ($1,755). Y3F Sport Appearance package for Z28 includes rocker moldings, front fascia moldings, rear fascia moldings, spoiler extension, 16-in. aluminum wheels and P235/55R16 all-season black sidewall tires ($1,348). WU8 SS performance and appearance package for Z28, includes 320-hp engine, forced air induction hood, a unique spoiler, 17-in. aluminum wheels, P275/40ZR17 Goodyear Eagle F1 tires, high performance ride & handling package and SS badging ($3,500). QCB P235/55R16 black sidewall tires on base Camaros ($132). QFZ P245/50ZR16 black sidewall all-season performance tires on Z28s ($225). QLC P245/50ZR16 black sidewall performance tires on Z28s ($225). CC1 transparent removable roof panels, includes locks, lockable stowage and sun shade ($995). N96 16-in. aluminum wheels on base Camaro ($275). N98 16-in chrome aluminum wheels on base Camaros ($775). N98 16-in. chrome aluminum wheels on Camaro Z28s ($500).

2001

1SA convertible with base equipment group, includes vehicle with standard equipment (no cost). 1SA hatchback base equipment group, includes vehicle with standard equipment; not available with 1SB (no cost). 1SB hatchback preferred equipment group 1 includes remote keyless entry, theft-deterrent alarm system, cruise control, fog lights, twin electric remote-control sport mirrors, power door locks, power windows with driver's side express down feature and remote hatch release; not available with 1SA ($1,170). 1SB convertible preferred equipment group 1, includes vehicle with standard equipment (no cost). 1SC Z28 hatchback preferred equipment group 2, includes vehicle with standard equipment; not available with 1SD (no cost). 1SD Z28 hatchback preferred equipment group 1 includes remote keyless entry, theft-deterrent alarm system, electronic cruise control, twin electric remote-control sport mirrors, power door locks, power windows with driver's side express down feature, remote hatch release; power six-way driver's seat, leather-wrapped steering wheel with redundant radio controls, leather-trimmed gear shift knob, leather-wrapped parking brake handle, rear carpeted floor mats and color-keyed body side moldings; not available with 1SC ($1,715). AG1 six-way power driver's seat ($270). AR9 leather accent bucket seats ($500). B35 rear carpet mats ($35). B84 body-color body side moldings on hatchback ($60). BBS Hurst performance shift linkage for Z28, includes short-throw shift linkage, requires six-speed manual transmission ($325). C49 hatchback rear window defogger ($170). CC1 transparent removable hatch roof panels, includes locks, lockable storage provisions and sunshades ($995). FE9 federal emissions requirements (no cost). GU5 3.23:1 ratio performance rear axle; requires MX0 automatic transmission and QLC or QFZ tires ($300). MN6 six-speed manual transmission in Z28, includes "skip-shift" feature (no cost). MX0 four-speed overdrive automatic transmission ($815). N96 16-in. silver cast-aluminum wheels ($275). NB8 California and Northeast states emissions override, requires FE9 (no cost). NC7 federal emissions override, requires YF5 or NG1 (no cost). NG1

Northeast states emissions override (no cost). NW9 traction control ($250). PW7 16-in. chrome cast-aluminum wheels on base Camaro, requires QCB tires ($975). PW7 16-in. chrome cast-aluminum wheels on Camaro Z28; not available with WU8 Camaro SS package ($725). QCB P235/55R16 black sidewall tires for base Camaro, requires N96 or PW7 wheels ($135). P245/50ZR16 Goodyear Eagle RSA all-season performance tires on Z28, recommended with NW9 traction control; not available with WU8 SS package ($225). P245/50ZR16 Goodyear Eagle GS-C performance tires on Z28; not available with WU8 SS package ($225). New Jersey cost surcharge ($93 to dealer no cost to buyer). U1S trunk-mounted 12-disc CD changer in base convertible and all Z28s, requires UNO ($595). U1S trunk-mounted 12-disc CD changer in base coupe, requires ULO or UNO ($595). UK3 leather-wrapped steering wheel in base coupe, includes leather-wrapped steering wheel rim, redundant radio controls, leather-trimmed gear shift knob and leather-wrapped parking brake handle, requires 1SB and ULO or UNO ($170). UK3 leather-wrapped steering wheel in Z28 coupe, includes leather-wrapped steering wheel rim, redundant radio controls, leather-trimmed gear shift knob and leather-wrapped parking brake handle, requires 1SC and included in 1SD ($170). ULO Monsoon 500-watts sound system in base coupe, includes Monsoon 500-watt sound system, ETR AM/FM stereo radio with seek-and-scan, digital clock, Auto Tone Control, cassette player, TheftLock, speed-compensated volume, eight speakers and auxiliary amplifier ($350). UNO Monsoon 500-watts sound system with CD player in base convertible and all Z28s, includes Monsoon 500-watt sound system, ETR AM/FM stereo radio with seek-and-scan, digital clock, Auto Tone Control, CD player, TheftLock, speed compensated volume, eight speakers and auxiliary amplifier ($100). UNO Monsoon 500-watts sound system with CD player in base coupe, includes Monsoon 500-watt sound system, ETR AM/FM stereo radio with seek-and-scan, digital clock, auto-tone control, CD player, TheftLock, speed-compensated volume, eight speakers and auxiliary amplifier ($450). V12 power steering cooler in Z28 ($100). WU8 SS Performance/Appearance package for Z28, includes 325-hp engine, forced-air induction hood, a specific SS spoiler, 17-in. aluminum wheels, P275/40ZR17 Goodyear Eagle F1 tires, a high-performance ride and handling package, a power steering cooler, a low-restriction dual outlet exhaust system, SS badging, a 3.23:1 ratio rear axle with the MX0 automatic transmission or a 3.42:1 ratio rear axle with the MN6 six-speed manual transmission; available for Z28s, but was not available with Y3F Sport Appearance package ($3,950). Y38 RS package, for base coupe, includes dual silver or black Heritage stripes on hood, roof and deck lid, RS interior and exterior badging and Z28-type exhaust system with silver painted dual outlets; not available with Y87 or Y3F (no cost). Y3F Sport Appearance package for base Camaros, includes front fascia extension, rocker panel moldings, spoiler extension, rear fascia molding, 16-in. silver cast-aluminum wheels and P235/55R16 black sidewall ties; not available with Y3B ($1,755). Y3F Sport Appearance package for Z28s, includes front fascia extension, rocker panel moldings, spoiler extension and rear fascia molding; not available with WU8 ($1,348). Y87 Performance Handling package for base convertible, includes Zexel Torsen limited-slip differential, dual outlet exhausts and sport steering ratio, requires QCB and N96 ($275). Y87 Performance Handling package for base coupe, includes Zexel Torsen limited-slip differential, dual outlet exhausts and sport steering ratio, requires 1SB, QCB and N96; not available with Y3B ($275). YF5 California emissions requirements (no cost). ($275)

2002

1SA convertible with base equipment group, includes vehicle with standard equipment (no cost). 1SA hatchback base equipment group, includes vehicle with standard equipment; not available with 1SB (no cost). 1SB hatchback preferred equipment group 1 including remote keyless entry, theft-deterrent alarm system, cruise control, fog lights, twin electric remote-control sport mirrors, power door locks, power windows with driver's side express down feature and remote hatch release; not available with 1SA ($1,170). 1SB convertible preferred equipment group 1, includes vehicle with standard equipment (no cost). 1SC Z28 hatchback preferred equipment group 2, includes vehicle with standard equipment; not available with 1SD (no cost). 1SD Z28 hatchback preferred equipment group 1 includes remote keyless entry, theft-deterrent alarm system, electronic cruise control, twin electric remote-control sport mirrors, power door locks, power windows with driver's side express down feature, remote hatch release; power sixway driver's seat, leather-wrapped steering wheel with redundant radio controls, leather-trimmed gearshift knob, leather-wrapped parking brake handle, rear carpeted floor mats and color-keyed body side moldings; not available with 1SC ($1,700). AG1 six-way power driver's seat ($270). AR9 leather accent bucket seats ($500). B84 body-color body side moldings on hatchback ($60). BBS Hurst performance shift linkage for Z28, includes short-throw shift linkage, requires six-speed manual transmission ($325). C49 hatchback rear window defogger ($170). CC1 transparent removable hatch roof panels, includes locks, lockable storage provisions and sunshades ($995). GU5 3.23:1 ratio performance rear axle; requires MX0 automatic transmission and QLC or QFZ tires ($300). MN6 six-speed manual transmission in Z28, includes "skip-shift" feature (no cost). MX0 four-speed overdrive automatic transmission ($725). NW9 traction control ($250). PW7 16-in. chrome cast-aluminum wheels on base Camaro ($725). PW7 16-in. chrome cast-aluminum wheels on Camaro Z28; not available with WU8 Camaro SS package ($725). QLC P245/50ZR16 Goodyear Eagle GS-C performance tires on Z28, not available with WU8 SS package ($225). R6M New Jersey cost surcharge ($93 to dealer no cost to buyer). U1S trunk-mounted 12-disc CD changer, requires UNO ($595). UK3 leather-wrapped steering wheel in base coupe, includes leather-wrapped steering wheel rim, redundant radio controls, leather-trimmed gearshift knob and leather-wrapped parking brake handle, requires 1SB and ULO or UNO ($170). UNO Monsoon 500-watts sound system with CD player in base convertible and all Z28s, includes Monsoon 500-watt sound system, ETR AM/FM stereo radio with seek-and-scan, digital clock, Auto Tone Control, CD player, TheftLock, speed compensated volume, eight speakers and auxiliary amplifier ($350). WU8 SS Performance/Appearance package for Z28, includes 325-hp engine, forced-air induction hood, a specific SS spoiler, 17-in. aluminum wheels, P275/40ZR17 Goodyear Eagle F1 tires, a high-performance ride and handling package, a power steering cooler, a low-restriction dual outlet exhaust system, SS badging, a 3.23:1 ratio rear axle with the MX0 automatic transmission or a 3.42:1 ratio rear axle with the MN6 six-speed manual transmission; available for Z28s, but was not available with Y3F Sport Appearance package ($3,625). Y38 RS package, for base coupe, includes dual silver or black Heritage stripes on hood, roof and deck lid, RS interior and exterior badging and Z28-type exhaust system with silver painted dual outlets; not available with Y87 or Y3F ($1,345). Y87 Performance Handling package for base hatchback, includes Zexel Torsen limited-slip differential, dual outlet exhausts and sport steering ratio, requires QCB and N96 ($275). Z4C 35th Anniversary package for Z28 convertible with the SS package, includes traction control, 12-disc CD changer, 17 x 9-in. custom black machine-faced aluminum wheels, black anodized brake calipers, custom silver embroidery on head restraints, ebony leather seating surfaces with pewter leather inserts and custom trophy floor mats, requires WU8 ($2,500).

Acknowledgments

If I could acknowledge everyone who helped me with the 50-odd automotive books I have compiled, there would be nothing between these covers but a list of names. Since I'm supposed to be an editor type (last week I didn't know what an editor does and now I are one), I guess I should be able to whittle this down to the essentials. First, let me thank Tony "Mr. Bow Tie" Hossain, who was onto the Camaro thing when I was still pushing Blue Flame sixes. Additional kudos go to a guy I've never met, except over the Internet, Scott Settlemire of GM. If anyone ever gets elected "King of Camaros," it will be Scott. Brian Earnest is an editor's editor (now literally) who took this book from the rough-draft stage to a finished product. And picture-man Jerry Heasley is right up there on my top five list. I love when Brian pays Jerry for another bunch of photos because I know it's going to take my book to a new level. Steve Smith and Bill Krause also deserve a nod for the original concept behind this project. I hope you all enjoy reading it. Please let us know when you spot one of those gremlins that seems to sneak into all books on automotive history.